FGF Studies in Small Business and Entrepreneurship

The aim of the FGF Studies in Small Business and Entrepreneurship is to showcase exceptional scholarly work in small business and entrepreneurship research. This Scopus listed book series has an interdisciplinary focus and includes works from management, finance, innovation, marketing, economics, sociology, psychology and related areas reflecting the breadth of different approaches to small business and entrepreneurship research. Volumes in the series may include

- Research monographs,
- Edited volumes, and
- Handbooks The FGF Studies in Small Business and Entrepreneurship

acknowledge that small business and entrepreneurship phenomena occur at various levels of analysis and hence the series is concerned with a plethora of levels including the analysis of individuals, organizations, networks, economies and societies. Through this, the book series serves as a vehicle to help academics, professionals, researchers and policy makers, working in the fields of small business and entrepreneurship, to disseminate and obtain high quality knowledge. The FGF Studies in Small Business and Entrepreneurship are published on behalf of the FGF e.V., the largest and leading association of entrepreneurship scholars in Germany, Austria and Switzerland. However, titles in this series are by no means restricted to the German-speaking countries, international proposals for inclusion in the series are extremely welcome. Proposals should be addressed to one of the editors-in-chief.

Harald Pechlaner • Hannes Thees •
Wei Manske-Wang
Editors

The Clash of Entrepreneurial Cultures?

Interdisciplinary Perspectives Focusing on Asian and European Ecosystems

Springer

Editors
Harald Pechlaner
Chair of Tourism/Center for Entrepreneurship
Catholic University of Eichstätt-Ingolstadt
Eichstätt, Germany

Hannes Thees
Chair of Tourism/Center for Entrepreneurship
Catholic University of Eichstätt-Ingolstadt
Eichstätt, Germany

Wei Manske-Wang
China Center
Management Center Innsbruck, The Entrepreneurial School®
Innsbruck, Austria

ISSN 2364-6918 ISSN 2364-6926 (electronic)
FGF Studies in Small Business and Entrepreneurship
ISBN 978-3-030-97049-9 ISBN 978-3-030-97050-5 (eBook)
https://doi.org/10.1007/978-3-030-97050-5

This Springer imprint is published by the registered company Springer Nature Switzerland AG
The registered company address is: Gewerbestrasse 11, 6330 Cham, Switzerland

Preface

Entrepreneurship enables development and innovation through creativity in taking entrepreneurial opportunities and risks. Flourishing entrepreneurship requires the recognition and design of specific context conditions around policy and finance, but also around institutions and culture. It is the specific culture with its local embeddedness where entrepreneurs develop and try to extend the system's boundaries and innovate. However, those actions and interactions oscillate between local and global conditions.

Although the past and present crises have challenged globalization (the economic and financial crisis, the climate crisis, the demographic change, or, most recently, the COVID-19 pandemic and the Russia–Ukraine war), it has stressed the interdependence of value chains globally. Especially the COVID-19 pandemic has brought globalization to a standstill, but more importantly, it has raised questions about secure production chains, crisis assistance, increased mobility, and sustainability. The sum of these major crises may have strengthened the bonds between some countries; however, the emerging challenges are pressing, and states frequently dispute issues, which are increasingly emerging unexpectedly and putting the resilience of countries and regions to the test; on the other hand, long-standing problems such as climate change are taking on a completely new meaning against the backdrop of changing conditions. Climate change and sustainable growth call for increased global cooperation and governance.

Ecosystems are dynamic and, to a certain extent, vibrant in the interplay of young and established companies, of ideas and concrete plans, of acquisitions and cooperation, of institutions and organizations, of private and public actors, and of politics, business, society, and culture. Ecosystems are complex and require special sensitivity on the part of policymakers. What is needed is a shared understanding of the basic principles of ecosystems. It is about a common understanding that different cultural areas can also enable different understandings of entrepreneurship and of entrepreneurial cooperation and that this is precisely what constitutes a value in its own terms. If this is at least partially expressed or becomes visible along the geographies between Europe and Asia, highly interesting opportunities can arise for companies and entrepreneurs.

While economic growth in its traditional meaning in Western Europe has slowed down, demanding more sustainable pathways and the inclusion of Eastern Europe, Asian countries are widely growing and still offer promising opportunities. Even so, in defining future directions, the EU seems in a lock-in. In contrast, China is leading the Asian century with the Belt and Road Initiative (BRI) and Regional Comprehensive Economic Partnership (RCEP). The BRI is initiating huge investments in connectivity across all continents, while the RCEP promotes regional integration in the Asia-Pacific region with the largest free-trade zone worldwide. As both regions—Asia and Europe—meet and even compete with their development approaches, a deep understanding is necessary to promote international cooperation on global challenges.

The connectivity between both regions in Eurasia has long been driven by a world-famous trade route: the Silk Road thousands of years ago, today being revived by the Belt and Road Initiative in a different shape. Asia was historically a sophisticated region of invention and civilization until it missed the Industrial Revolution—leaving this ground to Europe and the USA. Asia now has the ambition to retake technology leadership in the upcoming Fourth Industrial Revolution, seeing that they already have competitive advantages. Many indications support the emerging Asian position by its competitive countries: economic growth and technological improvement in China; the sustained innovative power of South Korea; the digital potential in India; and the innovation hubs Singapore and Vietnam with their emerging economy and supportive government—all of these make Asia a region of diversity and dynamism and, thus, a reason to take more into account in globalization, but also to recognize them as collaborators or competitors in Europe.

Although differences exist across Asia, the countries are widely promoting a different economic development model than that in Europe: more collective and strongly state-supported, but fast and innovative. The holistic thinking in most Asian countries is fundamentally distinct from the analytical thinking in Europe. What can Asia and Europe learn from each other in regard to supporting entrepreneurship? How shall they deal with their differences? How do entrepreneurial ecosystems develop under political capitalism, and how do they develop under liberal capitalism? What are the consequences of the clash of different understandings of governance of these ecosystems?

For those who are looking for answers and reflecting on these complex relations, this edited volume offers plenty of food for thought on building a bridge between Asia and Europe and rethinking meaningful entrepreneurial ecosystems with and for both Asia and Europe. Although there is a focus on German–Chinese relations, this comparison is based on the various understandings of entrepreneurship in the context of culture, politics, and economics, which are presented and discussed in the selected chapters.

Starting with the editor's introduction (Chapter "Introducing Central Questions in Entrepreneurial Ecosystems Across Cultures and Regions"), it becomes apparent that the complexity and sensitivity of global relations is rising, while Eurasia provides interesting ground for economic development but also for geopolitical tensions. These tensions lead to conflicts on the political level and also on a very local scale. Although the economic cultures are different across Eurasia, further cooperation provides vital ground for future collaboration. Harald Pechlaner, Hannes Thees, and Wei Manske-Wang call us to recognize and research the entrepreneurial ecosystem as an essential mediator in international relations that stresses complex linkages and governance.

China is undoubtedly a driving player in the globalization and economic growth pole. Understanding entrepreneurship in China from a Western perspective is still challenging. Against this background, Maximilian Scheu and Andreas Kuckertz (Chapter "Entrepreneurship in China: Autoethnographic Insights into a Pulsating Entrepreneurial Society") provide an autoethnographic account of the Chinese entrepreneurial landscape. They sketch a research path and provide important market understanding by analyzing and reflecting upon the business environment.

Sketching the differences between Asia and Europe is also key to the contribution of Haowen Chen (Chapter "Institutional Differences and Opportunity Exploitation: A Comparison of Managerial Ties Utilization in Asia and Europe"), who focuses on the institutional environments as a crucial factor of entrepreneurship. She proposes to take a global view and analyze entrepreneurial behavior in a particular setting between China and Germany. These institutional differences lead to significant differences in entrepreneurship, which need to be understood in detail. The West's mechanisms and theories do not necessarily follow the same rules in Asia, and vice versa.

Such an Asian–European understanding is desirable but hard to achieve, as Ulrich Bauer (Chapter "Mutual Incomprehension: Why Entrepreneurs from East Asia and Europe Do Not Understand Each Other: And It Is Getting Worse") highlights from a cultural perspective. The incomprehension from Westerners on how entrepreneurship is exercised in China is locked in outdated assumptions and lagging behind fast changes in the business environment. Analyzing specifics in Chinese culture helps us to overcome the inadequacies and shortcomings of Western views on China.

An initiative that could provide Asian–European connectivity and cultural exchange is the Belt and Road Initiative. Daniel Waite (Chapter "Economic Reactions to Global Development Strategies: Mapping Public Discourse in Germany on China's Belt and Road Initiative") analyzes the reaction strategies of stakeholders to the global initiative in German news articles. He utilizes game theory and innovative research questions to uncover that, currently, risks outweigh opportunities in the perception of various stakeholder levels.

With globalization, the analysis of entrepreneurial cultures has a long tradition and still delivers practical insights. In this regard, Jörg Büechl and Felix Haefner (Chapter "A Comparison of Entrepreneurial Culture in Germany and China") reflect on Hofstede's cultural dimensions to outline cultural differences between China and Germany.

Approaching specific markets, Gi Min Kim (Chapter "South Korea's Startup Ecosystem") provides an introduction into the specialties of the Asian market with a focus on South Korea's startup ecosystem, which still offers growth potential for multinational companies. Understanding the social and cultural aspects of South Korea is likewise important to implementing concrete measures to improve the business environment, but also to engaging in the South Korean market. The combination of financial and cultural factors in the entrepreneurial ecosystem is an important linkage here.

Lela Grießbach (Chapter "Peculiarities of Entrepreneurial Ecosystems in the Caucasus Countries: The Case of Georgia") investigates the peculiarities of the entrepreneurial ecosystem in the case of Georgia in the Caucasus region. Georgia has a strategic position at the interface between Asia and Europe and is thus trying to extend international relations with various partners. In domestic politics, Georgia has undertaken some significant endeavors to build up a business environment that bridges post-Soviet characteristics and Western-style market dynamics. In this challenging task, the Georgian ecosystem is still in its infancy.

The reasons for understanding Asian and European entrepreneurial cultures are manifold. One of them is to benefit from the exchange of knowledge. China's Belt and Road Initiative aims at knowledge transfer, but more so does the EU Connectivity Strategy. Both strategies meet in Central Asia, which is the premise for Justine Markisch (Chapter "Connecting Asia and Europe: Opportunities and Barriers for Knowledge-Oriented Regional Development in Central Asia") to analyze both strategies regarding their knowledge-oriented regional development. Her chapter contributes to theoretical discussions across the field of regionalism but also gives practical advice for governments and non-governmental organizations.

Another specific regional perspective is introduced by Gerhard Leypoldt (Chapter "Vietnam and Thailand: Southeast Asian Prospects for Corporate Cultures and Ecosystems in an Asian Century") in his contribution on Southeast Asia. He utilizes statistical data and personal experiences to give an understanding of how Vietnam and Thailand developed ecosystems in their respective environments of political and liberal capitalism. In this field, Gerhard Leypoldt delivers valuable practical insights for developing startup cultures and the role of women in the ecosystem.

As the information technology and knowledge economy raises the complexity of doing business worldwide, Xiao Han (Chapter "The Role of Strategic Alliances in Developing the Up-market Entrepreneurial Ecosystem") focuses on the role of strategic alliances. In ecosystems, those alliances are central and assist in collecting and assigning resources carefully. Therefore, Xiao Han calls us to consider scientific and technological resources, uniting actors and institutions to integrate science, technology, industry, and capital. She takes the example of the intelligent connected vehicles industry and the Chinese enterprise NIO to underline cooperation between various sub-ecosystems.

New industries are indeed emerging in the case of automated vehicles, but the work environment itself is changing even more quickly during the COVID-19 pandemic, requiring agility. Tatiana Lekýrová and Gabriela Antošová (Chapter "Agile at Scale Adoption: New Perspectives from a Solely Remote Environment") take the concept of agility, which combines innovative culture, consumer relations, and adaption to a changing environment, to assess virtual scaled agile transformation. In the case of a software company, they prove the relevance of online connectedness in a digital ecosystem with remote working, contributing to more innovative and dynamic thinking in companies.

In discussing regions and spaces along the geographies across Eurasia, the place becomes a focal factor. Angelika C. Messner (Chapter "Why and How Place Matters") offers fundamental thoughts about space, place, and knowledge regarding global transformations from a multidisciplinary perspective. Her contribution equals a journey from space to place, through "regions, people, populations, and countries"—designing thin lines in merging Eastern and Western thoughts. At the end of a mindful reading, the "Silk Road" is not a sequence of places with different regional histories, but a space of "comparisons and connections" with a deeper understanding "that knowledge is inseparable from place."

Concluding this preface, culture and mutual understanding are of utmost. Culture means to have a high sensitivity in the interpretation of contemporary social developments, to get an idea about the condition of space and society, and therefore to be able to envision possible futures. It is the basis for being able to interpret the needs of societies. This, in turn, breeds entrepreneurship. Ideas for solving societal problems and desires are the basis for it. Reading the book should, in a sense, make you sensitive to the many entrepreneurial opportunities when viewed through the lens of culture, but it should also draw your attention to a special space that you can only embrace as an entrepreneur if you view it with the necessary humility.

We dedicate this book to Prof. Jana Kucerova from Matej Bel University in Banska Bystrica, Slovakia. Unfortunately, she left us much too early. In many conversations, she emphasized the difficulties but also the importance of good relations between East and West. She taught us the sensitivity necessary for these relations.

Against the background of the various challenges in understanding entrepreneurial cultures and their particular ecosystems between Asia and Europe, we hope to provide the reader with multiple perspectives on an issue we strive for in globalization: mutual understanding.

Eichstätt, Germany Harald Pechlaner
Eichstätt, Germany Hannes Thees
Innsbruck, Austria Wei Manske-Wang

Contents

Introducing Central Questions in Entrepreneurial Ecosystems Across Cultures and Regions

Harald Pechlaner, Hannes Thees, and Wei Manske-Wang

Abstract Starting from the often-underestimated role that entrepreneurial culture has in international cooperation, this chapter aims to answer fundamental questions on future relations between Asia and Europe. Linkages between doing business, economic culture, and entrepreneurial ecosystems are introduced at the interface of local development and globalization. In this setting, this chapter recognizes the influence of Eurasia and the New Silk Road in thc ncxt phasc of globalization, which may foster regional connectivity. However, mere connectivity needs to be brought to life through entrepreneurial activities that promote local development without surpassing power relations and sustainability challenges. Going beyond the perspective of global value chains and multinational enterprises, socio-economic exchange becomes a focus, where different forms of capitalism meet across Eurasia, causing contrasts in doing business and creating severe conflicts if the necessary sensitivity in dealing with each other is missing. Entrepreneurial ecosystems—as strongly diversified networks—may act as a mediators in international cooperation with a dynamic and context-related approach. Based on the model of international entrepreneurial ecosystems, a research field emerges at the socio-economic and local–global interfaces.

Keywords Entrepreneurial Ecosystem · Economic Culture · Asia · Europe · International Cooperation

H. Pechlaner · H. Thees (✉)
Chair of Tourism/Center for Entrepreneurship, Catholic University of Eichstätt-Ingolstadt, Eichstätt, Germany
e-mail: harald.pechlaner@ku.de; hannes.thees@ku.de

W. Manske-Wang
China Center, Management Center Innsbruck, The Entrepreneurial School®, Innsbruck, Austria
e-mail: Wei.Manske-Wang@mci.edu

H. Pechlaner et al. (eds.), *The Clash of Entrepreneurial Cultures?*, FGF Studies in Small Business and Entrepreneurship, https://doi.org/10.1007/978-3-030-97050-5_1

1 What Roles Do Asia and Europe Play in Future Globalization?

Discussing the interactions between Asia and Europe means understanding socio-economic systems and concentrating on cooperation in a region that has been under-researched compared to intra-European or European–American relations. However, Eurasia, widely defined as the combined European and Asian continents, has come to the fore of globalization (Khondker, 2021). Globalization reflects the development of global value chains and the associated interconnection of economies and geographies (Steger, 2017). While focusing on a holistic type of globalization, the role and the form of globalization have been frequently discussed and, lately, also questioned during the financial and migration crises, COVID-19 pandemic, trade wars, and rising populism (Steger, 2021). In this time, various alternative concepts have evolved, such as Re-Globalization (Benedikter et al., 2022), Post-Globalization (Flew, 2020), and Inclusive or Sustainable Globalization (Liu & Dunford, 2016) or even De-Globalization (Witt, 2019). These concepts underline the struggle between global and national interests, but also that between traditional and alternative development approaches (Flew, 2020).

The COVID-19 pandemic has stressed global value chains, which contributes to the re-configurement of global economic and power structures. Through increased cooperation, trade agreements, and blocs on a regional level, a "world of regions" (Katzenstein, 2015) or the "regional architecture of world politics" (Acharya & Buzan, 2010) has evolved as regionalization has gained momentum. Regions are now central to global politics, as regional trade agreements or even deeper regional integrations arise (Koller & Voskresenski, 2019). However, the significance of this regionalization is still increasing, particularly in Asia. The RCEP (Regional Comprehensive Economic Partnership) is a recent example of that. Discussions about the future of international politics and economics are undoubtedly incomplete without non-Western regions (Voskresenski & Koller, 2019).

It is probably China that shapes the upcoming phase of globalization. One of the most prominent globalization projects is the New Silk Road (or officially the *Belt and Road Initiative*) driven by China. The New Silk Road is a bundling of corridors for transportation and logistics between Asia, Europe, Africa, and, increasingly, South America. This (physical) mobility of goods and commodities, labor, and capital brings non-physical mobility, such as that of information, knowledge, traditions, cultures, religions, values, and lifestyles. In the upcoming phase of globalization, a kind of borderless mobility of labor and capital is emerging due to increasing digitalization, with ownership of information incidentally becoming a central building block of platform capitalism (Pechlaner & Thees, 2020). The globalization project New Silk Road could become a game-changer in global connectivity and the interdependence of states and companies with emerging rules and conditions (Rolland, 2017; Pechlaner et al., 2020). As such, Eurasia provides the potential for further economic development but may become a field of experimentation for the major powers to prove their impact and their development models. We currently see

Chinese infrastructure investments, which are also followed by the EU, resulting in clashes where states need to steer interests carefully. Nevertheless, the clash of entrepreneurial cultures, economic systems, and political directions along with the NSR is full of potential for mutual understanding, learning, and finally, development. However, if the opposing models are too far apart and unilateral restrictions hinder cooperation and exchange, the NSR may not flourish or remain a china-driven, one-directional corridor.

2 In What Way Is the Economic Culture Influencing International Entrepreneurship?

Global political tensions require careful steering between globalization and regionalization (Koller & Voskresenski, 2019). It is not only politics that shapes these linkages, but also multinational companies and entrepreneurs across all countries. The cultural background of actors becomes especially relevant in global relations as it defines the entrepreneurs' behavior in their interaction with stakeholders (Freytag, 2014). The entrepreneurial culture defines the prevailing societal setting in a country in regard to doing business. It comprises values, beliefs, standards, attitudes, behavior, and practices according to innovation, creativity, risk-taking, and entrepreneurial opportunities (Dzingirai, 2020; Domingue et al., 2011), providing context for entrepreneurial ecosystems (Spigel, 2020). Conversely, entrepreneurial ecosystems also allow cultural dynamics to take effect, which in turn influence the entrepreneurial thinking and actions of individuals.

A unique feature of entrepreneurial culture results from the spatial foundation in the context of regional networks or location-specific characteristics and objectives (Muñoz & Kimmitt, 2019; McKeever et al., 2015)—place matters (see Chap. "Why and How Place Matters" in this volume)! This embeddedness of an entrepreneur in local interaction includes the political design of context conditions but, so far, has underestimated the global and systemic relationships. Thus, intercultural management and communication issues are fundamental to act in global value chains (Reidy, 2010; Huang, 2020). Successful ecosystems with an entrepreneurial character are fundamentally international because the ecosystem—as a perceived space of condensed economic activity—can bring together investors, founders, people with ideas, and representatives of established companies. Ecosystems are nodes and edges within and between which encounters and networking take place. The more and the more internationally oriented these are, the more likely it is that independent cultural dynamics and quality demands will emerge. Ecosystems highlight the interdependence of every systemic element and the whole system's efficiency (O'Connor et al., 2018). Therefore, the economic culture determines how cooperation and competition are perceived and practiced in terms of risk-taking, collectivism, future orientation, and power distance (Minkov & Kaasa, 2020). International cooperation thus means to combine cultural systems of a different history and partially diverging economic interests and social structures. The economic culture—from a Western perspective—perceives entrepreneurship as enabling development and innovation through creativity, taking entrepreneurial opportunities and risks. It aims to create products and services that consumers demand (Brouwer, 2002; Acs & Lappi, 2021). From a Chinese perspective, entrepreneurship and private enterprise development unleashed since the 1980s and became a driving force for economic development (He et al., 2019). From an international perspective, the concepts around international entrepreneurial culture discuss the embeddedness of a firm abroad, defined through seeking international opportunities (Gabrielsson et al., 2014; McDougall & Oviatt, 2000). Interestingly, the intensity of internationality emerges through a firm's life cycle but still profits from international learning and networking throughout all phases (Gabrielsson et al., 2014).

One socio-economic system to upscale entrepreneurship and entrepreneurial ecosystems is capitalism, which constitutes the market's and actors' roles (Robbins, 2014). There is a close connection between the expression of capitalism and the development of entrepreneurial ecosystems. Capitalism encourages to rethink established actor roles and patterns of economic activity frequently in order to adapt and optimize the economic system. Although entrepreneurial ecosystems are discussed worldwide, different interpretations evolve in different forms of capitalism. Capitalism presents a market-driven economy, as well as economic and entrepreneurial freedom as actors strive for prosperity in a broad field of tension toward the rule of law and the states' initiatives. The rule of law defines Western-style liberal capitalism, i.e., clearly regulated property relations and a related state that is relatively less influential but based on democratic principles. Private actors can make their own decisions. Political capitalism is characterized in particular by China, with unclear property relations and a lack of rule of law, but also by efficient bureaucracy geared for growth in a strong state (Milanovic, 2019; Robbins, 2014; Crawford, 2000). In the future, the accelerating digitalization and sustainability in local and global practices may assist in linking or even converging different economic cultures and capitalisms – specifically the liberal and the political capitalism, if issues on surveillance do not restrict the necessary entrepreneurial freedom. Given the evidence of the socio-economic system, the place, with its specific rules and conditions, shapes how entrepreneurs and companies act in the domestic market, but also in international markets.

3 What Are the Contrasts in Doing Business in Asia and Europe?

In terms of international entrepreneurship and management, it is important to cope with the mentioned cultural settings that define the particular space for adaption, creativity, product development, business regulation, and daily business routines.

Therefore, an understanding of complementarities and differences in Asian and European forms of capitalism and political structures can support mutual investments and cooperation.

Cultural exchange has always been a factor of globalization, triggering flows of people, finances, goods, and information, taking place on an individual level. Cultural globalization in this context shapes everyday life by the diffusion of commodities, ideas, and standardization. Culture causes and enables the dialogue that is so important for every business. The central driver is digitalization that then also increases global connectivity, and international travel and migration (el-Ojeili & Hayden, 2006; Thees et al., 2022). In general, differences in entrepreneurship between developed and developing/emerging countries evolve in four factors: rates of opportunity, economic structures, institutional development, and provision of entrepreneurial resources (Spigel, 2020). Elaborating on the cultural dimensions, as, for example, introduced by Hofstede (Minkov & Hofstede, 2012; Minkov & Kaasa, 2020), the roles of collectivism and ties among people are, in particular, different between Western European and East Asian countries, which could then also cause conflicts in business collaboration. Nevertheless, further context-specific and culture-driven examination is needed to elaborate cultural dimensions carefully (Thees et al., 2022).

What can be learned from recent history is that conflicts frequently emerge in international politics. Different institutions map conflicts across Eurasia, e.g., the Friedrich Ebert Stiftung (www.fes.isometric.site/fes), the Council on Foreign Relations (www.cfr.org/global-conflict-tracker), and the Crisis Group (www.crisisgroup.org/crisiswatch). In particular, the Friedrich Ebert Stiftung includes alliances and routes of the New Silk Road in defining regional impact. Summarizing the political conflicts, a line at the outer borders of the Chinese influence is visible, e.g., in the East China Sea or the Kashmir region. The Russia-Ukraine war adds a new dimension and has certainly caused an inherent impact on the ground of the New Silk Road, which confirms the indispensability of political stability. Economic disputes along with the New Silk Road arose in terms of investments and credits, transparency and procurement, and local impact (Sun & Hou, 2019; Mao et al., 2019; Himaz, 2021). Perception of these conflicts is visible in Eastern Europe, where financing of motorways in Montenegro or the Gwadar Port in Sri Lanka led to investment stops and new independencies, questioning China's debt diplomacy (Ishaque et al., 2018). A central point of criticism is that it is often impossible for local parties and third parties to support infrastructure construction or even transport operations with their own leadership and workforce. Such examples have led to reserved reactions. European companies are defensive in applying for Chinese projects, and even the EU needed a couple of years to define a response on the BRI that then also strengthened the rights of the business sector in international cooperation. However, those agreements may have different durability depending on the countries. As China sets a long-term oriented and normative strategy, the governments in western democratic countries change more quickly because of their short election periods, and with this, the commitment against the New Silk Road as well. Nevertheless, Asia–Europe cooperation has resulted in positive examples and interdependencies developed for both sides. Against the background of Chinese actions in 2021, it is questionable whether cooperation may increase or result in neutrality. Along with the Russia-Ukraine war, China is cautious in economic and political positioning. China follows its subtle political style with soft governance on the international level. However, internally, China is very determined and tough, including a zero Covid policy, which is challenging in Chinese megacities and a form of digital surveillance, that increases efficiency but is threatening individual freedom. The experiences of China with America under President Trump have shown that there are already international disruptions and no guarantee for supply chains to flourish. This has also caused China to focus inward and neighboring counties to become more independent. At the same time, a couple of countries have become even more dependent on the Chinese trade and political protection. Reflecting on relations between Russia, EU, China and the USA, the distribution of power, knowledge, and trust in the form of a balance between dependence and independence is crucial for a geopolitical and geoeconomic setting that supports entrepreneurial opportunities locally.

The culture of capitalism is embedded in cultures and places (Crawford, 2000), and that causes different forms of capitalism to interact or even clash (Milanovic, 2019). The New Silk Road is such a melting pot of different entrepreneurial and economic cultures, especially countries between the growth poles of East Asia and Western Europe. It becomes even more complicated when various forms of capitalism meet in third-party countries, e.g., in Central Asia. However, engaging in future cooperation along with the New Silk Road may increase regional integration.

4 How Can Entrepreneurial Ecosystems Mediate between Economic Systems?

As varieties of capitalism meet, they may benefit from each other as they focus on different entrepreneurship context conditions. Whether on a national or international scale, for entrepreneurship to flourish requires the recognition and design of specific context conditions around policy, finance, human capital, markets, supporting industries, institutions, and culture (Isenberg, 2011). The Entrepreneurial Ecosystem has gained increasing attention in scientific and practical discussions as an instrument to describe and promote such context conditions for entrepreneurial activities. It finally emphasizes the need for a proper context for entrepreneurship and individual aspirations to emerge and flourish. The entrepreneurial culture explains various processes within the ecosystem on societal norms, propensity for innovation, wealth creation, creativity, and entrepreneurs' status (Isenberg, 2011; Stam & van de Ven, 2019). The concept of entrepreneurial ecosystems exceeds former concepts in its stronger emphasis on the entrepreneurially active individual and interaction between actors, such as in startups, established enterprises, politics, or agencies. The output of the ecosystem can thus be an increase in economic activity, innovation, and startup

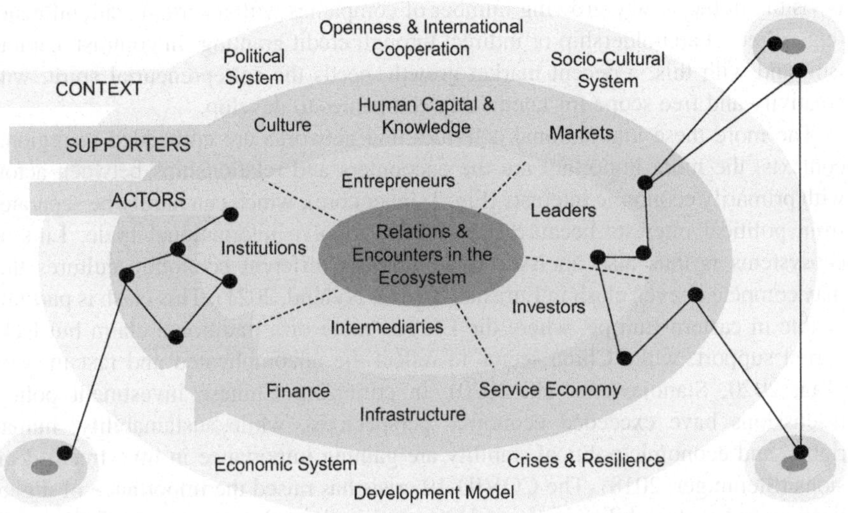

Fig. 1 Determinants of an international entrepreneurial ecosystem. Source: Own elaboration

generation, as well as increased sustainability. The ecosystem needs culture and creates culture. Economic culture meets the regional culture of the actors, and differences are often visible in the area of tension between international conventions and local customs and traditions. Ecosystems are successful when there is a quality requirement to accept these differences within the framework of an absorptive capital and, if necessary, to develop them further.

The potential of the ecosystem approach is to support local interests by focusing on local resources and entities. Although the context conditions of the ecosystem are shaped by political actions as well, the ecosystem remains a market-driven and flexible approach to foster entrepreneurship. On a local scale, ecosystems and related clusters are available across Eurasia (Brem & Nylund, 2021). The high-income countries and the newly industrialized countries certainly provide regional agglomeration of various industry sectors, such as tech, transportation, or energy, while the developing countries still struggle to introduce economic diversity and access to global value chains (Batsaikhan & Dabrowski, 2017). China, therefore, has started developing industrial zones that can act as predecessors for clusters and ecosystems (Hong Kong Trade Development Council, Belt and Road Portal, 2020). However, these industrial zones remain Chinese-driven and are within a different economic culture. The New Silk Road is thus a space where different systems meet. Although local ecosystems may emerge successfully, functioning across national borders remains marginal. Therefore, we introduce a first model on the international entrepreneurial ecosystem that considers the multiple relations of local and international systems (Fig. 1). The Chinese direction in allowing the development of free markets and entrepreneurship will become crucial. With its control-orientation, the Chinese government may threaten the opening towards market globalization in the past. This is visible in the slowly growing number of companies with a certain state influence (e.g., direct shareholdership or indirect through credit granting. In contrast, capitalism, and with this, a decent market growth, needs the entrepreneurial spirit, with creativity and free scope for talents and companies to develop.

The more these international activities and networks are embedded in regional contexts, the more important are the encounters and relationships between actors with primarily economic interests (Fig. 1, inner core), which can hardly be separated from political interests because they mostly involve international trade. Linking ecosystems is thus also an issue of combining different economic cultures that may compete or even clash in Eurasia (Brem & Nylund, 2021). This clash is partially visible in eastern Europe, where the EU has more of a traditional claim but lacks partial support, while China seems to reflect the uncomplicated and fast investor (Tan, 2020; Stanojevic et al., 2020). In criticizing Chinese investment policy, discussions have exceeded economic perspectives, while sustainability, human rights, and economic/political stability are gaining importance in investment decisions (Steininger, 2018). The COVID-19 crisis has raised the importance of digitalization and sustainability in the industry and in the political systems. Still, it will probably strengthen the state's role even in Western democracies. An orientation on sustainability and digitalization paired with economic culture plays a particular role in establishing entrepreneurial ecosystems along the NSR. In such a multidimensional and multidisciplinary setting, the entrepreneurial ecosystem also illustrates different understandings across cultures and in contrasting economies (Fig. 1, Context), which should finally complement greater sustainability in capitalistic activities. Ecosystems are networks of institutions, organizations, and actors with different demands and perceptions (Fig. 1, Actors). What is needed for balance is the narratives that make this balance possible. Different developments of capitalism produce different narratives for entrepreneurial and political success. The more it is possible to find agreement on the goals of economic and political action, and the more it is possible to develop narratives that find a fundamentally positive resonance even in different systems of capitalism and political governance, the more successful international cooperation will be. No matter how qualitatively demanding the infrastructures and institutions in the various countries and regions may be, it is the encounters and relationships that form the core of a functioning network—as illustrated in Fig. 1, the borders between the various circles need to be permeable and impact each other.

In addition, our understanding of globalization is challenged by current crises, but also by technological development and the use of artificial intelligence (Luo, 2021), with sometimes drastic changes in the understanding of state, law, property, and privacy, as well as collectivism and individualism (Milanovic, 2019). Political community and common good will take on new meanings, whereas digital entrepreneurial ecosystems evolve within strategic and transnational cooperation (Sussan & Acs, 2017). A multilayered network (Fig. 1, Exemplary Networks) becomes an ecosystem when there is a guiding idea and a somewhat similar underlying mood across the networks that not only holds the network as a whole together but also makes possible and provides the basis for dynamism. Along with innovation, then, it is the concept and understanding of quality that is one of the essential characteristics of an ecosystem. The quality of the encounter and the relationship is the core, followed by the quality of supporters, such as infrastructure and institutions. It is about the claim to create foundations for stability and prosperity in spaces, with the goal of quality of life, as well as competitiveness. Finally, the entrepreneurial ecosystems represent the interface of the mentioned developments that could lead to new understandings of entrepreneurship, stakeholder interaction, international collaboration (Fig. 1, Outer Points, illustrating other ecosystems) and competition, power relations, and political influence. The quality of dialogue is ultimately the core of the entrepreneurial ecosystem and at the same time a guarantor of dynamic further development. Hospitality plays an important role in economic exchange when it comes to creating trust. There is a crucial difference between a fundamental understanding of the "Silk Road" that demonstrates the possibility of bringing economic prosperity to the region and a peacemaking project. Innovation is of central importance, but so is quality, i.e., ambition, in order to be successful. For this, broad acceptance that goes far beyond economic success is a prerequisite. Especially along the corridors and routes of the New Silk Road, the diversity of priorities in infrastructure and institutions with the goal of political, economic, cultural, and social development becomes apparent.

5 Outlook on Entrepreneurship Research across Cultures and Regions

Building upon the previous sections and sketching the role of entrepreneurial cultures, a research agenda emerges in a special international setting. It becomes evident that understanding the particular entrepreneurial cultures, including those in less-developed economies, is essential for successful cooperation and the development of international ecosystems (Spigel, 2020). In general, ecosystem research is an emerging field that still requires conceptualization and explanation of cause and effect relations (Wurth et al., 2021). In particular, research across different cultural, institutional, and industrial settings seems valuable—aiming to provide international research and further elaborating a conceptual model. Such international research should surpass the typically regional and national entrepreneurship research as firms are often linked to international partners and facing international competition (Belitski et al., 2021; Wurth et al., 2021).

For ecosystem research, Wurth et al. (2021) suggest a research agenda including the streams of complex systems, structure, microfoundations, and context. Context focuses on the embeddedness of spatial levels and the interaction between them, but also the peculiarities of each regional system. This embeddedness is linked to the role of local entrepreneurship and the discussed Asian–European relations. During tense times, the desire to proceed with close contact between international researchers and Chinese researchers is understandable to fulfill the awareness-raising role of research. Nevertheless, the space for independent study and cooperation is getting smaller because of growing distrust and political tensions.

Besides a mere economic focus, in an interdisciplinary approach, the entrepreneurial ecosystems can be a system and mediator in various cultural, political, and socio-economic settings (Wurth et al., 2021; Liguori et al., 2018). This finally calls for research in international relations, management, economics, and cultural studies to address differences and commonalities in emerging international Asian–European ecosystems.

References

Acharya, A., & Buzan, B. (2010). Non-Western international relations theory. In *Perspectives on and beyond Asia*. Routledge.

Acs, Z., & Lappi, E. (2021). Entrepreneurship, culture, and the epigenetic revolution: A research note. *Small Business Economics, 56*(4), 1287–1307. https://doi.org/10.1007/s11187-019-00230-0

Batsaikhan, U., & Dabrowski, M. (2017). Central Asia–twenty-five years after the breakup of the USSR. *Russian Journal of Economics, 3*(3), 296–320. https://doi.org/10.1016/j.ruje.2017.09.005

Belitski, M., Caiazza, R., & Lehmann, E. E. (2021). Knowledge frontiers and boundaries in entrepreneurship research. *Small Business Economics, 56*(2), 521–531. https://doi.org/10.1007/s11187-019-00187-0

Benedikter, R., Gruber, M., & Kofler, I. (Eds.). (2022). *Re-globalization. New Frontiers of political, economic and social globalization*. Routledge.

Brem, A., & Nylund, P. A. (2021). Maneuvering the bumps in the new silk road: Open innovation, technological complexity, dominant design, and the international impact of Chinese innovation. *R&D Management, 51*(3), 293–308. https://doi.org/10.1111/radm.12451

Brouwer, M. T. (2002). Weber, Schumpeter and knight on entrepreneurship and economic development. *Journal of Evolutionary Economics, 12*, 83–105.

Crawford, D. (2000). Chinese capitalism: Cultures, the southeast Asian region and economic globalisation. *Third World Quarterly, 21*(1), 69–86.

Domingue, J., Galis, A., Gavras, A., Zahariadis, T., Lambert, D., Cleary, F., et al. (Eds.). (2011). *The future internet. Future internet assembly 2011: Achievements and technological promises*. Springer. (lecture notes in computer science, 6656). Available online at http://site.ebrary.com/lib/alltitles/docDetail.action?docID=10461652

Dzingirai, M. (2020). Design thinking perspective in entrepreneurship education. In N. Baporikar (Ed.), *Handbook of research on entrepreneurship development and opportunities in circular economy* (pp. 397–416). Business Science Reference (Advances in business strategy and competitive advantage (ABSCA) book series).

el-Ojeili, C., & Hayden, P. (2006). Cultural Globalization. In C. el-Ojeili & P. Hayden (Eds.), *Critical theories of globalization* (pp. 134–177). Palgrave Macmillan.

Flew, T. (2020). Globalization, neo-globalization and post-globalization: The challenge of populism and the return of the national. *Global Media and Communication, 16*(1), 19–39. https://doi.org/10.1177/1742766519900329

Freytag, A. (2014). *Entrepreneurship and culture. [Place of publication not identified]*. Springer.

Gabrielsson, M., Gabrielsson, P., & Dimitratos, P. (2014). International entrepreneurial culture and growth of international new ventures. *Management International Review, 54*(4), 445–471. https://doi.org/10.1007/s11575-014-0213-8

He, C., Lu, J., & Qian, H. (2019). Entrepreneurship in China. *Small Business Economics, 52*(3), 563–572. https://doi.org/10.1007/s11187-017-9972-5

Himaz, R. (2021). Challenges associated with the BRI: A review of recent economics literature. *The Service Industries Journal, 41*(7–8), 512–526. https://doi.org/10.1080/02642069.2019.1584193

Hong Kong Trade Development Council, Belt and Road Portal (2020). *Belt and Road Industrial Park*. Overseas Economic and Trade Cooperation Zones on the Belt and Road. Available online at https://beltandroad.hktdc.com/en/sme-corner/industrial-park, updated on 10/20/2021, checked on 10/20/2021.

Huang, J. (2020). *Sino-German intercultural management. Self-organization, communication and conflict resolution in a digital age*. Springer International Publishing AG (SpringerBriefs in Business Ser). Available online at https://ebookcentral.proquest.com/lib/kxp/detail.action?docID=6021190

Isenberg, D. (2011). The entrepreneurship ecosystem strategy as a new paradigm for economy policy: Principles for cultivating entrepreneurship. In *Babson Entrepreneurship Ecosystem Project, Babson College, Babson Park*. MA.

Ishaque, W., Ullah, A., & Safia. (2018). Spring 2018. *GPR, 3*(1), 120–128. https://doi.org/10.31703/gpr.2018(III-I).13

Katzenstein, P. J. (2015). *A world of regions. Asia and Europe in the American imperium*. Cornell University Press (Cornell studies in political economy).

Khondker, H. H. (2021). Eurasian globalization: Past and present. *Globalizations, 18*(5), 707–719. https://doi.org/10.1080/14747731.2020.1842085

Koller, B., & Voskresenski, A. D. (2019). Preface. In A. D. Voskresenski & B. Koller (Eds.), *The regional world order. Transregionalism, regional integration, and regional projects across Europe and Asia* (pp. xii–xiii). Lexington Books (Russian, Eurasian, and Eastern European politics).

Liguori, E., Winkler, C., Hechavarria, D., & Lange, J. (2018). Guest editorial. *JEC, 12*(2), 86–91. https://doi.org/10.1108/JEC-02-2018-0017

Liu, W., & Dunford, M. (2016). Inclusive globalization: Unpacking China's belt and road initiative. *Area Development and Policy, 1*(3), 323–340. https://doi.org/10.1080/23792949.2016.1232598

Luo, Y. (2021). New OLI advantages in digital globalization. *International Business Review*, 101797. https://doi.org/10.1016/j.ibusrev.2021.101797

Mao, H., Liu, G., Zhang, C., & Rao, M. A. (2019). Does belt and road initiative hurt node countries? A study from export perspective. *Emerging Markets Finance and Trade, 55*(7), 1472–1485. https://doi.org/10.1080/1540496X.2018.1553711

McDougall, P. P., & Oviatt, B. M. (2000). International entrepreneurship. The intersection of two research paths. *Academy of Management Journal, 43*(5), 902–906. https://doi.org/10.2307/1556418

McKeever, E., Jack, S., & Anderson, A. (2015). Embedded entrepreneurship in the creative re-construction of place. *Journal of Business Venturing, 30*(1), 50–65.

Milanovic, B. (2019). *Capitalism, alone. The future of the system that rules the world*. Harvard University Press.

Minkov, M., & Hofstede, G. (2012). Hofstede's fifth dimension. *Journal of Cross-Cultural Psychology, 43*(1), 3–14. https://doi.org/10.1177/0022022110388567

Minkov, M., Kaasa, A. (2020). A test of Hofstede's model of culture following his own approach. *CCSM* ahead-of-print (ahead-of-print). https://doi.org/10.1108/CCSM-05-2020-0120

Muñoz, P., & Kimmitt, J. (2019). Social mission as competitive advantage: A configurational analysis of the strategic conditions of social entrepreneurship. *Journal of Business Research, 101*, 854–861.

O'Connor, A., Stam, E., Sussan, F., & Audretsch, D. B. (2018). *Entrepreneurial ecosystems. Place-based transformations and transitions*. Springer International Publishing (38).

Pechlaner, H., Erschbamer, G., Thees, H., & Gruber, M. (Eds.). (2020). *China and the new silk road*. Springer International Publishing.

Pechlaner, H., & Thees, H. (2020). *Is the silk road a road of fear?* Challenges of Global Transformation | global-e (Re-Globalization, 20). Available online at https://www.21global.ucsb.edu/global-e/april-2020/silk-road-road-fear-challenges-global-transformation, updated on 4/28/2020, checked on 4/28/2020.

Reidy, R. W. (2010). Intercultural awareness; the new value chain principle. *Journal of Intercultural Management, 2*(1), 57–68.

Robbins, R. H. (2014). *Global problems and the culture of capitalism* (6th ed.). Pearson.

Rolland, N. (2017). China's "belt and road initiative": Underwhelming or game-changer? *The Washington Quarterly, 40*(1), 127–142. https://doi.org/10.1080/0163660X.2017.1302743

Spigel, Ben (2020): Entrepreneurial ecosystems. Theory, practice and futures. : Edward Elgar Publishing (Entrepreneurship footprints series). Available online at https://www.elgaronline.com/view/9781788975926.xml

Stam, E., & van de Ven, A. (2019). Entrepreneurial ecosystem elements. *Small Business Economics*. https://doi.org/10.1007/s11187-019-00270-6

Stanojevic, S., Bin, Q., & Jian, C. (2020). Sino-EU15 export competition in central and Eastern Europe: Is China crowding out exports from the EU15? *Eastern European Economics, 58*(3), 264–282. https://doi.org/10.1080/00128775.2020.1712554

Steger, M. B. (2017). *Globalization. A very short introduction. Fourth edition, fully updated. new edition*. Oxford University Press. (Very short introductions, 86).

Steger, M. B. (2021). The state of Globality in a (post)-COVID world. *New Global Studies, 15*(2–3), 117–143. https://doi.org/10.1515/ngs-2021-0003

Steininger, S. (2018). What's human rights got to do with it? An empirical analysis of human rights references in investment arbitration. *Leiden Journal of International Law, 31*(1), 33–58. https://doi.org/10.1017/s0922156517000528

Sun, J., & Hou, J. W. (2019). Monetary and financial cooperation between China and the one belt one road countries. *Emerging Markets Finance and Trade, 55*(11), 2609–2627. https://doi.org/10.1080/1540496X.2018.1540976

Sussan, F., & Acs, Z. J. (2017). The digital entrepreneurial ecosystem. *Small Bus Econ, 49*(1), 55–73. https://doi.org/10.1007/s11187-017-9867-5

Tan, A. (2020). China and Russia: Competition in Kyrgyzstan. In *Future Directions international*. Available online at https://www.futuredirections.org.au/wp-content/uploads/2020/01/China-and-Russia-Competition-in-Kyrgyzstan.pdf, checked on 10/20/2021.

Thees, H., Pechlaner, H., & Manske-Wang, W. (2022). A matter of system? Economic Cultures & Capitalism along China's new silk road. In R. Benedikter, M. Gruber, & I. Kofler (Eds.), *Re-globalization. New Frontiers of political, economic and social globalization*. Routledge.

Voskresenski, A. D., & Koller, B. (2019). *The regional world order. Transregionalism, regional integration, and regional projects across Europe and Asia*. Lexington Books (Russian, Eurasian, and Eastern European politics).

Witt, M. A. (2019). De-globalization: Theories, predictions, and opportunities for international business research. *Journal of International Business Studies, 50*(7), 1053–1077. https://doi.org/10.1057/s41267-019-00219-7

Wurth, B., Stam, E., & Spigel, B. (2021). Toward an entrepreneurial ecosystem research program. *Entrepreneurship Theory and Practice, 104225872199894*. https://doi.org/10.1177/1042258721998948

Harald Pechlaner holds the Chair of Tourism and is Head of the Center for Entrepreneurship at the Catholic University of Eichstätt-Ingolstadt, Germany. He is also Head of the Center for Advanced Studies of Eurac Research, Bolzano-Bozen, Italy. He holds an Adjunct Research Professorship at the School of Management and Marketing at Curtin Business School at Curtin University, Australia. He researches, teaches and publishes on destination governance/recovery, leadership and design, entrepreneurship, and global challenges for regions and destinations. He is President of AIEST (International Association of Scientific Experts in Tourism) and full member of the European Academy of Sciences and Arts.

Hannes Thees is a Ph.D. student at the Chair of Tourism and Center for Entrepreneurship, Catholic University of Eichstätt-Ingolstadt, Germany. He is also a Senior Analyst at the German Competence Center for Tourism. Besides a dedication to tourism development, his main research fields are the New Silk Road and its local implementation, entrepreneurial ecosystems, governance of regions and destinations, technological development in tourism, and regional cooperation.

Wei Manske-Wang is Professor for International Business and Head of China Center at the Management Center Innsbruck, The Entrepreneurial School in Innsbruck, Austria, and Head of China Center—A bridge between Europe and China for students, academia, industries and society, which was established at MCI in May 2021. Wei was born in Shanghai, PR China, she completed her bachelor's degree in Germanistik & Tourism in China and studied Business Administration with Honors and PhD in Economics in Germany. Wei has worked for a Bavarian "hidden champion" for 14 years and gained extensive insights into internationalization and led projects in Marketing, Sales, Strategy and R&D.

Entrepreneurship in China: Autoethnographic Insights into a Pulsating Entrepreneurial Society

Maximilian Scheu and Andreas Kuckertz

Abstract This chapter provides a unique perspective on the Chinese entrepreneurial landscape via insights that result from a combination of evidence drawn from the academic literature and the lead author's experience from living for over two years in China. That experience underpins an autoethnographic account of entrepreneurship in China. That account is accompanied by reflections on China's entrepreneurship-backed rise, the idea of mass entrepreneurship, and characteristics of China's environment that affect entrepreneurship. This paper thus offers readers a first impression of the reality of entrepreneurship in China. It also provides real-world entrepreneurial insights into China from a foreign perspective. Those general impressions could equip readers to identify promising research paths and understand differences to the Western system.

Keywords China · Entrepreneurship · Autoethnography

1 Introduction

China only opened up to foreign trade and investment in the late 1970s but has since developed from one of the poorest countries in the world to a leading nation for commercialization, innovation, and mass entrepreneurship. This ongoing development at a previously unknown pace prompted the emergence of various entrepreneurial ecosystems. Beijing, Shanghai, and Shenzhen are among the world's most promising examples (Startup Genome, 2019). They are the birthplace of numerous so-called unicorns—startups valued at more than a billion US dollars.

Nevertheless, from a Western perspective, knowledge of the emergence of China's entrepreneurial society, its entrepreneurial ecosystems, and its successful startups lags far behind the knowledge of Western counterparts (Cao & Shi, 2020). Generally, one should view "entrepreneurship in transition economies. . .through a

M. Scheu · A. Kuckertz (✉)
University of Hohenheim, Entrepreneurship Research Group, Stuttgart, Germany
e-mail: maximilian.scheu@uni-hohenheim.de; andreas.kuckertz@uni-hohenheim.de

H. Pechlaner et al. (eds.), *The Clash of Entrepreneurial Cultures?*, FGF Studies in Small Business and Entrepreneurship, https://doi.org/10.1007/978-3-030-97050-5_2

different lens than one grounded in Western assumptions and values" (Puffer et al., 2010, p. 460). This is especially the case for China owing to its different values and systems (Tan, 1996; Chen, 2001). Chinese super startups, such as Meituan, DJI, Ele. me, or pinduoduo, to name but a few, are barely known beyond China's borders, at least not in the West. However, those enterprises were founded in the previous two decades and are now worth billions of dollars and successfully serve hundreds of millions of customers. Confronting Western experts on entrepreneurship with the names of such Chinese startups or locations famed for entrepreneurship such as Zhongguancun (a specific district of Beijing primarily known for innovation and entrepreneurship) seldom elicits any recognition.

This chapter aims to reduce that knowledge gap and contribute to the academic literature by sharing first-hand experience and knowledge about China's entrepreneurial ecosystems, particularly in the greater Shanghai area. Our approach should be considered autoethnographic (Adams et al., 2015); that is, the lead author's reflection on the direct experience of the entrepreneurial ecosystem of Shanghai is allied with insights from the broader literature familiar to the remainder of the author team. Having studied at a Chinese university with a focus on innovation and entrepreneurship, the lead author engaged with the entrepreneurial ecosystem of Shanghai by conducting research, hosting and facilitating entrepreneurial events, and working with a startup. During that time, he has undertaken several steps of the entrepreneurial process, spent countless hours with both Chinese entrepreneurs and those of other nationalities and entrepreneurship facilitators, and worked as a consultant advising a Chinese startup for several months. That specific experience permits the author to offer a sophisticated and—from a Western perspective—unique view on entrepreneurial activity in China.

Consequently, this chapter offers the Western reader a nuanced picture of China's entrepreneurial landscape and a glimpse of the map of China's innovation landscape. Moreover, it provides real-world insights and entrepreneurial perspectives on China from a foreign point of view. We share the most impactful and lasting impressions, clearly distinctive from the Western (entrepreneurial) experience. Finally, these general impressions may point the reader to promising areas of research that deserve more comprehensive investigation. The many conversations among the author team on Chinese entrepreneurship and how it differs from the Western experience led to delimiting the focus of this chapter to three main topics and combining prior literature with individual experience. Those topics are the rise of entrepreneurship in China, the emerging phenomenon of entrepreneurship for the masses, and environmental dynamics, each of which we explore below.

2 China's Entrepreneurial Rise and the Emergence of its Entrepreneurship Culture

If we are to understand the entrepreneurial rise of the country, we must at least review the events of the last century in China. Entrepreneurship is a relatively new phenomenon in China's long history. In particular, the turbulent first half of the twentieth century in the country brought extensive political and economic changes. When the Republic of China followed the imperial dynasties and overthrew existing institutions, private businesses and companies emerged, just to be overthrown again following the accession to power of the Chinese Communist Party (CCP) in 1949. It took almost 30 years before the government reformed economic policy and prompted the re-emergence of private businesses. Since that time, entrepreneurial growth has occurred in several waves. Dai et al. (2019) describe three types of entrepreneurs in China who have appeared since the advent of the open door policy introduced by Deng Xiaoping in December 1978. We argue that this categorization should be extended to include a fourth type: those who follow the most recent developments in China's entrepreneurial landscape.

The first generation of Chinese entrepreneurs founded their businesses immediately after the reforms in 1979, despite the legal environment still being in flux (Huang, 2012; Dai et al., 2019). Low entry barriers characterized these businesses, which rarely required much capital or technology, but met everyday demands for goods and services such as selling agricultural products, operating as street vendors, or setting up barbershops. These businesses were either a community-owned township and village enterprise (TVE) or privately owned and run *getihus* (Dai et al., 2019; Park & Shen, 2003; He et al., 2019).

The succeeding generation of Chinese entrepreneurs started more complex and technology-driven enterprises in the 1980s and 1990s. These entrepreneurs were frequently well-connected to the government, highly decorated members of the military or the CCP, or managers of state-owned enterprises who privatized them and developed them to work more efficiently. These entrepreneurs set the example for following generations by establishing industrial ventures that entered complex sectors. Famous examples from this period familiar to a Western audience would be Huawei and Lenovo.

As TVEs increasingly became private firms in the 1990s and *getihus* became legal enterprises (Park & Shen, 2003), the entrepreneurial rise of private firms throughout society started. The third generation of entrepreneurs built companies around the start of the new millennium. Those firms were characterized by their innovativeness and their success in establishing new markets and industries. Prominent examples are early internet entrepreneurs like Jack Ma or Robin Li,[1] whose companies have since strongly influenced the whole country and have become entrepreneurial role models for people throughout China. That period saw a

[1] Jack Ma is the founder of the Alibaba Group; Robin Li is the founder of Baidu.

paradigmatic shift toward Western entrepreneurial values such as independence, individualism, and risk-taking on Chinese businesspeople (Ralston et al., 1999). This shift of values favoured the development of China's entrepreneurial spirit.

We suggest updating Dai et al.'s (2019) historical account and argue for adding a fourth type or generation, generation Z, to that classification system. Many of today's entrepreneurs in China were born during or after the 1980s. One group of this generation, the millennials in the Tier 1 cities like Shanghai, Beijing, or Shenzhen, is well equipped with resources that allow them to act entrepreneurially. Some prominent members of this group grew up in families that had profited during China's economic expansion in the 1980s and were thus relieved of the onus of escaping the poverty that hindered their predecessors. In contrast, these younger generations enjoyed a good education, and their members are frequently the only descendant of the family due to the CCP's longstanding one-child policy. The entrepreneurial role models of the prior generation inspire them, and they prioritize lifestyle and meaningful work over job security and income alone. As a result, they have the freedom to act entrepreneurially. The other group, those from less privileged households, sees the opportunity for upward social mobility offered by being self-employed and earning an income considerably above the average level that is necessary to keep pace with the dramatic increase in living costs in Tier 1 cities.[2]

3 Top-Down Mass Entrepreneurship and the Competition for Entrepreneurship

China's entrepreneurial rise was not only a result of a paradigmatic shift of values but also a political decision. The government's top-down approach to fostering entrepreneurship and the support of private value creation through entrepreneurship contributed to this entrepreneurial rise.

Mass entrepreneurship[3] was a key objective in the CCP's thirteenth 5-year plan in 2015 and remained so in the fourteenth 5-year plan. As such, "the Chinese government is spending significant amounts of money aiming at developing ecosystems for entrepreneurship across China" (Chen et al., 2020, p. 2). While some criticized the government for failing to provide the necessary institutional environment for entrepreneurship before the twenty-first century (Zhou, 2014), the fundamental change of policy regarding economic development with the dismantling of trade restrictions and the increase in private ventures led to the rapid growth of the Chinese economy (Jian et al., 2021). Although there is still a difference between rural and urban areas, the institutional environment generally supports entrepreneurship (Luo & Chong,

[2] Chinese Tier 1 cities have housing costs that might exceed those of, for instance, New York, Paris, or London.

[3] "Everyone is an entrepreneur, creativity of the masses" (大众创业, 万众创新)

2019). Furthermore, the central government has set a goal of becoming a global innovation leader by 2035 through the promotion of technology. The provinces, cities, and even districts compete to contribute to reaching that goal. Hence, the authorities implement institutional intermediaries to support the emergence of innovative ventures. Specifically, innovation and science parks promote flourishing ecosystems and are frequently run by the government (Armanios et al., 2017).

When the lead author first became involved in Chinese entrepreneurial society, the competition to attract startups and innovation had already become noticeable between the entrepreneurial ecosystems and within single ecosystems of a city. Government officials were competing for entrepreneurial talent to promote their favoured ecosystem or district, establishing high-tech parks in almost every district of the larger cities. They attract entrepreneurs by offering benefits like free-tax offers or free office space, among other incentives, for startups. Moreover, build-measure-learn cycles are far shorter in China if a new form of technology is deemed attractive. Large ecosystems like those of Shanghai, Shenzhen, or Beijing directly report to the central government rather than to an intermediary provincial government. That allows for the swift implementation of special rights. Government can administer new policies faster, tailor them to a particular area, and an ecosystem can be pushed systematically in a promising direction. Shenzhen served as a test ecosystem for new mobility and consequently became a global leader in electromobility. Beijing developed a robust ecosystem for artificial intelligence startups; Shanghai is strong in e-commerce and gaming, among others. There is no single entrepreneurial ecosystem equivalent to the United States' Silicon Valley. Instead, China developed different ecosystems with different strengths. One thing all Chinese ecosystems have in common, however, is the strength of large numbers. Ongoing urbanization means all of China's business hubs are metropoles that house millions of people. Therefore, a single entrepreneurial ecosystem has enormous potential to experiment with business models, serve customers, and create a critical mass of early adopters of new technologies.

4 The Environment: Huge Markets and Incredible Speed

Speed characterizes the Chinese entrepreneurial environment to a large degree, as can be deduced from the lead author's experience:

I was working with a Chinese startup in Shanghai. They were new to the city and looking for an office location. On a Saturday, we went to see different locations of which none was suitable. Then, I coincidentally saw an attractive studio on Weixin[4] *close by. From contacting the agent to signing the contract, it took only 3 hours. On Sunday, they started to remodel the place; a week later, the company opened up a*

[4]WeChat, Chinese all-rounder smartphone application.

fully decorated and ready-to-operate office space. I was intrigued by the speed of China once again.

China has the largest domestic market globally, and the purchasing power of that market of 1.38 billion people is increasing, giving rise to unique dynamics and rules. There are sufficiently large niche markets for any business, and the competition for successful business models is fierce. Although China's institutional system does have its voids (Zhang et al., 2016) and bureaucracy remains a challenge for private firms (Ahlstrom & Ding, 2014), bureaucratic processes have eased over the last years. Nevertheless, China is very bureaucratic in many regards, and the freedom to do business has room for improvement (World Bank, 2020).[5] A setting that allows rapid changes that the central government does not trigger might not seem appealing to entrepreneurs; however, in China, the situation feels like a wholly different story.

The phenomenon of China speed (Zhong & Krosinsky, 2020) is a crucial characteristic of Chinese entrepreneurship. Informal institutions work at a fast pace. The use of digital resources, permanent reachability, and the publicly debated 996 work ethic[6] in startups (Li, 2019) set the competitive frame for entrepreneurs. The overall speed must be high to stay at the competitive edge. The market is constantly changing, and startups have to keep pace with these changes to reach their customers. This speed also brings many opportunities. Chinese customers are inquisitive about new technologies and early adoption. Products do not need to be perfectly fine when they launch; instead, customers support the development process. If an entrepreneur cannot quickly refine the product to meet the customers' wishes, a competitor will do so. Hence, we argue that the market size brings about the dynamics that accelerate entrepreneurial processes and galvanize the whole ecosystem. Technology adoption is very high as the Chinese have leapfrogged some steps deemed essential in the West.[7]

Moreover, the sheer size of Chinese ecosystems means there is a high density of the components of a single entrepreneurial ecosystem (e.g., following Spigel, 2017). Major Chinese cities have extensive infrastructure, research facilities, multinational enterprises (MNEs), talent, entrepreneurial facilitators, and customers. The whole demographic structure of these ecosystems differs from Western ones. A business model requiring a critical mass will find it easier to develop in a Chinese mega-ecosystem than in the more fragmented ecosystems of the West. Shanghai serves as a great example because, with around 25 million inhabitants, it is one of the largest metropolises both in China and the world. With its history characterized by elements of foreignness and business for over 150 years, Shanghai is the most international and business-driven city in China. More than 700 MNEs have their Chinese or Asia-

[5] The ease of doing business generally has ameliorated within the legislative period of PRC chairman Xi Jinping from being ranked 91st in 2012 (World Bank, 2012) to 31st in 2019 (World Bank, 2020) globally.

[6] 996—from 9 am to 9 pm, 6 days a week.

[7] E.g., mobile payment. Mobile payment technology is widespread throughout China, while not everybody has a debit card.

Pacific regional headquarters in Shanghai (Xinhua, 2019), making it mainland China's financial and business capital. The entrepreneurial ecosystem hosts most foreign startups countrywide and is particularly strong in service, e-commerce, and software (Gothe et al., 2019). According to Startup Genome (2019, p. 145), Shanghai hosts several thousand angel investors, several hundred research institutions, and more than 3000 software startups, making it one of the most favourable environments for new technology ventures globally.

5 Concluding Thoughts on China's Entrepreneurial Landscape

The surrounding institutions affect entrepreneurship (Welter, 2011) and entrepreneurial ecosystems. China's entrepreneurial culture and entrepreneurial ecosystems are developing in both endogenous and exogenous terms. Governmental policies foster innovation and encourage the establishment of new firms to change the country to become an international pacesetter for new technology, meaning considerable support is directed to developing world-class entrepreneurial ecosystems. The endogenous development comes about through the changing perception of entrepreneurship within society. The younger generation gives the impression of rarely addressing the consequences of failing while the opportunity cost of founding an enterprise seems lower than in the West. Instead, individuals with the courage to become an employer and exploit an opportunity are admired. The wish for independence that goes along with being responsible for one's own firm seems stronger in China than in Europe. The possibility to make it from rags to riches motivates nascent entrepreneurs from less developed areas.

The power of large numbers catalyses this new entrepreneurial culture when paired with governmental support on all levels. Chinese entrepreneurial hotspots are mega-cities with millions of people. That combination allows business models that require rapidly acquiring a critical mass to work even as a city-based business. Moreover, the competition is agile and forces entrepreneurs to act and react quickly. Therefore, we assume that China's entrepreneurial ecosystems will produce more impactful startups, and internationalization to and from China will increase in the future. In addition, China is actively establishing new markets and firms abroad to serve its vision of reactivating the Silk Road, the so-called Belt-and-Road-Initiative (Pechlaner et al., 2020). Therefore, it will be even more critical to strengthen the competencies around entrepreneurship in China from a Western perspective.

Acknowledgements This research results from the Research Area "Innovation, Entrepreneurship, and Finance (INEF)" at the University of Hohenheim's Faculty of Business, Economics, and Social Sciences.

References

Adams, T. E., Holman Jones, S., & Ellis, S. (2015). *Autoethnography: Understanding qualitative research*. Oxford University Press.

Ahlstrom, D., & Ding, Z. (2014). Entrepreneurship in China: An overview. *International Small Business Journal, 32*(6), 610–618.

Armanios, D. E., Eesley, C. E., Li, J., & Eisenhardt, K. M. (2017). How entrepreneurs leverage institutional intermediaries in emerging economies to acquire public resources. *Strategic Management Journal, 38*(7), 1373–1390.

Cao, Z., & Shi, X. (2020). A systematic literature review of entrepreneurial ecosystems in advanced and emerging economies. *Small Business Economics, 57*, 75–110.

Chen, M. J. (2001). *Inside Chinese business: A guide for managers worldwide*. Harvard Business School Press.

Chen, J., Cai, L., Bruton, G. D., & Sheng, N. (2020). Entrepreneurial ecosystems: What we know and where we move as we build an understanding of China. *Entrepreneurship and Regional Development, 32*(5–6), 370–388.

Dai, S., Wang, Y., & Liu, Y. (2019). The emergence of Chinese entrepreneurs: Social connections and innovation. *Journal of Entrepreneurship in Emerging Economies, 11*(3), 351–368.

Gothe, M., Zheng, B., & Ramos, O. (2019). A foreign startups guide to China. In the race for innovation. German Chamber Ticker. Shanghai. *Business Journal of the German Chamber of Commerce in China, 2019*(4), 15–16.

He, C., Lu, J., & Qian, H. (2019). Entrepreneurship in China. *Small Business Economics, 52*, 563–572.

Huang, Y. (2012). How did China take off? *Journal of Economic Perspectives, 26*(4), 147–170.

Jian, J., Fan, X., Zhao, S., & Zhou, D. (2021). Business creation, innovation, and economic growth: Evidence from China's economic transition, 1978–2017. *Economic Modelling, 96*, 371–378.

Li, X. (2019). The 996. ICU movement in China: Changing employment relations and labour Agency in the Tech Industry. *Made in China Journal.* Available at https://madeinchinajournalcom/2019/06/18/the-996-icu-movement-in-china-changing-employment-relations-and-labour-agency-in-the-tech-industry/.

Luo, B., & Chong, T. T. L. (2019). Regional differences in self-employment in China. *Small Business Economics, 53*, 813–837.

Park, A., & Shen, M. (2003). Joint liability lending and the rise and fall of China's township and village enterprises. *Journal of Development Economics, 71*(2), 497–531.

Pechlaner, H., Erschbamer, G., Thees, H., & Gruber, M. (2020). *China and the new silk road–Challenges and impacts on the regional and local level.* Springer Nature.

Puffer, S. M., McCarthy, D. J., & Boisot, M. (2010). Entrepreneurship in Russia and China: The impact of formal institutional voids. *Entrepreneurship Theory and Practice, 34*(3), 441–467.

Ralston, D. A., Egri, C. P., Stewart, S., Terpstra, R. H., & Kaicheng, Y. (1999). Doing business in the 21st century with the new generation of Chinese managers: A study of generational shifts in work values in China. *Journal of International Business Studies, 30*(2), 415–427.

Spigel, B. (2017). The relational Organization of Entrepreneurial Ecosystems. *Entrepreneurship Theory and Practice, 41*(1), 49–72.

Startup Genome. (2019). *Global startup ecosystem report 2019.* Available at https://startupgenome.com/reports

Tan, J. (1996). Regulatory environment and strategic orientations in a transitional economy: A study of Chinese private enterprise. *Entrepreneurship Theory and Practice, 21*(1), 31–47.

Welter, F. (2011). Contextualizing entrepreneurship-conceptual challenges and ways forward. *Entrepreneurship Theory and Practice, 35*(1), 165–184.

World Bank. (2012). *Doing business 2013: Smarter regulations for small and medium-size enterprises*. World Bank Publications.

World Bank. (2020). *Doing Business 2020: China's Strong Reform Agenda Places it in the Top 10 Improver List for the Second Consecutive Year.* Available at https://www.worldbank.org/en/

news/press-release/2019/10/24/doing-business-2020-chinas-strong-reform-agenda-places-it-in-the-top-10-improver-list-for-the-second-consecutive-year

Xinhua (News agency). (2019). *Shanghai home to over 700 regional headquarters of multinational corporations*. Available at https://www.chinadaily.com.cn/a/201909/15/WS5d7e022ca310cf3e3556b7cd.html

Zhang, M., Gao, Q., Wheeler, J., & Kwon, J. (2016). Institutional effect on born global firms in China: The role of sun Tzu's the art of war strategies. *Journal of Asia Business Studies, 10*(1), 1–19.

Zhong, H., & Krosinsky, C. (2020). China speed: Modern China's work ethic and sociology. In *Modern China*. Palgrave Macmillan.

Zhou, W. (2014). Regional institutional development, political connections, and entrepreneurial performance in China's transition economy. *Small Business Economics, 43*(1), 161–181.

Maximilian Scheu is a researcher and doctoral student with the University of Hohenheim's Entrepreneurship Research Group. His research interests are international entrepreneurship, institutional influences, and entrepreneurial ecosystems—particularly in cross-cultural and cross-border settings. Maximilian Scheu spent several years in Asia, which helped his research to include current topics of cross-border innovation and entrepreneurship exchange between developed and emerging economies.

Univ.-Prof. Dr. Andreas Kuckertz is head of the Entrepreneurship Research Group at the University of Hohenheim. For FGF e.V., the largest academic association in the German-speaking countries focusing on entrepreneurship, innovation, and SMEs, he has been serving as president since October 2018. He is Associate Editor of the Journal of Business Venturing Insights. International research visits have taken him to the Queensland University of Technology, Turku School of Economics, University of Vaasa, and Cass Business School, among others.

Institutional Differences and Opportunity Exploitation: A Comparison of Managerial Ties Utilization in Asia and Europe

Haowen Chen

Abstract This chapter discusses how differences in distinct institutional environments affect the vital entrepreneurial activity of utilizing managerial ties for opportunity exploitation. Focusing on the comparison between Asia and Europe provides an opportunity for researchers to see entrepreneurs operating in the same global market with strong and consistent rules and, in this case, to examine how the differing institutional settings affect the behavior of entrepreneurs in different markets.

This chapter adopts an institutional theory perspective to investigate entrepreneurial behavior in two regions of the world with disparate institutional environments and enormous regional differences—Asia and Europe. Two typical countries are chosen, China, the largest emerging country in Asia, and Germany, the largest economy in Europe. A comparative study of the differences provides insight into the impact of cultural context and institutional environment on entrepreneurial behavior. The study finds that institutions in these two different environments lead to significant differences in entrepreneurial practices.

By exploring and comparing the relationship between managerial ties and opportunity exploitation in Asia and Europe, this chapter intends to provide a better theoretical understanding of the different behavior patterns of entrepreneurs in divergent institutional contexts.

Keywords Managerial ties · Opportunity exploitation · Institutional theory perspective

1 Introduction

The core of entrepreneurship is opportunity exploitation. To facilitate the opportunity exploitation, existing research has emphasized the importance of utilizing informal institutions such as managerial ties. Geletkanycz and Hambrick (1997)

H. Chen (✉)
Economics and Management School, Wuhan University, Wuhan, China

H. Pechlaner et al. (eds.), *The Clash of Entrepreneurial Cultures?*, FGF Studies in Small Business and Entrepreneurship, https://doi.org/10.1007/978-3-030-97050-5_3

define managerial ties as "executives' cross-border activities and their related interactions with external entities." Based on relationships with different stakeholders, existing research generally distinguishes managerial ties as ties with other firms (including customers, suppliers, and peers), and ties with government (involving relationships with government officials at all levels) (Peng & Luo, 2000). The core logic behind the value of managerial ties is that firms with managerial ties can more easily access resources, such as information flows and political support, from external stakeholders, and therefore firms can improve opportunity identification and hence firm performance (Luk et al., 2008).

We further propose that the effort of managerial ties as informal institution in influencing opportunity exploitation is likely to be contingent on the formal institutions affecting firm's behavior in the process of resource development. The existing literature suggested that managerial ties become less efficient when market forces have a larger influence on business decisions and outcomes (Peng, 2003), following market efficiency logic that is operative in developed European countries such as German where formal market mechanisms (e.g., formal rules for engaging in competition, and free market forces governing the competitive rivalry, actions, and outcomes) are mature, and social norms (normative) place more emphasis on the roles of formal institutions.

However, in some Asian countries, such as China, where the process of economic transformation has provided more market opportunities, social norms place more emphasis on informal institutions, and managerial ties can complement, or even partially replace, formal institutions. In this context, Chinese firms may emphasize the leverage of managerial ties more than German firms. Thus, the mechanisms for using managerial ties to promote opportunity utilization may differ between Germany and China.

Why we choose China and Germany for this comparative study? Because China is the largest economy in Asia, and Germany is the largest economy in Europe, both of which are very representative. China's economic development since the "reform and opening up" has attracted world attention, and Chinese entrepreneurs have become a force to be reckoned with in the world market. Influenced by thousands of years of Confucian culture, Chinese entrepreneurs have a unique attitude toward managerial ties, and today, with the deep development of the market economy, it is worth paying attention to the use of managerial ties for opportunity exploitation by Chinese entrepreneurs. Germany, on the other hand, has a similarly tortuous history, having experienced political wars, regime changes, state transformations and map changes, and the entrepreneurs as an elite class has been deeply affected. The German entrepreneurs' sense of competition and crisis is deep in their bones, and the German entrepreneurs are also known for their craftsmanship, so we are also curious about the German entrepreneurs' focus on managerial ties and how to use them for opportunity exploitation.

What's more, since 2016, China has become Germany's largest global trading partner for 3 years, with bilateral trade accounting for nearly one-third of my trade with the European Union, and Germany has maintained its position as China's largest trading partner in Europe for 44 years. As of 2018, Germany has the highest amount of investments and projects in China among EU countries. Likewise, in terms of Chinese investments in EU countries, Germany is also at the top of the list. China and Germany are important economic and trade partners of each other.

In short, in order to effectively exploit market opportunities, firms need to use managerial ties for opportunity exploitation depending on the institutional environment (Lovett et al., 1999). However, existing research has largely ignored this issue, so two important questions remain: How do ties with other firms and ties with government affect opportunity exploitation? What are the differences between Germany and China in terms of the use of managerial ties for opportunity exploitation? To answer these questions, we integrate institutional theory into entrepreneurship research to enrich our understanding of the contingencies that influence the impact of managerial ties on opportunity exploitation.

2 The Comparison Between Germany and China in Institutional Perspective

From an institutional theory viewpoint, cultural, social norms, and regulation are three key institutional forces which can influence entrepreneurial activities. Both cultural values and social norms as informal institutions are likely to influence formal institutions such as regulations and/or interact with them to affect a firm's strategic choices (Holmes et al., 2012).

1. Cultural

Ancient China pioneered a great agrarian civilization, which is characterized by a self-sufficient agricultural environment, an emphasis on natural cycles, a strict hierarchical order and legal rituals, stability, static, worship of power, and exclusion of risk. The ancient agricultural countries advocated strongman politics and hierarchical order to ensure that orders would be followed thoroughly, that the population would continue to reproduce, and work more.

The ancient Europeans did not have a fertile two-river valley and were forced to wander around for business, one of the very important ways was by sea. The risks of shipping were much greater than farming, so they gradually developed an open, outward-looking, dynamic, and unstable maritime culture, which was the opposite of agrarian culture, and at the same time, they were more receptive to risks and uncertainties, and more daring to take risks and keep contracts (doing business with strangers by contract). Marine culture, with the uncertainty and openness of technology, is highly compatible. Forced to fight for their lives against the sea, Europeans are more interested in freedom, in exploring nature, and in interacting and cooperating with people.

2. Social norms

China has been deeply influenced by Confucianism for thousands of years. Confucianism advocates and upholds hierarchy from the ideological point of view. East Asian intellectuals are deeply influenced by Confucian ideology and culture, blindly pursuing "face (Mianzi)" and hierarchical status, unwilling to admit academic mistakes, and blind faith in authority. The establishment of anti-authority courage and ideology requires the maintenance and establishment of a democratic system, and the establishment of a democratic system is a mutually reinforcing relationship with the formation of democratic consciousness.

China has a special term to describe the relationship between people—Guanxi. Guanxi has existed in China for a long time and is woven like a fine fiber into every person's social life and every aspect of Chinese society. It is embedded in Chinese culture, which has a history of more than 5000 years. Ever since Confucius recorded the hierarchy of social rules, values, and authority in writing in the sixth century BC, Chinese society has functioned like a clan network. Guanxi functions in a series of concentric circles, with close family members at the center and relatives, classmates, friends, and acquaintances arranged at the periphery in order of Guanxi's proximity and level of trust. Guanxi is used to achieve the desired outcome when situations beyond one's capabilities arise (Redding & Ng, 1982).

The cultural basis of Guanxi is Chinese collectivism. Park and Luo (2001) argue that Guanxi is the concept of using connections to obtain help in personal contacts, and they identified "Mianzi" and "Renqing" as two Chinese philosophies related to Guanxi from a Chinese cultural perspective. In order to cultivate and expand a viable Guanxi, a certain level of face (Mianzi) must be maintained (Yeung & Tung, 1996). In essence, reciprocity—an idea inherent in Guanxi—comes from Renqing (human feeling) (TSui & Farh, 1997). When a person does not consider the responsibility of reciprocity, he loses face, hurts the feelings of the people involved (e.g., friends and family), and ultimately poses a danger to Guanxi. In short, Guanxi is a personal relationship, and is instrumental, reciprocal, transferable between subjects, and intangible (Park & Luo, 2001).

The managerial ties described in this paper are also based on the existence of Guanxi. The social networks formed by managers of enterprises, managers of other enterprises, and government officials exist as a channel mechanism for enterprises to compensate for institutional defects and obtain scarce resources. The norms of trust and reciprocity established between firm managers and managers of other firms and government officials, on the other hand, serve as an informal governance mechanism that plays a key role in coordinating and facilitating cooperative collective action among firms and government.

The reason why Europe was able to lead in science and technology in modern times lies firstly in the rise of the Renaissance movement and secondly in the establishment of democracy in various countries. The German sociologist Max Weber, in his famous work "The Protestant Ethic and the Spirit of Capitalism," pointed out the value of the Reformation to the rise of capitalism. The new doctrines and ideas that emerged from the Protestant ethic, such as the spirit of present-day asceticism and the pursuit of realistic living, were highly compatible with the accumulation of capital and pragmatic enterprise required by capitalism. The Protestant ethic gave birth to a by-product that gave people a legitimate secular purpose in the pursuit of self-interest, thus motivating them to gradually escape ignorance and work for personal gain. Protestants choose to "eat comfortably" and pursue the pleasures of this life, while Catholics prefer to "sleep soundly" and cultivate the blessings of the next. Weber finally summarized the ideological basis for the rise of the capitalist market as rationalism. Rationalism in the West was the driving force behind the rise of modern science, free markets, and democracy.

3. Regulation

The great polemic between Keynes and Hayek was the battle between government interventionism and free market thinking. This polemic continues to this day, and the battle between the visible hand and the invisible hand remains fierce. In the perception of many, China favors government interventionism, while Europe is more like the free market. By government intervention, we mean direct government intervention in the economy, such as running state-owned enterprises, raising tariffs, providing financial subsidies, monopolizing markets, etc. Government intervention, with a strong personal touch, will hinder the play of the free market and violate economic laws. However, it is incomplete to simply assume that China is purely government interventionist. China has been market-oriented for more than 40 years and has fully established a market economy. But the huge size of the country and the lack of balanced development between regions have led to different perceptions of the role of the formal and formal institutional complement—the managerial ties—among entrepreneurs in different regions.

3 Ties with Other Firms and Opportunity Exploitation

For Chinese firms, a weaker market system negatively affects their ability to take advantage of new market opportunities. Firms often need to use ties with other firms as an alternative to formal market mechanisms (Zhang & Li, 2010). For example, capital allocation in emerging market is less efficient, so firms can use ties with other firms to obtain needed capital. First, given the significant turbulence and primitive regulations in emerging economies like China, firms need more resources for many purposes, one of which is to exploit opportunities. Second, uncertainty and high business risks are ubiquitous in these economies, and competition is sometimes more unpredictable than in market economies such as Germany (Gu et al., 2010). Due to the imperfect legal system, unfair competition exists in China, and firms rely more on ties with other firms to overcome the weaker formal institution in order to identify and exploit opportunities. Third, because German economic policy tends to favor short-term consumption over long-term investment, opportunities are more concentrated and perhaps easier to identify and exploit. In general, German firms have access to more resources from the market (e.g., information resources from an efficient stock market) for exploiting market opportunities. Therefore, we argue that the positive impact of ties with other firms on opportunity exploitation is greater in China than in Germany.

Ostrom (2005) introduces the concept of institutional polycentrism, arguing that there are multiple institutional centers of power. Therefore, institutional systems are complex and multi-layered (Batjargal et al., 2013; Dau, 2013). For example, the formal systems associated with markets may differ in different regions of the same country. Therefore, it is useful to examine whether ties with other firms have the same impact in regions within a country with more developed market systems as in regions with less developed market systems, which share similar cultural values and social norms. Existing research based on the logic of market efficiency suggests that in highly efficient markets, management ties may have less impact on information flows and transactions. However, due to the prevalence of relational social norms, the effect of ties to other firms remains strong in cultures with efficiently functioning regulations and other mechanisms. However, even in a country like China, firms operating under the same traditional culture and social norms must contend with different levels of market efficiency. The unique institutional attributes of each market system cause them to use these relationships in different ways to take advantage of market opportunities.

As China has increasingly implemented policies to reform and open its markets, the market economy system and market regulations have become more sophisticated, but these changes have been greater in the coastal regions than inland areas. This is partly because China began implementing these reforms first in the coastal regions, where cross-border transactions are easier to conduct. As a result, there are more market opportunities in the coastal regions. To take advantage of these market opportunities, firms use contacts with other firms to obtain resources and timely information, such as new customer preferences, and to identify market trends, including market changes. Moreover, these resources can be used more effectively in markets where there are more opportunities. Thus, in coastal China, cultural values, social norms, and market rules combine to produce a positive impact on opportunity development from ties with other firms.

In contrast, in regions with less developed market systems, such as inland China, market opportunities are much more limited and, therefore, ties with other firms play a weaker role in exploiting market opportunities. Thus, while Chinese culture and social norms emphasize the positive role of ties with other firms, greater influence from the government and weaker market forces make ties with other firms less efficient in these regions. In other words, the positive effects of ties with other firms on opportunity exploitation are stronger in China's coastal regions than in China's inland regions.

4 Ties with Government and Opportunity Exploitation

In a market economy like Germany, ties with the government may have a positive effect on opportunity exploitation, but to a lesser extent. First, existing research provides competing arguments for the relationship between firms and government in a market economy. For example, Hillman and Hitt (1999) examine the process of political strategy formulation and suggest that firms with higher perceived or actual dependence on government policies are more likely to use their ties with government to promote their business operations. Moreover, other studies have shown that market economies usually have a strong legal framework to constrain government power. Thus, compared to emerging economies such as China, governments in market economies generally do not have as much power to allocate resources or enact policies that interfere with the functioning of the market.

Second, German firms try to establish linkages with the government, but more often than not, they lobby the government to enact laws and regulations that are favorable to their industry and even, where possible, to specific firms. Of course, the level of these linkages and lobbying efforts vary from industry to industry. For example, there are some industries that are more dependent on government procurement (e.g., national defense), while others are less dependent on government. Companies that rely on government contracts emphasize their ties with the government to help secure new contracts, while often investing little time and effort in exploiting other new market opportunities. Other firms invest heavily in lobbying efforts to protect their current market leadership and/or market share (e.g., through favorable laws or regulations, such as import restrictions), focus on their current markets, and rarely invest much time and effort in exploiting new market opportunities. Thus, the role of government contacts in leveraging opportunities can be helpful, but generally in a more limited way. Third, because Germany is a political democracy, top government officials change frequently (e.g., every 4 or 8 years). The turnover of officials makes it more difficult for firms to establish long-term relationships with government agencies. Political action in Germany is expensive, and therefore, establishing ties with the government is expensive for firms. Therefore, we propose that relationships with the government have a positive but limited impact on the development of opportunities in Germany.

Chinese firms can benefit by leveraging their ties with the government (Zhou et al., 2008). These ties can help firms gain access to scarce resources that can be used to identify and exploit lucrative opportunities. From the perspective of traditional Chinese culture, firms' ties with the government are key resources, and the prospect of economic growth based on government orientation is a remnant of the planned economy, which in turn influences Chinese firms' strategic decisions. For this reason, Chinese firms tend to use their ties with the government to help them exploit opportunities. However, progressive economic reforms have deeply altered China's market system, and greater market efficiency has affected the value of ties with the government.

In regions with less developed market economy systems, such as inland China, the imprint of norms and value systems inherited from the centrally planned economy remains strong. The market systems in these regions contain more remnants of planned economies, and most firms in these regions still value and emphasize their interface with the government. Businesses in these regions attempt to build personal relationships with local government officials based on a traditional relationship culture. Although local government is encouraged to deregulate business and to reduce its direct involvement in business activities, it still controls a significant portion of strategic resources and has considerable power to approve projects and allocate resources. As a result, managers tend to maintain a disproportionate relationship with government officials because market mechanisms play a weaker role in these areas. In such cases, it is more difficult for firms to obtain resources from the market and thus pursue and exploit new market opportunities without government help. Close ties with the local government can help firms obtain scarce resources such as land, capital, and advance information about industrial planning or relevant policies and regulations, all of which facilitate the exploitation of potential economic opportunities. In general, relationships with the government have had a positive effect on exploiting opportunities in China's interior.

During the economic reforms of the 1980s, the Chinese government established special economic zones in coastal areas to attract foreign direct investment, and these areas gradually developed more Western-style market characteristics and sophisticated infrastructure support, resulting in a more stable competitive environment. As a result, the market economy system in these regions is more mature than inland China, increasing the impact of market efficiency. In these regions, the value of ties with the government becomes more complex.

When the ties with the government rise from low to moderate levels, firms can obtain favorable government support, such as facilitating linkages between the firm and other entities, supporting the development of efficient logistics, and ensuring smooth collection of payments from other firms. In such cases, firms need to spend only a modest amount of resources to maintain linkages with government officials and entities, and can therefore devote more resources to identifying and exploiting opportunities in the marketplace. Thus, establishing and maintaining modest ties with the government can help a business gain government legitimacy without raising suspicions of corruption or nepotism.

Beyond a certain point, however, the strength of the relationship with government will reduce a firm's ability to take advantage of opportunities. First, establishing and maintaining too close ties with government incurs substantial costs, and the resources generated by government ties often require political reciprocity. The requirement for reciprocity may cause firms to limit their opportunity-seeking activities primarily to government-designated activities. Second, firms with overly intensive relationships with government officials tend to experience inertia due to their over-reliance on government help, even when there are significant changes in the environment. Inertia not only reduces the probability of independent problem identification and resolution, but also hinders the introduction and utilization of new ideas. As a result, the efficiency of opportunity development is reduced. Third, companies must invest significant resources to maintain these relationships, and are therefore likely to be locked into less efficient relationships and their outcomes. The value of ties with government depends heavily on the power and success of the government officials involved, and these relationships may lose their value or become a liability if officials are ousted or leave to work elsewhere. Especially as the market system becomes more developed (more open and less dependent on government direction and control), market transaction costs are lower and market self-regulation has a greater impact on business decisions. As a result, firms can find and exploit more opportunities in the market than they can from government guidance. Thus, we conclude that the ties with government have an inverted U-shaped effect on the utilization of opportunities in coastal China.

5 Conclusion

This chapter presents a comparative study of Chinese and German entrepreneurs' use of managerial ties for opportunity exploitation from an institutional theory perspective. We find that the positive effect of ties with other firms to opportunity exploitation is stronger for Chinese entrepreneurs than for German entrepreneurs, and that this positive effect is stronger in the more economically developed coastal areas of China than in the inland China. In the case of ties with government, German entrepreneurs also use this relationship appropriately for opportunity exploitation, while Chinese entrepreneurs choose to maintain moderate ties with government, where either too distant or too close ties with government are detrimental to opportunity exploitation.

Of course, many of these issues have not been fully discussed in this chapter—as they are rarely addressed in the existing literature—but nonetheless they remain critical. Some literature suggests that the role of guanxi is diminishing as China's market-oriented reforms progress (Tan et al., 2009), but the profound impact of cultural will not disappear in just a few decades, and indeed such Guanxi-oriented managerial ties continue to act as a lubricant or even a catalyst in business activities. And as Chinese entrepreneurs expand their territory, the impact of Guanxi culture may spread around the world in the footsteps of Chinese entrepreneurs. In future studies, more convincing evidence to show the changes of managerial ties in Chinese business activities may lead to new theoretical breakthroughs. One of the most pressing issues is that there should be more empirical studies in the future to further prove the speculations derived from theoretical derivations, and a major limitation of the current empirical literature is the U.S.-centric bias. More empirical research on Asian-European comparisons is to be expected and is a severe challenge for empirical research in the coming years.

References

Batjargal, B., Hitt, M. A., Tsui, A. S., Arregle, J.-L., Webb, J. W., & Miller, T. (2013). Institutional polycentrism, entrepreneurs' social networks and new venture growth. *Academy of Management Journal, 56*(4), 1024–1049.

Dau, L. A. (2013). Learning across geographic space: Pro-market reforms, multinationalization strategy, and profitability. *Journal of International Business Studies, 44*(3), 235–262.

Geletkanycz, M. A., & Hambrick, D. C. (1997). The external ties of top executives: Implications for strategic choices and performance. *Administrative Science Quarterly, 42*, 654–681.

Gu, F. F., Hung, K., & Tse, D. K. (2010). When does guanxi matter? Issues of capitalization and its dark sides. *Journal of Marketing, 72*, 12–28.

Hillman, A., & Hitt, M. A. (1999). Corporate political strategy formulation: A model of approach, participation, and strategy decisions. *Academy of Management Review, 24*, 825–842.

Holmes, B., Miller, T., Hitt, M. A., & Salmador, M. P. (2012). The interrelationships among informal institutions, formal institutions, and inward foreign direct investment. *Journal of Management*. https://doi.org/10.1177/0149206310393503

Lovett, S., Simmons, L. C., & Kali, R. (1999). Guanxi versus the market: Ethics and efficiency. *Journal of International Business Studies, 30*, 231–247.

Luk, C., Yau, O., Sin, L., Tse, A., Chow, R., & Lee, J. (2008). The effects of social capital and organizational innovativeness in different institutional contexts. *Journal of International Business Studies, 39*, 589–612.

Ostrom, E. (2005). *Understanding institutional diversity*. Princeton University Press.

Park, S. H., & Luo, Y. (2001). Guanxi and organizational dynamics: Organizational networking in Chinese firms. *Strategic Management Journal, 22*(5), 455–477.

Peng, M. W. (2003). Institutional transitions and strategic choices. *Academy of Management Review, 28*, 275–296.

Peng, M. W., & Luo, Y. (2000). Managerial ties and firm performance in a transition economy: The nature of a micro-macro link. *Academy of Management Journal, 43*, 486–501.

Redding, S. G., & Ng, M. (1982). The role of 'face' in the organizational perceptions of Chinese managers. *Organization Studies, 3*(3), 201–219.

Tan, J., Yang, J., & Veliyath, R. (2009). Particularistic and system trust among small and medium enterprises: A comparative study in China's transition economy. *Journal of Business Venturing, 24*, 544–557.

Tsui, A. S., & Farh, J. L. L. (1997). Where guanxi matters: Relational demography and Guanxi in the Chinese context. *Work and Occupations, 24*(1), 56–79.

Yeung, I. Y. M., & Tung, R. L. (1996). Achieving business success in Confucian societies: The importance of Guanxi (connections). *Organizational Dynamics, 25*(2), 54–65.

Zhang, Y., & Li, H. (2010). Innovation search of new ventures in a technology cluster: The role of ties with service intermediaries. *Strategic Management Journal, 31*, 88–109.

Zhou, K. Z., Poppo, L., & Yang, Z. (2008). Relational ties or customized contracts? An examination of alternative governance choices in China. *Journal of International Business Studies, 39*, 526–534.

Haowen Chen received the Ph.D. degree in management from Xi'an Jiaotong University, Xi'an, China. She is currently an Assistant Professor in the Department of Technical Economics and Innovation Management, Economics and Management School, Wuhan University. She has authored or coauthored many research papers in refereed journals such as Industrial Marketing Management, Asia Pacific Journal of Management, etc. Her current research interests include technology and innovation management, and entrepreneurship.

Total Incomprehension: Why Entrepreneurs from Europe Do Not Understand China: And It Is Getting Worse

Ulrich Bauer

Abstract After considering possible sources for the analysis, it is shown how Western thinking has globalized itself through colonialism, and is now regarded by Westerners as "global normality." In China, this is seen completely differently.

Next, the long-term Chinese strategy to achieve technological world domination is described alongside hard and arbitrary Chinese interventions in their economy, the lack of a rule of law, and the increasing technical and economic detachment from the Western world (decoupling). In this context, entrepreneurs are now mainly needed as "useful idiots" (Lenin) to build and secure Chinese independence and later supremacy.

Finally, attention is drawn to the mostly inadequate training courses for entrepreneurs that instead of tough challenges prefer to give gentle references to a culture that has already passed.

Keywords Intercultural competencies · Chinese world domination

The lack of European understanding that China "functions" very differently from all other non-Western countries, let alone Western countries, is enormous. Incomprehension beyond functional communication is overwhelming. Speechlessness prevails, which both sides mostly are not even aware of. This is mainly due to the ignorance of our own Western assumptions, to the refusal to take seriously the Chinese claim to technological world domination in the first place, and to rapidly changing conditions in China as well as often-outdated trainings to prepare for possible cooperation.

U. Bauer (✉)
Hochschule Kempten–University of Applied Sciences, Kempten, Germany
e-mail: ulrich.bauer@hs-kempten.de

H. Pechlaner et al. (eds.), *The Clash of Entrepreneurial Cultures?*, FGF Studies in Small Business and Entrepreneurship, https://doi.org/10.1007/978-3-030-97050-5_4

1 Introduction

Entrepreneurs should go where they can quickly and efficiently implement their ideas. Does the cultural and historical environment play any role at all? Isn't it just best to go where the gold rush mood promises the greatest and fastest successes? Then China would be your choice.

This contribution focuses on China. While, after decades of economic and legal harmonization in Europe, one may speak of a common area of action with often-similar conditions, this is not the case in Asia. India, China, or the Muslim Republic of Malaysia, for example, are so fundamentally different in legal, economic, cultural, and political terms that it would be thoughtless and unconsidered to speak of "an Asian sphere of action." The growing military and economic threat from China to all neighboring countries makes a hegemonic overpowering of East Asia by the Chinese conceivable (Zhang, 2015). One must rather expect that the Western world will strengthen its contacts with Asian democracies (India, Japan, Indonesia, South Korea, etc.) in order to contain the Chinese dominance. Hence, a peaceful and constructive strengthening of common interest and convergences in Asia is becoming increasingly unlikely.

The ecosystem for every entrepreneurial effort consists of a framework of conditions by the respective state, of legal, infrastructural, and other hard facts, the educational system and the qualification of employees, the financing options, and many other visible factors. In addition, there are a few invisible factors that can promote, prevent, or even damage the starting of a new business. Surprisingly, they are often not taken into account. Even the catastrophic failure of the Western world 2021 in Afghanistan was not due to military, economic, legal, or perhaps infrastructural challenges. It was because of these invisible factors.

"The ignorance of the prevailing social, cultural and political realities in Afghanistan has contributed significantly to the mistakes at the strategic, operational and tactical level," says a report by the US Inspector General for Reconstruction in Afghanistan (Sigar, 2021:71). What applies to the military also applies to companies: one concentrates usually on the visible, on the presentable successes, on quick results. How can it be that so many smart people in companies, in the military, in governments, etc., regularly ignore the invisible factors, even though this has long been known (Hall, 1959) to be important and (often) crucial? How can it be that large sums of money are invested without knowing the social, cultural, and historical framework of action? The reasons for these obvious misjudgments are certainly diverse: one's own knowledge and methods are often grossly overestimated, one believes that what worked at home must work everywhere, one does not appreciate complex factors that cannot be expressed in simple numbers, one looks for fast success instead of long-term developments. Three crucially important issues are particularly rarely taken into account: firstly, one usually does not recognize one's own biases when dealing with a culturally different economic ecosystem—be it for entrepreneurs or otherwise—because one does not even know reasons for and the genesis of one's own biases and has never heard anything about it. Secondly: especially with China, many are not sufficiently informed and naively underestimate how systematically Chinese politics are striving for technological world domination

(Hamilton & Ohlberg, 2020) and to what extent China is already quietly influencing Western discourses and decisions (Weber, 2020). India doesn't, Japan doesn't, Indonesia doesn't, but China does. So cope with it. Thirdly, most training courses for business travelers to China are conducted with outdated material, metaphysical concepts, and without critical examples. You learn how to hand over a business card instead of dealing with the stealing of intellectual property or cyber espionage. Censored media do the rest.

It would be valuable if a consideration like this could include a Chinese perspective. However, the first Chinese universities have now deleted "academic freedom" from their statutes and replaced it with "loyalty to Xi Jinping's thinking" (Weber, 2020). So official studies are increasingly aligned with the party line. Something like this should sound familiar to German entrepreneurs—it was similar in Europe 80 years ago.

In anthropology, the distinction emic-etic was introduced for this change of perspective in 1954 (Headland et al., 1990), but always with the reservation that the person who created a description "from the outside" (etic) only required the perspective "from the inside" (emic) as an informant. The two perspectives are never of equal value in cultural research, because that would be naive in view of the author's inevitable bias, as well as the often questionable role of emic informants.

In fact, three options would be possible as a Chinese perspective: (a) Chinese authors in China, (b) Chinese authors abroad, and (c) non-Chinese authors who have lived in China for a very long time.

Since China is a totalitarian dictatorship in which an estimated two million Internet censors alone can nip any free expression in the bud, and another two million government employees constantly praise the party and all official decisions (internet trolls that form the famous 50-cent-army) you don't expect free expressions in China in writing. The way to the prison camps is short. Therefore, this source cannot be used sensibly unless you want to become a propaganda organ of the Chinese dictatorship (Hamilton & Ohlberg, 2020).

The question of whether overseas Chinese could be an emic source of information is even more complicated. First, it does not mean anything to the quality as a source that someone is Chinese. That would lead to an argument like "Only blondes can write about blondes." It is also known that Chinese authorities abroad approach their citizens and demand that they cooperate. "There is a hitherto little understood lively scene of *united front* organizations [. . .], largely targeting and catering to the Overseas Chinese community, delivering a unified message about the motherland and uniting the diaspora ideologically. The influence thus exerted seems focused [. . .]" (Weber, 2020:3). Authors who can evade such pressure are considered here as long as they write in English. However, many of these free authors personally have a very critical relationship with China, which stems from memories of the terror of the Cultural Revolution, among other things.

Finally, there are Western managers and authors with an affinity for China who live in China and may have taken a Chinese perspective. Many of them stay in China because they have come to terms with the system, with spying and controls, and are foregoing a critical analysis of the situation. It is said that they pay a high price for it. Jamil Anderlini, editor-in-chief of POLITICO Europe and a good expert on the situation on site, judges: "The Stockholm syndrome, named after a notorious robbery in the Swedish capital in 1973, is a phenomenon in which the victim of kidnapping or hostage-taking develops feelings of trust, affection or sympathy for their captor. It is a condition that afflicts much of the corporate world and some governments when it comes to their dealings with the Chinese Communist party" (Anderlini, 2021).

2 Western Ignorance

Let us begin with the first issue: the extensive ignorance of our own, culture-bound perspective on the world. This problem applies to Westerners as well as Chinese, albeit for completely different reasons. For reasons of space, we will only take a closer look at the Western perspective here. As an entrepreneur from the Western world, one knows about important global institutions, the World Bank, the UN, the World Monetary Fund (WMF), the World Intellectual Property Organization (WIPO), etc. All are structured according to Western legal concepts, all apparently apply worldwide. Many further global institutions also seem to have universalized Western thinking in economic, political, and legal aspects. This may lead to the dangerously wrong impression that Western modernity has successfully universalized itself all over this planet and all dance to the music of the Enlightenment. Is that really so?

The title of this book makes a complicated reference to Huntington's well-known title of "The Clash of Civilizations" (Huntington, 1996). Complicated because our book—in contrast to Huntington's—bears the title "Culture," and because the concepts of "culture" and "civilization" are both highly complex and there is still no solid consensus on their interpretation to this day. In addition, they often are incorrectly translated as *false friends* in various European languages, let alone Chinese.

Even if Huntington's book has been (and still is) heavily criticized for many good reasons, and even if its simplification to concentric cultural circles with lively changing criteria (sometimes religious, then geographical, then again historical) is catchy, but certainly not consistent, so it does contain thoughts that are worth considering, which we shall take up here.

Huntington writes that "the West" must also take into account values of other cultures in order to avoid new global conflicts. He strongly emphasizes that it would be a mistake to equate modernization with Western culture or Westernization. The values of the West are not being recognized as universal values in most other cultures. We understand the term "West" not as "culture," but as a series of massive leaps in rationality that began with the Renaissance 1450 and developed through Protestant reforms 1550, the Enlightenment 1750, and the French Revolution 1789 to the idea of inalienable, *individual* human rights. This gradual introduction of reasoning replaced religious or merely power-driven reasons for action and led toward an increasingly objective, rational organization of the (Western) world. Rule *of* law instead of rule *by* law, norm-driven differentiated organizations, a self-universalizing structure of modern statehood, and a high formal rationality of its institutions were evolving subsequently. This gradual process took five centuries and has only taken place in this form in Europe (Winkler, 2019). It has subsequently been exported to North America (and Australia, New Zealand, etc.) through colonization since the seventeenth century. In eighteenth-century Europe, a large number of individual rights developed (free speech, democracy, property, inviolability of the home, confidentiality of letters, freedom of study and teaching, etc.). These rights are taken for granted and demanded in the "West." However, only around 10% of all people on this planet live in this context.

In the twentieth century, especially in the aftermath of the Second World War, the organizational forms, economic models, legal structures, and institutions of these 10% then became the template and global model for practically all world organizations such as the UN, UNESCO, WHO, WTO, OECD, etc. The 90% of people who historically do not belong to the "West" have joined these institutions in their respective countries. In this way, the illusion could arise that this rational, objective, and differentiated organizational model of the Western world, which guarantees so many rights for individuals, would apply to all and would also be desirable for all. From the point of view of most people in the world (90%), neither is the case. The idea that global modernity was a somehow universal, Western modernity is just a Western illusion.

For Westerners it may be very difficult to accept that the fortuitous historical dynamics of the nineteenth and twentieth centuries, which made the values of such a small minority binding for the entire world, will not last forever. This is even truer as the international agreements that are so important, for example, for entrepreneurs (protection of intellectual property, freedom of thought, etc.) breathe a Western spirit and were also signed by China and others, but are in situ not implemented in the spirit, they are meant to be.

The illusion of having globalized one's own values goes hand in hand with the uncomfortable embarrassment of having to admit that one cannot achieve this personally in the place. So it is not surprising that entrepreneurs who work in China prefer to remain silent about their problems with surveillance and control. In their daily operations, many of these companies face intellectual property theft, unpredictable and predatory policymaking, intrusive surveillance by secret police, and the threat of exit bans or employee arrest arising from ordinary business disputes (Anderlini, 2021). Because Beijing has punished so many companies and countries for a range of perceived political slights, many entrepreneurs in China keep quiet. But they tend to blame politicians, media, or human rights groups in their home countries for antagonizing their oppressors.

3 Chinese Policy: Striving for Technological World Domination

During the past 2000 years, China has been the largest or second largest economic power on the planet about 90% of the time (Maddison Project, 2021), and mostly the largest political power as well. It was not until the nineteenth century that this changed and led to a rapid and deep crash. Today's Chinese leadership wants to regain old glory and is ready to act actively, hard, and systematically against the Western model of thinking and acting.

While Western entrepreneurs, almost drunk with enthusiasm for China, rave about the infinite possibilities, the largest market in the world and the lack of the oh so annoying regulations regarding human rights, the environment, labor law, etc., they probably overlook that the least suspected, but mostly simple naively assumed protection of their ideas and activities is not guaranteed at all in China. In any case, the Chinese state will not guarantee such rights, neither for Westerners nor for Chinese. Since the beginning of 2020, the number of brutal political interventions by the Communist Party in economic activity has even increased significantly. China is state capitalist. Many companies are owned by the state (Grünberg, 2021). There is neither a free market nor a neutral legal framework for it. The private sector that it authorizes is widely controlled. If you want to be a successful entrepreneur, you have to be a member of the party (as a Chinese) and, as a foreigner, at least approve and praise all orders without criticism. Foreign companies have to accept that party members take a seat in their Chinese branches. The distinction between "public" and "private" that we know in Europe does not exist in China. In the early 2000s, it looked as if China was liberalizing its economy both internally and externally. In the West, it was hoped that this would lead to political reforms, in keeping with the motto "change through trade." That has proven terribly naïve (Grünberg, 2021). With the crackdown on fintechs (2019), on crypto currencies (2020), or on online games for young people (2021), the party has shown that they can intervene quickly and hard in the market by decree. There have been such options in Germany before, too, but that was 75 years ago.

While other countries in Asia accept the globalized Western standards as beneficial, some even actively promoting them, China has been taking a different path since the turn of the millennium. Thirty years after the end of the bipolar world, a new bipolar world is emerging: China and its vassals against the West. In the digital world, this can already be seen as a widely completed development: all countries in this world will have to decide in the future which digital world they want to belong to: Google or Baidu, WhatsApp or Weixin, Amazon or Alibaba, Infineon or Huawei, etc. China operates a targeted strategy to shut out Western competitors from the strategically most important fields: decoupling (European Chamber, 2020).

The Berlin think tank *Mercator Institute for China Studies* (MERICS), perhaps the best source of information about China today, has worked with the European Chamber of Commerce in Beijing to produce a study that drastically describes this systematic decoupling from the West (European Chamber, 2021). China is interested in entrepreneurs as long as their ideas can be used for Chinese goals. For more than 15 years, China's leaders have advanced extensive industrial policies in an attempt to develop self-reliance in critical technologies and seek global dominance in high-value-added industries. The now infamous China Manufacturing 2025 (CM2025) initiative, which aims to substitute global competitors in ten strategic technologies, was just the most visible expression of a deeply engrained and extensive support system that protects China's own industry against entrepreneurs from outside.

For entrepreneurs with a view to China, two strategies are of particular importance: (1) innovation decoupling—research and development (R&D); standards will be defined in Beijing in the future; and (2) digital decoupling—data governance, network equipment, and telecommunications services controlled by the Communist Party. Both strategies—in connection with the very problematic Chinese patent system—mean that entrepreneurs can only do what the communist party allows, and only as long as it allows it. The decision to hinder or damage Western entrepreneurship in China is usually implemented administratively, or Chinese competitors are allowed to out-boot their Western partners, to take over their knowledge, and to use their training on site until they are no longer needed. Western victims usually walk away silently. It is neither sensible nor really possible to legally defend oneself against the influence of the party and political interests. Firstly, there is no strict civil law in China (the civil law implemented in early 2021 mainly deals with family law, inheritance law, etc.) (Civil Code, 2020), secondly, there are no independent courts, and thirdly, after that, one would probably no longer have any opportunities to do business in China. However, one also has to realize that the Chinese market is not as big as China likes to claim. Around 500 million Chinese live on a level with Europeans—the two markets are rather comparable. The rest of them live in poverty or extreme poverty, despite all government propaganda (Welthungerhilfe, 2021).

In contrast to all other Asian countries—and in contrast to Europe—China has a clear, long-term strategy. The country is a dictatorship with a controlled state capitalism. It can best be understood by looking at the German Third Reich. Similarities are stunning. The almighty party cultivates an extensive leadership cult, organizes industry according to strategic goals, and uses the spineless legal system to achieve its goals. Anyone who expresses themselves critically in public disappears into camp detention. In addition, there is a lot of agitation in the Chinese media against anyone who is even timidly critical of the system. Hence, hardly anyone would utter anything that runs counter to the official party line.

4 Preparation for Entrepreneurs Going to China

The number of training courses currently offered for international engagement in general, be it economic, legal, or—this is the normal case—cultural preparations, is enormous. The training offered is based on the assumption that there are reliable framework conditions and that above all technical-practical questions (financing, logistics, accommodation, personnel recruitment, local building permits, and the like) have to be addressed and that cultural challenges (how to negotiate, how trust is built, etc.) are important. That's not enough for China. The usual training courses do not assume that one would like to become entrepreneurially active in a dictatorship that has explicitly set itself the goal of technological world domination (Hass, 2021), and whose controlled state capitalism has all kinds of non-tariff obstacles at its disposal and also takes the freedom to ignore international institutions and agreements whenever that is useful. What works well on a large scale ("Hong Kong? There's no such thing as an internationally binding contract!"), works even better on a small scale. Entrepreneurs who are inadequately informed and lose a lot in China are unlikely to admit it publicly. Therefore, there is also a serious lack of real and true examples for the actual challenges when planning the content of trainings. The rule is that problems are whitewashed, and afterwards nobody wants to admit that they should have been better informed beforehand.

The qualification of the trainer usually consists of more or less personal experience and occasionally (good) language skills that are anecdotally prepared and supplemented with facts about the country. The usual management speak is rarely about risks, but mainly about opportunities. Western self-censorship then meets Chinese censorship—both complement each other. That is not enough for China. Instead of dealing with hardware Trojans that Chinese semiconductor manufacturers build into the devices of Western entrepreneurs (Ender et al. (2020)), one learns to eat with chopsticks. Instead of dealing with the 36 stratagems (hide the dagger behind the smile) of everyday Chinese business (von Senger, 2006), you will learn something about the seating arrangements in Chinese negotiations. Instead of analyzing the influence of the Chinese Communist Party on banks, companies, and authorities, one learns a little calligraphy.

The topicality of the training usually leaves a lot to be desired. While the Chinese themselves like to rave about their 2000-year history, one should rather concentrate on the last 2000 days, so fast is change in China. Most of what structurally applies to training courses on India, Japan, Singapore, or Korea (business protocol, negotiation, small talk, drafting contracts, etc.) is not sufficient for China. In contrast to all other Asian countries, it is necessary to explain a dictatorship with deep, daily interventions in economic activity and that ownership structures (also in joint ventures) are by no means always clear. Companies as big and professional as Yahoo have been forced out of the Chinese market by outsourcing their stake in the joint venture to a new (Chinese only) company without Yahoo even realizing it in time (Scheuer, 2018). We don't like to talk about such occurrences, but that can happen to any entrepreneur.

People have a basic need to find their way around the world. Orientation systems learned in childhood and adolescence help. In the first years of life, a person acquires values and routines, as well as a social role. This process is called *enculturation*, and its goal and result is that a person understands his world and can deal with it in the same way as other people in the respective culture do. During the enculturation process, people acquire "handy tools" with which they can orientate themselves in the world without much thought. However, we are usually not aware of our values, our ideals, and our heroes, and therefore behave according to patterns that are not clear to us. Most training courses ignore dealing with those Western preconditions, which can quickly become a dangerous self-handicap for entrepreneurs in China. In addition to the naive belief in the universalized Western values such as contractual loyalty, legal compliance, and honesty, these are above all historical values and ideals: the white knight, the Ten Commandments, the ideal of the honorable merchant, etc. We learned such values in a Western childhood, we expect them elsewhere and if others do not behave accordingly, we do not know what to do (Thomas, 2006). Very few training courses really help with the necessary relativization of such personal values. However, this relativization would be the prerequisite for becoming entrepreneurially successful in an ecosystem that is characterized by completely different values. In many cases Westerners react to this with a "deficit hypothesis," i.e., they assume that the other has to develop further. That is not enough in China. Here you have a counterpart who has developed *differently* and aggressively rejects Western values. Hardly anyone in the West has learned to deal with it. This attitude in China represents the Chinese elite, the party, and the dictatorship. We do not know how the Chinese people would decide if ever asked. However, a look at Taiwan can provide first clues.

If you actually grapple with the fact that we are facing an opponent of system in China, then the argument that "others" would do equally bad things is tempting. This rhetorical figure is known as "what-aboutism" and it promotes a dangerous argumentative leveling of the difference in values. This is exactly one of the aims of Chinese propaganda. Dictatorship should be on an equal footing with democracy. This is also where an entrepreneur has to decide what values he has. It is not about "totalitarian China" wanting to subjugate the "free West." There is more than one China, and a distinction must be made between the people and the party. However, the Chinese party leadership wants to maintain absolute dictatorial power in its own country and to maximize its security by expanding its influence to the entire world. At least that is how it can be read in the official party programs (Pillsbury, 2015).

5 Media, Censorship, and the Chinese View

Entrepreneurs are well informed above average. That is part of their success. However, it is not all clear what enormous sums China is investing in manipulating Western public opinion and in creating manipulated "knowledge." No other Asian country, no other country in the world at all does something like this (Hamilton & Ohlberg, 2020). China strategically uses the economic hardships of Western publishers in order to buy platforms in serious guise for its propaganda. In the USA, but also in Germany, large sums of money flow into advertisements and inserts in renowned newspapers and magazines (*Handelsblatt*, *Financial Times*, *Wall Street Journal*, etc.). One can already see from the titles that this is about manipulating decision-makers and entrepreneurs. The fact that the quality of the texts in these advertisements or inserts does not meet the standards of the leading media hardly plays a role in their impact. Instead, it is the permanent repetition of the Chinese government's manipulative narratives that are supposed to nestle in the subconscious of the recipient. Without a critical classification, they can increasingly develop into "valid arguments" and change points of view. Then, propaganda has already achieved its goal. While many managers still believe that the opening-up policy has continued to develop since Deng Xiaoping, Xi Jinping set the course as early as 2017. He declared that the goal for 2049 (the 100th anniversary of the PRC) was that China would "become a leading global power." Part of that plan includes building a "world-class" military than can fight and win wars (Guardian, 2017).

In China itself, all information has been censored and manipulated for years. The Great Firewall isolates China from the rest of the world, more than two million censors (in addition to very sophisticated technical filters) delete every critical comment on social media in real time (Strittmatter, 2020). Newspapers only write what the party wants, and dissatisfaction becomes diverted into nationalist fantasies of great power, and, among other things, bashing foreigners, their products, and their brands. Without exception, all media are controlled and words such as "separation of powers" or "civil society" are added to the index.

Conversely, the Chinese also find it difficult to understand Western entrepreneurs. From their point of view, Westerners are not only naive and stupid—for example because they adhere to contracts without need—but they are often crude and primitive, for example because they openly address problems. In addition, Europeans frequently are perceived as late colonialists who believe that they can successfully sell their own (Western) values to the entire world as "modernization." However, human rights, freedom of thought and speech, the untouchability of the home or individual freedoms are not a modern success in China. Above all, they disrupt what is considered harmony in China. If everyone accepts a clear hierarchy, at the top of which was historically an emperor and is now the one-party dictatorship, then that is harmonious. Individuals and their ideas can be dispensed with quickly if they contradict this harmony. This is what entrepreneurs should think about before going to China.

At the same time, like the Germans before 1945, more and more younger Chinese are deeply convinced of their own superiority. Their claim to superiority is not based on racism, but on history, which from their point of view is more convincing and justified. Just as in Germany from 1933 onwards there should be an edition of "Mein Kampf" in every household, so today all young Chinese learn "Xi Jinping's thoughts." Universities have put "loyalty to Xi Jinping's thinking" in their statutes (Strittmatter, 2020). The neo-fascist leader cult around Xi combines the narrative of the superior world leader with the (quite understandable) rejection of historical insults. The injuries and humiliations that the West has inflicted on the Chinese—especially their elite—have been horrific indeed. Accordingly, most Chinese have no sympathy for the overstretching of Western concepts to global institutions in the twentieth century, and so China has long been building parallel institutions that will sooner or later openly question the claim to sole representation of the UN, WHO, WTO, Interpol, UNESCO, etc. In doing so, China is pursuing a twofold strategy: while at the same time it is developing its own alternatives, it is also taking over board seats (with votes primarily from Africa) in all international institutions and setting the agenda there (Rogin, 2020). The fact that China today is on the board of the UNHCR means that human rights, massacres in Tibet, mass detainment for Uyghurs, and many other topics are no longer officially addressed. The fact that China is on the board of the WHO has changed the global discussion about COVID significantly and systematically prevented an analysis. The fact that China was able to secure the vice-chairmanship of the World Intellectual Property Organization

(WIPO) in 2021 should give entrepreneurs pause for thought (Rogin, 2020). Today, no important decision can be made in the EU any longer without Chinese approval. Optionally, Portugal, Hungary, or another country that is already dependent on China can be activated as a blockade. This growing power gives self-confidence and, in case of doubt, leads to criticism of the Chinese approach being dismissed: "You are just jealous of the great Chinese success!" Recent studies show that although young Chinese are given access to uncensored information, the majority do not want to read it at all (Strittmatter, 2020). Satisfaction with one's own narrative of glory and superiority is now as great in China as it has been in Europe for two hundred years. Additionally, the party has a multitude of organizations that brainwash and manipulate information and censor the media in China, for Chinese overseas, and the rest of the world. Today, China is more economically capitalist, but politically more communist than it was 20 years ago. That is too little understood in the West. A cooperation on an equal footing only arises when it comes to concrete, practical questions. Entrepreneurial conversation with a Chinese counterpart becomes difficult, even if Western entrepreneurs sometimes don't notice that due to a lack of sensitivity (Liang 2014).

Let's summarize: Most companies' reporting systems imply that successes are loudly cheered, but there prevails an embarrassing silence about the theft of knowledge, data, patents, and experience. This leads to wrong assessments (Office of the United States Trade Representative, 2018). China encourages theft of ideas. The regulatory framework for this in China protects Chinese companies from Western charges, but also protects the Chinese market from Western ideas and, conversely, ensures that Chinese companies can operate worldwide, even if the origin of their ideas is not clear.

Westerners rate their own civilizational progress as exemplary and believe that everyone in the world would like to take on this. That is a terrible misunderstanding. Further, they can hardly imagine that their own values, which prevail in all global institutions, are now being attacked head-on. The idea of a new bipolar world is uncomfortable and scary.

China's will and ability to spy, to generate long-term benefits from manipulative interference in the economy, and to curtail people's freedom are not only underestimated in the West. Rather, one does not want to admit what does not fit into a Western image of justice, freedom, and human rights. In Beijing's economic strategy, intellectual property theft is a feature, not a flaw. The honorable businessman, the fulfilled contract, the pride in one's own reliability—all of this is stupid from the Chinese point of view. There is no historical basis for such ideals in China—there are other ideals instead. Looking for recognition in the world of entrepreneurs, however, one has to speak of courage and resilience, perseverance, and success. Western entrepreneurs, used to being in a safe environment in Europe, will find it hard to believe how severe the repression can become elsewhere.

Anyone who criticizes the Chinese party dictatorship exposes himself. People in the West are quickly referred to as "anti-Chinese," which is not only absurd in terms of the matter, but also reproduces the claim of the Chinese Communist Party to allegedly represent the interests of all Chinese. One may reasonably doubt that. Anyone who rejects criticism of China in this way is serving dictatorship.

Many Western entrepreneurs and companies have been successful in China over the past few decades. They were also needed there for the modernization, but that doesn't mean that they will still be successful there in the future when they are no longer needed. At the moment, China is closing again, and faster than it had ever opened. Many do not want to admit that. As long as entrepreneurs with their ideas, their commitment, and their technology are useful to the Chinese in catching up to the West technologically, militarily, and economically, and, in perspective, overtaking the West and eventually dominating it, they are welcome there and can be very successful. If these conditions no longer exist, there will be no reliable Chinese rule of law and no international institution to protect or save Western entrepreneurs.

The current development is so fast and disruptive that one can hardly dare to make predictions. What is certain, however, is that no additional research is required—the situation is well documented and is being researched further by well-informed specialists and institutions such as the European Chamber of Commerce in China, MERICS, and others. Many well-researched books are available. The problem seems more the attitude of Western entrepreneurs. Caught up in self-enamored fantasies of success, they seem to refuse to imagine an environment without the rule of law, a dictatorship with spies, arbitrariness, theft of ideas, instructions from the party, great corruption, and the sure will to rule the world one day.

References

Anderlini, Y. (2021). *Western Companies in China succumb to Stockholm Syndrome*. Financial Times May 2021. Retrieved July 23, 2021, from https://www.ft.com/content/51e1a437-3aca-42ed-8403-2a05b338622b

Civil Code. 2020 *of the People's Republic of China (Adopted at the Third Session of the Thirteenth National People's Congress on May 28, 2020)*. Retrieved July, 2021, from http://www.npc.gov.cn/englishnpc/c23934/202012/f627aa3a4651475db936899d69419d1e/files/47c16489e186437eab3244495cb47d66.pdf

Ender, M. et al. (2020). *Max Planck institute for security and privacy: Starbleed a full break of the bitstream encryption of Xilinx 7-Series Fpgas*. Retrieved from https://www.usenix.org/system/files/sec20_slides_ender.pdf

European Union Chamber of Commerce in Beijing. (2020). *The annual report*. Retrieved from https://www.europeanchamber.com.cn/en/publications-archive/916/Annual_Report_2020

European Union Chamber of Commerce in Beijing & MERICS. (2021). *Decoupling: Severed ties and patchwork Globalisation*. Retrieved from https://www.europeanchamber.com.cn/en/publications-decoupling

Grünberg, N. (2021). Party-state capitalism under xi: Integrating political control and economic efficiency. In: MERICS (ed.) The CCP's next century: Expanding economic control, digital governance and national security. Retrieved July, 2021, from https://merics.org/en/party-state-capitalism-under-xi-integrating-political-control-and-economic-efficiency

(The) Guardian. (2017). *Xi Jinping speech: Five things you need to know*. Retrieved Oct 18, 2017 from https://www.theguardian.com/world/2017/oct/18/xi-jinping-speech-five-things-you-need-to-know

Hall, E. T. (1959). *The silent language*. Doubleday.

Hamilton, C., & Ohlberg, M. (2020). *Hidden hand: Exposing how the Chinese Communist Party is reshaping the world*. Hardie Grant.

Headland, T., et al. (1990). Emics and Etics: The insider/outsider debate. *Frontiers of Anthropology, 7*.

Huntington, S. (1996). *The clash of civilizations and the remaking of world order*. Simon & Schuster.

Liang, Y. (2014). Culture-specific perspectives of intercultural competence/Kulturspezifische Perspektiven interkultureller Kompetenz. *Interculture Journal., 13*(22), 45–55.

Maddison Project. (2021). *The Maddison historical statistics*. Retrieved Aug, 2021, from https://www.rug.nl/ggdc/historicaldevelopment/maddison/?lang=en

Hass, R. (2021). *Stronger. Adapting America's China strategy in an age of competitive interdependence*. Yale UP.

Office of the United States Trade Representative. (2018). *Report into China's Acts, Policies, and Practices Related to Technology Transfer, Intellectual Property, and Innovation*. Retrieved from https://ustr.gov/about-us/policy-offices/press-office/press-releases/2018/march/section-301-report-chinas-acts

Pillsbury, M. (2015). *The hundred-year Marathon: China's secret strategy to replace America as the superpower*. Holt.

Rogin, J. (2020). *Putting China in charge of the world's intellectual property is a bad idea*. Washington Post. Retrieved Jan 30, 2020 from https://www.washingtonpost.com/opinions/global-opinions/putting-china-in-charge-of-the-worlds-intellectual-property-is-a-bad-idea/2020/01/30/51c1b688-43a6-11ea-aa6a-083d01b3ed18_story.html

Scheuer, S. (2018). *Der Masterplan. Chinas weg zur HighTech-Weltherrschaft*. Herder.

von Senger, H. (2006). *The 36 stratagems for business: Achieve your objectives through hidden and unconventional strategies and tactics*. Cyan Books.

SIGAR–Special Inspector General for Afghanistan Reconstruction. (2021). *What we need to learn: Lessons from twenty years of Afghanistan reconstruction*. Report August 2021. Retrieved Aug, 2021, from https://www.sigar.mil/pdf/lessonslearned/SIGAR-21-46-LL.pdf

Strittmatter, K. (2020). *We have been harmonised: Life in China's surveillance state*. Custom House.

Thomas, A. (2006). *Handbook of intercultural communication*. V&R.

Weber, R. (2020). *"Unified message, rhizomatic delivery: a preliminary analysis of PRC/CCP influence and the united front in Switzerland"*, Synopsis–China in Context and Perspective, 18 December 2020 Retrieved from https://sinopsis.cz/wp-content/uploads/2020/12/switzerland-rhizome.pdf

Welthungerhilfe. (2021, July). China hat die Armut ausgerottet. Wirklich? In: *Entwicklungspolitik & Agenda 2030*. Retrieved from https://www.welthungerhilfe.de/welternaehrung/rubriken/entwicklungspolitik-agenda-2030/china-erklaert-das-ende-der-armut

Winkler, H. A. (2019). *Werte und Mächte: Eine Geschichte der westlichen Welt*. Beck.

Zhang, F. (2015). *Chinese hegemony: Grand strategy and international institutions in east Asian history*. Standford UP.

Prof. Dr. Ulrich Bauer Undertook training in mechanical engineering (welder & turner) and spent several years as an assembly manager working worldwide on construction sites. Later, he studied anthropology, linguistics, history, cultural geography and archaeology amongst others. Master's degree in hermeneutics (philosophy); doctorate in applied linguistics. Has held various positions as managing director of educational institutions; longer academic stays abroad; in total 15 years outside Europe, much of that in East Asia. Since 2010 professor for intercultural communication at the University Kempten. Has travelled to more than 100 countries, about 50 of them professionally. Living today on an isolated farm on the slopes of the Alps.

Economic Reactions to Global Development Strategies: Mapping Public Discourse in Germany on China's Belt and Road Initiative

Daniel Waite

Abstract In this chapter, China's Belt and Road Initiative (BRI) is selected as a case study to analyze reaction strategies to Global Development Initiatives (GDIs). For this purpose, a framework of reaction levels to categorize stakeholders and a spectrum of reaction options are introduced in a theoretical model. Theoretical concepts, focusing on Game Theory, are brought forward in connection to the analysis. Qualitative Data Analysis of German news articles on the BRI is the methodology selected to generate results through a mix of deductive and inductive research. Results show the suitability of applying Game Theoretical concepts to forecast and analyze reactions of different stakeholder groups to GDIs. Signaling of self-declared Pareto-optimum choices can be observed in relation to GDI reaction strategies of influencing other actors. This setting can be matched best by the concept of the Coordination Game. Furthermore, a reduction of leeway for reacting to a GDI is visible when reducing the stakeholder level viewed. On a practical level, risks of the BRI are seen to outweigh opportunities significantly for German stakeholders. A clustering of identified themes in the sources shows a high level of risk adverseness of all stakeholder levels analyzed in relation to the initiative.

Keywords Belt and Road Initiative · Germany · Reaction · Global development initiative · Discourse analysis

1 Introduction

China's Belt and Road Initiative (BRI) can be characterized as the present's largest and most relevant international development project from a global perspective. The initiative, consisting of the land-based Silk Road Economic Belt and the 21st Century Maritime Silk Road, aims to create connectivity and cooperation between

D. Waite (✉)
WFI–Ingolstadt School of Management, Catholic University of Eichstätt-Ingolstadt, Ingolstadt, Germany
e-mail: daniel.waite@alumni.ku.de

H. Pechlaner et al. (eds.), *The Clash of Entrepreneurial Cultures?*, FGF Studies in Small Business and Entrepreneurship, https://doi.org/10.1007/978-3-030-97050-5_5

China and regional economies along its path (Belt and Road Portal, 2019; Syed & Ying, 2019).

Established in 2013 and also referred to as "One Belt, One Road" (OBOR), the BRI's corridors span from China to Europe via Central Asia on land. China's ports along the South China Sea are the starting point for the Maritime Silk Road, which leads to Europe's Mediterranean harbors via Southeast Asia, the Indian subcontinent, and Eastern Africa (Cai, 2017). Due to the scope of the initiative, it is referred to as "China's project of the century" and "Xi Jinping's most important foreign policy" (Berlie, 2020, p. 19).

Launched by Chinese President Xi Jinping at a time "when Chinese foreign policy has become more assertive," the BRI must also be viewed in the context of geostrategy, as well as geoeconomics (Cai, 2017). Criticism focuses on the risk of increasing economic dependency of participating countries toward China and the resulting rise of China's political and economic influence along the Belt and Road—potentially resulting in a competition of entrepreneurial cultures and ecosystems (Stam & Van de Ven, 2021).

From a perspective of nations and other economic actors outside of China, challenges arise concerning possible reactions toward the BRI as a global development initiative: How are risks of participation perceived in comparison to the potentially expected significant gains? And does the promise of economical benefit outweigh the threat of growing dependence on China?

Possible reaction options and strategies of economic and political stakeholders in response to large-scale global development projects therefore define the theoretical purpose of this study: to contribute to a better understanding of reactions and reaction strategies of various stakeholders toward Global Development Initiatives (GDIs) in general, with the Belt and Road Initiative serving as an object for empirical research.[1] The stakeholders taken into account range from governments and international organizations to firms and individual economic actors.

The subject of German stakeholders' attitudes toward the Belt and Road Initiative was selected to serve as the element of qualitative research within this chapter. The methodology used is software-based Qualitative Data Analysis (QDA) with the software NVivo, extracting and analyzing German-language news articles on the topic of the Belt and Road Initiative. Utilizing QDA software enables a large number of sources to be analyzed for reaction strategies, opinions, and sentiments, which can then be mapped into an overview of public discourse on the BRI.

In conclusion, the research question was defined as follows:

---

[1] See Fig. 1

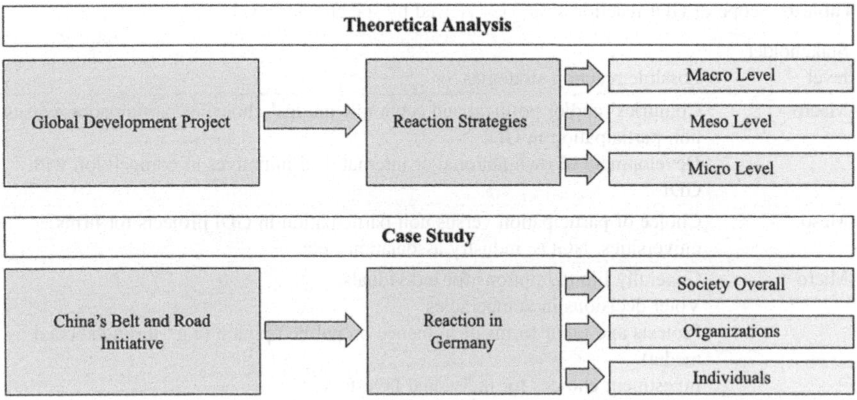

Fig. 1 Model of research approach

How do economic actors and stakeholders react to global development strategies? What kind of reactions and reaction strategies can be identified on a macro-, meso- and micro-level?Due to the nature of research through Qualitative Data Analysis, no specific hypotheses to be tested are defined prior to conducting the analysis (deductive research). In contrast, the evaluation of news articles is utilized with the goal of discovering new theories on the subject of reaction to large-scale development initiatives. While a certain framework is set before beginning the research process, hypotheses are primarily discovered and critically evaluated through performing inductive empirical research.

2 Theoretical Background

The fact that global development initiatives cannot exclusively be examined from a perspective of economics is easily understood when taking a historical example into account: The Marshall Plan was not viewed to be driven purely by economic motives. In fact, the Soviet Union perceived the plan "as an attempt to use American economic power to undermine the newly established Soviet sphere of influence" in Eastern Europe (Parrish, 1995).

This historical example underlines the relevance of global development initiatives in a geostrategic and political context. While the implications of the dawning BRI are not fully known yet, it is very likely that they will affect Europe on all stakeholder levels for the years to come.

Table 1 Scope of GDI reaction strategies viewed by stakeholder level

Stakeholder level	Possible reaction strategies
Macro	Countries' and/or political and economic unions' choice of participation versus non-participation in GDI Development of own national or international initiatives in competition with GDI
Meso	Choice of participation versus non-participation in GDI projects for firms, universities, NGOs, industry associations, etc.
Micro	Generally limited options for individuals Voter decisions in democracies Protests and other forms of influence on public opinion (e.g., through social media) Investment choices for individual investors

While the macro-level reaction is characterized by high-level policy decisions on reaction to the applicable GDI as a whole, meso-level reaction is limited to certain aspects of the initiative (e.g., individual projects for firms or research partnerships for universities).

Due to the potentially significant effect of the BRI on its various stakeholders, it is important for all parties involved to analyze possible reaction strategies toward the initiative. In practice these strategies generally seek to achieve an optimal reaction that serves the interests of the stakeholder. Depending on the level of the stakeholder, different options for reaction are available (Table 1).

In the context of this chapter's theoretical analysis, the choice between *participation* and *non-participation* in a global development initiative was identified as highly relevant. Translated to a general economic setting, this could be seen as an evaluation of *cooperation* versus *non-cooperation*, a central element of concepts related to Game Theory.

2.1 Game Theory

By applying the structural conditions of Game Theory to GDI reaction strategies, a possible range of options is shown in the conceptual overview of Fig. 2. The options depicted are not mutually exclusive, as in reality the game setting does not only consist of a single, but of infinite moves. And a reaction strategy might even consist of cooperation and non-cooperation in the same move and different fields of actions (e.g., cooperation in research vs. non-cooperation in economic topics).

In the overview, full-scale and formal engagement defines the most cooperative options in reaction to a nation faced with a GDI. Less cooperative, but still an overall friendly reaction lies in limited or conditional engagement, which is matched by opposition to project clusters on the non-cooperative side. Nations engaged in these kinds of reactions may include or exclude certain clusters from participation in the initiative. On the inward-facing sides of the cooperation/non-cooperation-axis lies limited opposition or small-scale engagement. Opposition or engagement can be

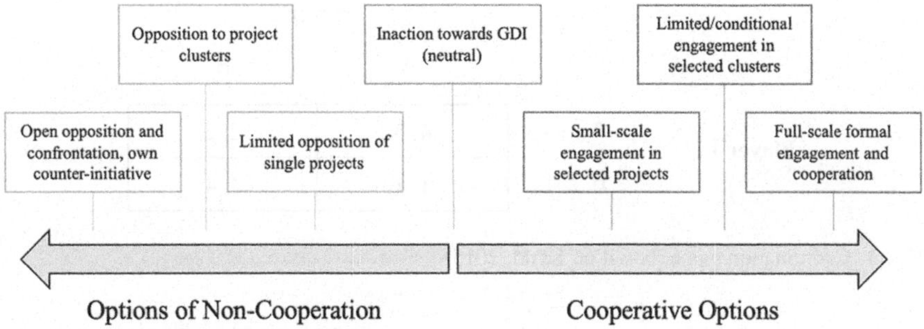

Fig. 2 Overview of GDI reaction options

characterized on a lower level than clusters, related only to single projects of the initiative.

2.1.1 Game Theory and Political Concepts

The 2 × 2 normal form[2] of games, found for example in the Prisoners' Dilemma, can be widely applied to various political settings, such as nuclear deterrence and the security dilemma (Kydd, 2015, p. 36). Three central assumptions of the rationalist international relations theory are selected to serve as a base for future game theoretical analyses:

1. "States are the most important actors. State actions determine war and peace, and set the conditions under which economic activity takes place. [. . .]."
2. "States interact in a context of anarchy. This implies that states may fight each other if they wish, but it also means that they cannot make commitments that they do not wish to keep in the future. [. . .]."
3. "States are rational. [. . .] [This can] be understood as an assumption that states make decisions based on their evaluations of the consequences of their actions, rather than via an evaluation of the appropriateness of the behavior" (Kydd, 2015, p. 2).

Furthermore, Kydd (2015, pp. 30-34) postulates that states can be seen as unitary actors with identifiable preferences, defined as *national interest*, focusing on the following four key items:

- Territory
- Power
- Security
- Wealth

[2] See Figs. 3 and 4

		Player 2 A	Player 2 B
Player 1	A	4, 3	2, 2
	B	1, 1	3, 4

Fig. 3 Coordination game (based on Kydd, 2015)

		Player 2 A	Player 2 B
Player 1	A	$b_1 + r_1 + r_2, b_2 - c_2$	r_1, r_2
	B	$r_2 - c_1, r_1 - c_2$	$b_1 - c_1, b_2 + r_1 + r_2$

Fig. 4 Coordination game: general notation (based on Kydd, 2015)

2.1.2 The Coordination Game

From the various game theoretical concepts suitable to be applied to economic or political contexts, the *Coordination* game was selected to serve as a theoretical framework for the following discussion of QDA results.

In this game, two players have to agree on a common strategy in order to receive higher payoffs, compared to contrary strategies (e.g., through adopting common standards). Kydd (2015, pp. 46-47) explains that, even though there are two Nash equilibria in Coordination, "both are Pareto superior to the non-equilibrium outcomes, and neither is Pareto superior to the other."

To bring the example of this game into a standard setting, b_i is defined as coordination benefit, r_j is additional revenue through coordination, and c_i is the cost of transition to the other side's technology (Kydd, 2015, p. 47). Both sides will not choose the other player's technology since:

$$r_j - c_i < b_i + r_i + r_j \tag{1}$$

The author further notes that "both sides will be [...] willing to cooperate rather than stick to their own technology if:

$$b_i - c_i > r_i[\ldots]."$$

3 Methodology

For the purpose of measuring reactions to China's BRI in Germany, 100 news articles were selected for coding by the QDA software. These articles were extracted online by using the Google News search algorithm and the search terms are shown in Table 2.

The validity of this approach was established through a pre-test sample: Of the first ten results shown, the majority seven dealt with the impact of the BRI on Germany, while the other three were either related to foreign policy issues outside of and not related to Germany or travel and tourism topics.

The other two search terms selected for data extraction were *Belt and Road Initiative Germany* and *Belt and Road Initiative reaction*.

Prior to extracting the articles selected for the case study, a framework of codes within the QDA software was prepared for this task. All codes shown below, except for the sub-items *Opportunities* and *Risks*, were created using a deductive approach, taking into account the theoretical background of the research question and before performing the analysis on the news articles.

1. *Evaluation of the initiative*

- Opportunities
  - Infrastructure development
  - Cultural exchange
  - New business partnerships with China
  - Establishment of research networks
  - Economic growth:
  - Of the own economy
  - Globally
- Risks
  - No inclusion of non-Chinese businesses
  - Human rights violations
  - Ecological aspects
  - Division of the EU member states
  - Increasing Chinese geopolitical influence, political system rivalry
  - Indebtedness to China
  - Economic dependence on China

Table 2 Search term overview for QDA data extraction

Search term	Number of articles captured
Belt and Road Initiative	32
Belt and Road Initiative Germany	33
Belt and Road Initiative reaction	35

2. *Historical analogies*

    - Historical Silk Road
    - Marshall Plan

3. *Reaction strategies*

    - Reaction levels

        - Macro
        - Meso
        - Micro

    - Game theory

        - Non-cooperation
        - Cooperation

Dividing the high-level code structure into three parts, the main focus lies on the first part, *Evaluation of the Initiative*. By assigning quotes from the extracted news articles to the sub-sections of Opportunities and Risks, an overview is given on the perception of the BRI in Germany.

The sub-items of *Evaluation of the Initiative* were created through an inductive approach: During the process of coding the new articles in the QDA software, these codes were created based on the content of the articles in scope.

The second main item in the code overview enables the creation of an overview of *Historical Analogies* in the selected news sources. Comparisons of the BRI and the U.S. Marshall Plan draw criticism in China (Shang, 2019; Wang, 2015). In contrast, the parallels between trade gains and other opportunities along the ancient Silk Road are stressed prominently in official reports (National Development and Reform Commission of the People's Republic of China, 2015). Examining reactions in Germany on this topic is relevant, as a conclusion can be made if public opinion favors one of these options more than the other.

Point number three, Reaction strategies, incorporates the stakeholder levels introduced previously. In support of a central aspect of the research question, the analysis of reaction strategies on the three levels (macro, meso, and micro) is performed. All quotes relevant to this part of the question are summarized in the corresponding codes.

Connecting the Qualitative Data Analysis process to the theoretical concepts, the parent code *Game Theory* is introduced. The two options, *Cooperation* and *Non-cooperation*, represent the most important options for action in basic game theoretical concepts.

4 Results of Qualitative Analysis

4.1 Evaluation of the Initiative

An overview of the number of references listed in Tables 2 and 3 quickly shows a first result of the Qualitative Data Analysis: While a total of 65 references were identified matching opportunities of the BRI Initiative, more than double this number, 136, were found in reference to risks of the initiative.

This imbalance highlights a general trend within the sources, which could indicate a tendency toward seeing more disadvantages than advantages in the initiative, hence supporting a cautious reaction strategy. Another possible explanation lies in the nature of the sources. News articles as important sources of information in democratic societies generally tend to critically question all kinds of private and public activities. In opposition to uncritically following official narratives as this might be the case in authoritarian regimes. So widespread criticism of the initiative needn't necessarily be equal to the opinion of the general public, while it nevertheless aims to provide valid points for critical reasoning in regard to the propagated advantages of the BRI.

4.1.1 Opportunities

Viewing opportunities linked to China's BRI Initiative, economic growth dominates the news sources in terms of frequency of reference. A total of 29 references are made to this topic in the data set, 14 of these instances relating to the own economy participating in the initiative (own economy denoting mostly Germany, but in some cases also other affected countries, e.g., Italy). Eight articles purely reference global

Table 3 References for BRI opportunities in QDA

Code	Number of references
Infrastructure development	18
Cultural exchange	5
New business partnerships with China	12
Establishment of research networks	1
Economic growth:[a]	29
Of the own economy	14
Globally	8
Total[b]	**65**

[a]Not mutually exclusive related to the sub-items. Codes can be assigned to the code *Economic growth* and one of the sub-points *or* only to the top level, implying *Economic growth* in general (globally and locally)

[b]*Economic growth* included in total, sub-points (*Of the own economy, Globally*) are counted within the preceding line

economic development with no specific focus on the own economy. This means that seven references are directly allocated to the top level, economic growth in general. One of these articles focusing both on own (local) and global economic growth can be exemplarily quoted as follows:

> According to the Ifo Institute, Germany's exports to China could increase by EUR 11.4 billion and imports from the [country] could increase by EUR 13.8 billion over the next few years due to the reduced trade costs and the infrastructure measures of the Belt and Road Initiative. But Germany's foreign trade could also increase with the member states of the New Silk Road. (Bosse, 2020)

Economic growth is mainly projected onto infrastructure development projects along One Belt, One Road: enabling cheaper transportation and more efficient flows of goods, as well as the opportunities of entering new markets.

Infrastructure development is the theme identified with the second highest number of references (18). Along the routes of One Belt, One Road, several infrastructure development projects for roads, railroads, ports, airports, and more form the backbone of the initiative (Belt and Road Portal, 2019; Fang & Nolan, 2019). The following quote gives an example for a reference in this code:

> The cities and regions at the starting and ending points also benefit from this rail route: The city of Duisburg is planning the settlement of 300 Chinese companies; and there are also plans for new logistics centers in Nuremberg, Hof, Bayreuth, Regensburg, Straubing, as well as in Dresden and Chemnitz. The spillover effects on the regions are considerable. (Lichter, 2019)

4.1.2 Risks

> During the last economic summit in Davos, the CEO of Siemens, Joe Kaeser, is said to have warned: 'The Chinese One Belt, One Road is going to be the new WTO.—like it or not'. (Bonschab, 2018)

In the evaluation of risks viewed from Germany's perspective in reaction to the BRI,[3] *Increasing Chinese geopolitical influence/political system rivalry* clearly leads the reference count, which is more than double as high as the total count of references for *Opportunities*.[4]

The analyzed articles state the opinion that China primarily uses the BRI in a bid to increase its global influence, even to the extent of achieving global dominance. This shall not only be achieved by economic, military, and political advances, but also by offering an alternative to the Western democratic political and societal systems.

Generally, the BRI is seen as a one-sided project to project Chinese visions of capitalism and trade onto its global trade partners in these coded sources, while

---

[3] See Table 4

[4] See Table 3

Table 4 References for BRI risks in QDA

Code	Number of references
No inclusion of non-Chinese businesses	22
Human rights violations	8
Ecological aspects	7
Division of the EU member states	12
Increasing Chinese geopolitical influence, political system rivalry	41
Indebtedness to China	22
Economic dependence on China	24
Total	**136**

allowing them no room for participation or multilateral establishment of common standards and agreements.

Perception of this behavior has increased since beginning of the global COVID-19 crisis (Manske-Wang & Pechlaner, 2020). China, as the point of origin of the pandemic (World Health Organization, 2020), is said to try to profit from its consequences in the form of increased political and societal influence by establishing a "Medical Silk Road" and offering aid to affected countries (e.g. Italy):

> The COVID-19 crisis could possibly become a new gateway for China's strategy of the New Silk Road. (Brantner, 2020)

4.2 Reaction Strategies

4.2.1 Reaction Levels

Taking a simple quantitative overview of the codes establishes a number of interesting facts: 32 references are made to macro-level options, whereas only half the number (15) match meso-level options. Again, less than half of the results of the next higher level (5) are relevant to the micro level. This indicates a strong focus and dominance of macro-level evaluation of potential options for action and reaction within the representatively selected German news articles.

Reaction options and corresponding sources found in the Qualitative Data Analysis process decrease when moving from the highest to the lowest stakeholder level. Voter behavior as possible course of action on the micro level is not explicitly brought forward in the sources.

4.2.2 Game Theory

Analysis of the selected news sources shows a strong trend to quotes supporting *Non-cooperation* toward the initiative: 33 references in 24 sources. This supports the previously established fact that more *Risks* than *Opportunities* are focused upon in

German news sources with regards to the BRI, as only 22 references in 18 sources advocate for Cooperation with One Belt, One Road.

Generally speaking, codes in the category of *Game Theory* do not constitute a form of "signaling" of a desired behavior aimed at a stakeholder group. Due to the nature of the news sources analyzed, these provide readers with information as a base for a following decision-making process on how to react to the BRI.

The following quote serves as an example of *Cooperation* in the results:

> The question arises as to whether it makes sense to use the rhetoric of systemic competition against the BRI instead of joining the negotiating table with China and influencing the basic rules of the initiative. (Bonschab, 2018)

For the case of a coded quote in the category of *Non-Cooperation*, an example can be shown by the following extract:

> However, the reactions [to the BRI] of many representatives in the West are rightly restrained. They do not want non-transparent, undemocratic and brutal state capitalism to conquer the world. (Marschall, 2019)

4.3 Historical Analogies

In this category of codes, a total of seven references are made to the Historical Silk Road, focusing on the legendary image of the ancient Silk Road:

> [The BRI] arouses longings: of the Orient, of caravans and of Marco Polo. Be-cause China wants to expand its influence not only on land but also at sea, the 'Silk Road of the Seas' is added. It stretches from the Chinese east coast over the Indian Ocean to the front door of Europe and the African west coast. (Hein, 2018)

The Marshall Plan is brought up more often, seven times. These references either compare the Marshall Plan's planned investment amounts to the BRI's or are critical in nature:

> While some observers, [. . .], compare the BRI with the Marshall Plan, others see it as an attempt by Beijing to create financially dependent vassal states. (Kaufmann, 2020)

5 Discussion

While the case study using QDA focused on German stakeholders' reaction to the BRI, the research question was designed to answer the general question of reaction strategies of various economic actors on different stakeholder levels to Global Development Initiatives. Translating the findings of the analysis of the previous chapter onto the theoretical level, a number of interesting observations can be made.

As a result of the QDA process, it was established that reaction options generally decrease when moving from a higher to a lower level. This is reflected in the distribution of results, with the number of references decreasing by over 50%

when moving to the next lower level. This would imply little room for action on the micro level (individuals), when answering the research question on reaction options to GDI per stakeholder level.

The range of reaction options to Global Development Initiatives presented in Fig. 2 can also be found mapped in the review of QDA results. Although all of the options are included in the results, the distribution of results on the scale from *Non-cooperation* to *Cooperation* is rather mixed. There is no possibility to establish a clear classification of an item, e.g., full-scale formal engagement or limited opposition, to a stakeholder reaction level. The levels (macro, meso, and micro) inhibit a diverse group of attitudes and reaction options within each other, sometimes even within a single source. This represents the process of weighing risks and opportunities of the initiative necessary to make an effective decision on how to react to this kind of GDI.

In contrast, taking a closer look at the reaction levels in connection with the theoretical concepts introduced in this chapter, it can be found that the matching of reaction levels to the respective theoretical frameworks is supported by the case study.

On the macro level, stakeholders affected by the BRI, as the GDI studied, are shown to be situated in a situation similar to the set-ups of the Prisoners' Dilemma as well as the Coordination Game.

In this context, Chinese communication narratives can be seen as trying to convince macro-level stakeholders (i.e., heads of state) of cooperation with the initiative. This process of convincing the other player is performed by emphasizing the *win-win* potential of One Belt, One Road. *Win-win* implies opportunities that can be profited from when cooperating. Viewed in light of game theory, this can be seen as signaling a *Pareto Optimum* to stakeholders.

6 Conclusion

6.1 Summary and Implications

Results of the Qualitative Data Analysis for the case study of Germany and China's BRI showed that leeway available for reacting to the initiative decreases when the stakeholder level is reduced (i.e., from macro to meso or micro). While the clear distinction of stakeholder levels for analysis of reaction strategies was challenged, it was still found to be overall suitable for the purpose, also confirmed through empirical research. Extraction and analysis of the data revealed an overall critical view of the BRI, with the category of Risks dominating over Opportunities.

Furthermore, game-theoretical approaches were found suitable for decision-making processes on a macro level. Hereby it is important that actors (i.e., players in a theoretical sense) perform a careful analysis to match their situation to one of the theoretical concepts available. For the case of Germany and the BRI it was established that the Coordination game matched the observed set-up most precisely.

Next to measuring expected payoffs through comparing risks and opportunities of engaging in the initiative, it is important that players collect information on other players' (expected) behavior. This behavior can be influenced by means of reacting to players' coordination efforts (e.g., within the EU in the case of Germany and the BRI). Other players' signaling of optima must also be carefully analyzed and taken into account in the reaction planning process (e.g., China's communication of a win-win situation as Pareto optimum).

Micro-level reactions were found to be highly connected to the macro level, due to voters' influence on this level in democracies. Furthermore, the role of individuals as investors is to be considered in reaction to Global Development Initiatives.

6.2 Limitations and Future Research

Limitations of research lie in the issue of news development over time, as future developments cannot be taken into account.

The current situation surrounding the dynamic development of the COVID-19 crisis and its connection to China's BRI (Manske-Wang & Pechlaner, 2020) is another limitation that needs to be taken into account when viewing the results of this paper. As future events surrounding the global health crisis are difficult to forecast, reaction strategies to the initiative on all stakeholder levels could also be affected in an unknown way.

Future research could focus on the role of political and economic unions[5] in reaction to Global Development Initiatives such as the BRI. As the discussions on the topic continue on all stakeholder levels in the EU member states, an interesting aspect for future research could lie in applying theoretical concepts such as Game Theory to the complex mechanisms within the union. As many countries currently shift away from multilateral decision-making processes in international politics, this aspect could be highly relevant for future research.

References

Belt and Road Portal. (2019). *Six years of "belt and road"!* Retrieved April 24 from https://eng.yidaiyilu.gov.cn/qwyw/rdxw/105854.htm

Berlie, J. A. (2020). *China's globalization and the belt and road initiative*. Springer.

Bonschab, T. (2018). *Drei Gründe, warum der Westen seine Einstellung zur neuen Seidenstraße überdenken sollte*. https://makronom.de/chinas-belt-and-road-initiative-drei-gruende-warum-der-westen-seine-einstellung-zur-neuen-seidenstrasse-ueberdenken-sollte-25977

Bosse, T. (2020). *Die Seidenstraße erfreut sich neuer Beliebtheit*. https://www.dvz.de/rubriken/land/detail/news/die-seidenstrasse-erfreut-sich-neuer-beliebtheit.html

[5] E.g., the European Union or NATO

Brantner, F. (2020). *Die EU nach Corona–Europa wird zum Wurmfortsatz der Neuen Seidenstraße.* https://www.cicero.de/wirtschaft/europa-corona-bonds-eu-deutschland-italien-spanien-china
Cai, P. (2017). *Understanding China's belt and road initiative*. Lowy Institute For International Policy.
Fang, C., & Nolan, P. (2019). *Routledge handbook of the belt and road*. Routledge.
Hein, C. (2018). *Chinas langer Weg nach Westen.* https://www.faz.net/aktuell/wirtschaft/der-handelsstreit/seidenstrasse-chinas-langer-weg-nach-westen-15605201.html
Kaufmann, D. (2020). *Chinas neue Seidenstraße ohne Europa?* https://www.dw.com/de/chinas-neue-seidenstraße-ohne-europa/a-52030207
Kydd, A. H. (2015). *International relations theory*. Cambridge University Press.
Lichter, J. (2019). *Deutschland sollte offiziell Partner werden.* https://www.handelsblatt.com/politik/konjunktur/research-institute/handelspolitik-mit-china-neue-seidenstrasse-deutschland-sollte-offiziell-partner-werden/24280410.html
Manske-Wang, W., & Pechlaner, H. (2020). *Corona: Krönung Chinas zur Weltmacht? Die Maskendiplomatie Chinas und die neue Seidenstraße der Gesundheit.* Retrieved 20 June from https://blogs.eurac.edu/covid-19/china-seidenstrasse/
Marschall, B. (2019). *"Neue Seidenstraße": Vorsicht gegenüber China.* https://rp-online.de/politik/deutschland/neue-seidenstrasse-vorsicht-gegenueber-china_aid-38411417
National Development and Reform Commission of the People's Republic of China. (2015). *Vision and actions on jointly building silk road economic belt and 21st–century maritime silk road.* Retrieved May 10 from https://en.ndrc.gov.cn/newsrelease/201503/t20150330_669367.html
Parrish, S. (1995). Soviet reaction to the Marshall plan: Opportunity or threat? *Problems of Post-Communism, 42*(5), 18–24.
Shang, H. (2019). *The belt and road initiative: Key concepts*. Springer.
Stam, E., & Van de Ven, A. (2021). Entrepreneurial ecosystem elements. *Small Business Economics, 56*(2), 809–832.
Syed, J., & Ying, Y.-H. (2019). Introduction: Diversity, convergence and opportunities along the belt and road. In *China's belt and road initiative in a global context* (pp. 1–19). Springer.
Wang, Y. (2015). The belt and road initiative is by no means the Chinese version of the Marshall plan. *Qiu Shi, 12*.
World Health Organization. (2020). *Coronavirus disease (COVID-19) pandemic*. https://www.euro.who.int/en/health-topics/health-emergencies/coronavirus-covid-19

Daniel Waite holds a M.Sc. degree in business administration after graduating from the Catholic University of Eichstätt-Ingolstadt, Germany. Corporate Social Responsibility in controversial industry sectors as well as the economic impact of sustainability on commercial aviation defined the focus of his previous research. In his professional career, he has worked for an aviation consultancy firm in the Middle East. Currently, he is employed by a major European aerospace and defense company, supporting the deployment of Value Management methodology in current and future product development.

A Comparison of Entrepreneurial Culture in Germany and China

Joerg Bueechl and Felix Haefner

Abstract Progressive globalization and an interdependent network of international projects increase the importance of analyzing entrepreneurial cultures. Among the most important cooperations between Europe and Asia are the economic interactions between Germany and China, which are the regions' largest economies. A cross-cultural investigation of different entrepreneurial cultures reveals capacities and barriers of the joint development of innovation-driven cooperations. This chapter offers an overview of the current state of research, followed by an outline of cross-cultural differences on the basis of Hofstede's, (*Asia Pacific Journal of Management* 1:81-99, 1984b) cultural dimensions. Further, we juxtapose the role of the entrepreneur from both a Chinese and a German perspective. We close with critical remarks and call for future research to address important research gaps.

Keywords China · Germany · Entrepreneurship · Cross-cultural management

1 Introduction and the State of Research

The people within a company, their personal relationships with one another, and their different cultural backgrounds are becoming increasingly important. Specifically, the members of an organization, including their personal networks, constitute an essential part of international cooperation and networks that are needed to foster effective collaboration. Understanding one another's individual values, characteristics, and preferences is of fundamental relevance in the global context. The role of culture has attracted increasing attention when investigating entrepreneurial actions, as researchers such as Hayton and Cacciotti (2013) attest.

J. Bueechl (✉)
Tuebingen University, Tübingen, Germany
e-mail: joerg.bueechl@uni-tuebingen.de

F. Haefner
Aalen, Germany

H. Pechlaner et al. (eds.), *The Clash of Entrepreneurial Cultures?*, FGF Studies in Small Business and Entrepreneurship, https://doi.org/10.1007/978-3-030-97050-5_6

Over the last few decades, the interest in scientific progress and the development of entrepreneurial actions on the basis of different cultures have steadily grown. The connections between cultural values and entrepreneurial thinking have been of particular interest to scholars and managers. Because culture-specific systems of orientation trigger opportunities, motivations, conditions, and modes of action, researchers agree that cultural characteristics, values, as well as backgrounds, strongly shape and influence the notion of entrepreneurship in individual countries (Thomas, 2003; Hayton & Cacciotti, 2013).

The effects of national cultures on entrepreneurship have been the subject of research for almost 70 years; however, on a mainly conceptual level (Schumpeter, 1934). Structured empirical scientific evidence was generated about 20 years ago (Hayton et al., 2002). As early as 1930, scholars were focusing on what is now known as entrepreneurial culture on a national level (Weber, 2001). The basic constituents of entrepreneurial motivation are primarily determined through a historical and respective social development processes which shape a nation over time, but also by contemporary political circumstances. The degree of openness, the ability to subsidize, as well as the degree of innovation of a nation also contribute to development. The literature divides these facets into three categories. The first category is the social context under investigation of entrepreneurial thinking, which deals with society, the network, and market conditions. Cultural values form the second category. These are often of central interest, because culturally determined characteristics shape a person and their respective behavior from birth (Hayton & Cacciotti, 2013). Specifically, members of a culture engage in a continuous sense-making process through a socialization process in which they collect and process information of their daily lives subconsciously from early on, and which is rooted in collective and culturally relevant social rules and norms (Thomas et al., 2010).

The interdependence between national culture and entrepreneurial characteristics and traits has been extensively investigated, as business, sociology, and psychology scholars attest (Hayton et al., 2002). Specifically, researchers highlight the moderating role of culture in the relationship between contextual factors and entrepreneurial outcomes (Hayton et al., 2002), as well as the impact of culture on related technical innovations (Schumpeter, 1934) and the economic development (Birley, 1987) of countries.

Now the selected literature has been reviewed, we will demonstrate the impact of culture in China and Germany on entrepreneurship. We chose these countries for investigation for conceptual reasons. Both countries are prominent economies in Asia and Europe, with extensive mutual trading activities resulting in ongoing intercultural collaboration. Furthermore, both countries account for different tendencies with respect to their corresponding cultural dimensions.

2 Intercultural Differences

Compared to Germany, the body of entrepreneurship research in the Chinese context is still relatively limited and fragmented, because entrepreneurship has been mainly regarded as a state matter in the socialist economic system. However, since the 1990s, over 10 years after the Opening Reform *Gaige Kaifang*, there has been structural and increasing support for start-ups, especially for founders of the upper class, who have close ties to government officials and thus profit from their social capital (Heberer, 2000).

Ongoing digitalization helps to make predictions about future market and client behaviors, and enables the identification of business opportunities which have led to a newly emerging, dynamic, and more open start-up scene on a global scale. However, these dynamics are also heavily impacted by several other factors, such as economic (e.g., monetary and fiscal policy instruments), socio-cultural (e.g., governance, human capital, and recognition of entrepreneurial actions), and above all, political influences. In this regard, good governance is of top priority for the Chinese environment (Xie et al., 2019). In China, as well as in Germany, the government exerts its influence in various ways, such as through regulatory mechanisms, or by the promotion of carefully defined key industries (Kretschmer, 2021). For instance, China is currently pursuing the "Manufacturing 2025" plan, which fosters the expansion of ten key industries, including aerospace and maritime equipment, equipment for new energies, and biopharma and medical products (Froese et al., 2019). Another recent development in China is the introduction of centralized registration processes of market participants in combination with simplified market exit procedures (Yue, 2021). In addition, start-ups are also supported by financing models, such as grants or low-interest loans in the early stages of their business development (Hemmert et al., 2019). Simultaneously, entrepreneurs in China are under high pressure, due to limited copyright protection, censorship restrictions, and market entry barriers because of high minimum capital requirements (Mattheis, 2014). The lack of comprehensive enforcement of policies and regulations has resulted in systematic corruption, which has often been based on cronyism. As an effort to counteract this problem, the Chinese government, under party leader Xi Jin Ping, rolled out a widespread anti-corruption campaign in 2012. However, recent research demonstrates the lasting negative effects of corruption on the performance of small entrepreneurial firms, leading to higher financing costs, lower sales growth, and inefficiencies in labor and capital allocation (Gianetti et al., 2021). Whereas the level of corruption in Germany is relatively low, there are numerous economic, social, and cultural factors that impede the support for start-ups and entrepreneurship. Looking toward more entrepreneurship-friendly countries like the US, Germany could promote its socio-cultural interactions in the form of entrepreneurial groups and networks, entrepreneurial hubs, and governmental assistance to increase trust and decrease personal risk (Richter et al., 2018). Furthermore, testimonials of famous German entrepreneurs could help to increase the recognition of entrepreneurs, while decreasing the stigma of failure (ibid).

In order to assess and evaluate the role of culture in an entrepreneurial context, it is important to develop an understanding of entrepreneurship first. Regarding entrepreneurial culture, entrepreneurs share various characteristics. For example, entrepreneurs tend to be particularly good at dealing with uncertain situations, due to their emotional stability. They also have a pronounced need for autonomy, as well as having extraordinary analytical or problem-solving skills. From an academic perspective, entrepreneurial traits can be described as "the need for achievement," an "internal control compulsion," a "problem-solving orientation," a "willingness to take risks," and "assertiveness" (Müller & Gappisch, 2005).

Different approaches exist toward describing what culture is about. Whereas culture can be understood as a universal phenomenon, cultural scholars apply different approaches to define culture: it can be defined as "the human-made part of the environment" (Triandis, 1998, p. 306), as well as "the collective programming of the mind" (Hofstede, 1991). One globally accepted definition is given by the combination of Herbig (1994) and Hofstede (1980), in which characteristics and values are comprehensively described. They define culture as "a set of shared values, beliefs, and expected behaviors." In this context, shared values, which are deeply rooted and sometimes unconscious, shape society, political institutions, and technical systems. To the same extent, they reflect common values and thereby reinforce social beliefs (Hayton et al., 2002). Because the members of a specific culture take an active part in its development, culture includes any tangible and intangible aspects of our daily lives, and is "always manifested in a system of orientation typical to a country, society, organization or group" (Thomas et al., 2010, p. 19).

We follow numerous cross-cultural researchers by applying Hofstede's model of cultural dimensions and country scores for our Chinese–German comparison within an entrepreneurial context. Specifically, we focus on the four dimensions: power distance, individualism/collectivism, masculinity, and uncertainty avoidance.

The first dimension considers the power distance index (PDI). It measures the extent to which unequally distributed power is expected and tolerated. A high PDI score would indicate that the specific society accepts an unequal, hierarchical distribution of power. A low PDI score, on the other hand, accounts for a low tolerance toward unequally distributed power.

The term "individualism vs. collectivism" defines the position within the society and whether the self-image of individuals is defined by an "I" or a "We." A high score indicates a more individualistic society; whereas a low score signals the interdependence of the individual with the collective.

Masculinity versus feminity takes into account society's preference for performance, attitudes toward gender equality, and behavior. Masculine characteristics are performance, heroism, assertiveness, and material reward for success. Feminine characteristics, which are explained by a low score, would be cooperation, modesty, care for the weak, and quality of life (Hofstede, 1984a, b).

Uncertainty avoidance considers in which way unknown situations and unexpected events are dealt with. A high uncertainty avoidance index shows low tolerance for uncertainty and risk taking. A low index, on the other hand, accounts for high tolerance for uncertainty and ambiguity (Yoo et al., 2011).

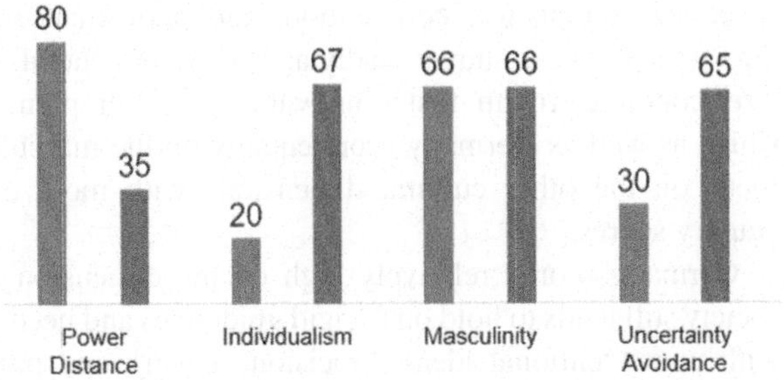

Fig. 1 Cultural dimensions: China (blue) and Germany (violet)

In order to analyze the differences between the two countries under investigation, the four relevant cultural dimensions of the two respective countries China and Germany are compared with the help of Fig. 1.

Researchers widely assume that entrepreneurial actions take place in cultures which score low in power distance, low in uncertainty avoidance, high in individualism, and high in masculinity (George & Zahra, 2002). In the next step, we evaluate each dimension for their entrepreneurial implications in the chosen cultural contexts.

In terms of the power distance index, China scored very high. This means that low power differentials are generally rejected. Equal rights for all individuals are not that important. Employees accept commands and execute them from their superiors. The German value was comparatively low and therefore reflects a lower tendency toward power distance. Control is unpopular, competences should be shown if they were based on it. High power differentials are generally rejected. It is assumed that low power distance leads to a better access to resources, more entrepreneurial initiatives, and opportunities than high power distance (Radziszewska, 2014). However, empirical studies testing these assumptions are inconclusive. There is even one study which indicates that Germans show a lower entrepreneurial motivation than their high power distance counterparts (Bouncken et al., 2009).

With a rather high value on the individualism scale, Germany belongs to a rather individualistic society. Individuals are expected to care mainly for themselves and their immediate family members. This corresponds to a loose social structure. In their working life, a contract is based on mutual advantage. Chinese society is rather collectivistic. This is reflected in strong family connections in which people also care about distant relatives. In his comparative US–American–Chinese study with a focus on the implications of individualism on entrepreneurship (next to openness-to-change and self-enhancement), Holt (1997) revealed no significant cultural differences. Also, Tan (2002) identified mainly universal entrepreneurial traits, such as innovativeness, proactiveness, and aggressiveness in his comparative US–American–Chinese study. In their cross-cultural study, Moriano et al. (2012) also found no strong effects of individualism in Germany on entrepreneurial intentions compared to their collectivistic countries under investigation.

With a value of 66, both countries reflected a rather masculine society. It is quite success oriented, which describes the phenomenon “living to work.” The focus of success is on justice, competition, and performance. Status, which is achieved through success, is shown gladly and often. In general, masculine countries emphasize economic growth, foster innovation, and entrepreneurial thinking. Because both China as well as Germany score equally on the masculinity dimension, we instead focus on the other cultural dimensions with more extensive differences in the country scores.

Germany scored relatively high on the dimension uncertainty avoidance. The society still tends to hold on to rigid guidelines and needs more time to acquaint itself with unconventional ideas. Precision at work and punctuality are required, with safety playing an important role. Compared with China, the German culture is a rather uncertainty-avoidant one. In China, depending on the individual situation, rules can be deviated from for the sake of practicality. In their cross-cultural study, Hancıoğlu et al. (2014) confirmed that in high uncertainty avoidance cultures (such as in China), entrepreneurship flourishes more and develops better than in low uncertainty avoidance cultures (such as Germany), where the risk factor could slow down the start-up endeavors.

Overall, it can be said that across the board (with the exception of uncertainty avoidance) the relationship between cultural dimensions and entrepreneurship is at best inconclusive. While Hofstede's cultural dimensions are widely applied in cultural research, scholars also point out numerous limitations with regard to his concept, in the areas of cultural homogeneity, national divisions, political influences, the amount of dimensions, or statistical integrity (Shaiq et al., 2011). Consequently, alternative concepts have been developed, such as the GLOBE study a more comprehensive and theoretically sound approach (House et al., 2004). Other cross-cultural entrepreneurship researchers, however, question the causal dynamics between Hofstede's cultural dimensions and the concept of entrepreneurship. Specifically, they suggest that Hofstede's constructs are not even key drivers of entrepreneurship and therefore call for further measures, such as regulatory, cognitive, and normative aspects to shed more light on entrepreneurship across cultures (Hayton et al., 2002; Hunt & Levie, 2002). In a similar vein, researchers point out that cultural dimensions were initially established in the context of formal organizations and are not specific enough to be applied to new business contexts (Busenitz & Lau, 1996). Yet it was important for us to shed more light on the relationship between cultural dimensions and entrepreneurship, because the bulk of cross-cultural studies on entrepreneurship applies Hofstede's dimensions.

3 The Entrepreneurial Role in a Cultural Context

In addition to the general cultural context, the societal view and perceived role of entrepreneurs can shed more light on the inhibiting and facilitating factors of the start-up process. One way is to look at the leadership culture or leadership ideals of the culture as a key influence on entrepreneurship. The entrepreneurial activity here corresponds primarily with outward-facing leadership, where the leader is proactive, builds positive relationships, and is inspirational to others. The leader is charismatic, people oriented, and team oriented. This is opposed to self-protective, non-participative leadership, in which the leader acts egocentrically, according to their own advantage. Classic characteristics are paternalism and saving face, which is considered neutral in Confucian Asian culture. In German culture, self-protective leadership is viewed rather negatively. However, entrepreneurs must still exhibit self-protective attributes. Entrepreneurship is a proactive and performance-oriented behavior. The closer the cultures are to charismatic leadership, the higher the perceived legitimization of entrepreneurs (Stephan & Pathak, 2016, p. 508). Another important factor influencing the role of the entrepreneur is social status. In China, entrepreneurs are incorporated into a traditional, far-reaching value system through widespread religious practice (Froese et al., 2019, p. 253). The teachings of Confucius are still significant, and highlight constant virtues and the ideal of (hierarchical) human relationships. For business life, the relationship "sovereign and subject," as well as "obligation and submission" is central. This has given rise to a management style that is primarily paternalistic (Fan, 2000, p. 4). It also coincides with *Zhong-Yong* mentality, which helps one to look at things from different perspectives, focuses on accepting contradictions, avoiding extremes, and ensuring harmony (Ma et al., 2018, p. 324). It can exert a positive impact on team building and on maximizing the opportunities stemming from *guanxi* (close, Chinese network, with a high degree of loyalty), ultimately resulting in higher company performance. It also helps to reduce uncertainty, as profound *guanxi* provides better information density and more resources (Ma et al., 2018, p. 336). Successful entrepreneurs in China place great emphasis on social and political interactions with internal and external organizations (colleagues, competitors, and government officials) (Cong et al., 2017, p. 29). Simultaneously, Confucianism results in a higher perceived pressure to assume social responsibility as a company. As an overall rule, it can be claimed that the higher the social status of a company, the higher its social commitment and political networking (Liu et al., 2021, p. 651).

In interviews with Chinese entrepreneurs, it became evident that they themselves portray the role of the entrepreneur as something academic, almost exalted, and perceive it as a selfless calling to improve society. This leads to tensions, because the entrepreneurial role overshadows the role in the family environment, which is also rated very highly in China (Bell et al., 2019, pp. 46–47; Cinar et al., 2018, p. 217). The fear of Chinese of setting up a business is not as large as before, because entrepreneurial role models among acquaintances and education have a positive influence. Last, founders find themselves in a paradox in the Chinese cultural context. Capitalist entrepreneurship is seen as strongly individualistic to the point of egoistic behavior (Obschonka, 2017, p. 70). It can be assumed that people for whom Confucian values are less prevalent can develop an active entrepreneurial culture more quickly (Obschonka et al., 2019, p. 961).

In comparison, one could assume that the role of entrepreneurs in Germany, as a Western country, is much less contradictory. However, this is not the case. A special feature of German entrepreneurship is the *Mittelstand*, which is characterized by strong regional roots and a sense of social responsibility (Pahnke & Welter, 2019,

p. 351), as well as an attitude of trust and reciprocity (Pahnke & Welter, 2019, p. 355). The perception of entrepreneurs in German society is rather contradictory, because entrepreneurship is seen as playing a driving role; while entrepreneurs are seen as careless or irresponsible, rejecting the much safer and smarter occupations and failing to live up to the expectation of contributing to the German economy (Kalden et al., 2017, p. 96). The general attitude of Germans toward the entrepreneur does not tend to be appreciative. Success is rarely attributed to hard work. Simultaneously, failure almost happily leads to a stigma attributed to personal mistakes and overestimation. Those who succeed should compensate society for the privilege and take social responsibility (Kalden et al., 2017, p. 98). The envy and great social stigma of failure is a major discouraging factor. In addition, the great risk that entrepreneurs take rarely receives the recognition it deserves, but instead leads to a debt of obligation. German culture seems to promote stability more than change, which is why the social status of entrepreneurs is significantly reduced (Kalden et al., 2017, pp. 99–100). Despite Germany's economic strength, start-up rates are still lower than in other economies (Kalden et al., 2017, p. 91).

4 Conclusion

The aim of this chapter is to give a brief overview of the Chinese and German entrepreneurial landscape and to draw comparisons. We started by portraying the current state of research, where we highlighted how the investigation of entrepreneurship from a cultural perspective has long been on the agenda of scholars, but that it was not until 20 years ago, that structured empirical efforts have been undertaken. Then, we teased out the intercultural differences of entrepreneurship in China and Germany, where we drew on one of the most commonly applied concepts in cross-cultural management: Hofstede's cultural dimensions. While these work very well in describing what culture is all about and how one country differs from another, it has been pointed out that they are not necessarily well suited to explain cross-cultural phenomena in the field of entrepreneurship (Hayton et al., 2002), and researchers should also look beyond and incorporate additional manifestations of culture (George & Zahra, 2002). Furthermore, it is also useful to separate culture from other aspects, such as cognitive dispositions and human characteristics, to better understand the different underlying processes and dynamics (Busenitz & Lau, 1996; Tan, 2002). Aside from these relevant factors, there is a profound misconception regarding the transferability of Western concepts in the Asian context: Barkema et al. point out that "our knowledge about management and organizations in the East remains relatively limited or colorized with a Western lens" (2015: 460). This observation is a call for further research to engage in more theory building, particularly by identifying and analyzing the impact of emic concepts, such as *guanxi*, but also by assessing the transferability of Western concepts, such as good governance. In a similar vein, the associations with specific concepts and phenomena, and resulting behaviors that impact the entrepreneurial mindset and actions, such as cronyism, need to be investigated in a culture-sensitive manner (Kidd & Richter, 2003).

We closed with a juxtaposition of the entrepreneurial role in both the Chinese and the German context. Interestingly, the entrepreneurial role in either cultural context cannot be understood as a simple, one-dimensional phenomenon, but is accompanied by a great deal of contradictional signals. Overall, the literature on cross-cultural entrepreneurship is still limited and fragmented. Consequently, more empirical investigations are needed to shed light on the underlying dynamics and processes of entrepreneurship, to build more context-based theory, and thus to resolve existing inconclusive results and contradictions.

References

Barkema, H. G., Chen, X. P., Luo, Y., & Tsui, A. (2015). West meets east: New concepts and theories. *Academy of Management Journal, 58*, 460–479.

Bell, R., Liu, P., Zhan, H., Bozward, D., Fan, J., Watts, H., & Ma, X. (2019). Exploring entrepreneurial roles and identity in the United Kingdom and China. *The International Journal of Entrepreneurship and Innovation, 20*, 39–49.

Birley, S. (1987). New ventures and employment growth. *Journal of Business Venturing, 2*, 155–165.

Bouncken, R. B., Zagvozdina, J., Golze, A., & Mrozewska, A. (2009). A comparative study of cultural influences on intentions to found a new venture in Germany and Poland. *International Journal of Business and Globalisation, 3*, 47–65.

Busenitz, L. W., & Lau, C. M. (1996). A cross-cultural cognitive model of new venture creation. *Entrepreneurship Theory and Practice, 20*(4), 25–40.

Cinar, E. M., Du, Y., & Hienkel, T. (2018). Chinese entrepreneurship attributes: A comparative GEM data analysis. *Journal of Entrepreneurship in Emerging Economies, 10*, 217–248.

Cong, C., Dempsey, M., & Xie, H. M. (2017). Political skill, entrepreneurial orientation and organizational justice. *International Journal of Entrepreneurial Behavior & Research, 23*, 20–34.

Fan, Y. (2000). A classification of Chinese culture. *Cross Cultural Management–An International Journal, 7*, 3–10.

Froese, F. J., Sutherland, D., Lee, J. Y., Liu, Y., & Pan, Y. (2019). Challenges for foreign companies in China: Implications for research and practice. *Asian Business & Management, 18*, 249–262.

George, G., & Zahra, S. A. (2002). Culture and its consequences for entrepreneurship. *Entrepreneurship Theory and Practice, 26*, 5–8.

Gianetti, M., Liao, G., You, J., & Xu, Y. X. (2021). The externalities of corruption: Evidence from entrepreneurial firms in China. *Review of Finance*, 629–667.

Hancıoğlu, Y., Doğan, Ü. B., & Yıldırım, Ş. S. (2014). Relationship between uncertainty avoidance culture, entrepreneurial activity and economic development. *Procedia-Social and Behavioral Sciences, 150*, 908–916.

Hayton, J. C., & Cacciotti, G. (2013). Is there an entrepreneurial culture? A review of empirical research. *Entrepreneurship & Regional Development, 25*, 708–731.

Hayton, J. C., George, G., & Zahra, S. A. (2002). National Culture and entrepreneurship: A review of behavioral research. *Entrepreneurship Theory and Practice, 26*, 33–52.

Herbig, P. (1994). *The innovation matrix: Culture and structure prerequisites to innovation.* Quorum.

Heberer, T. (2000). Privater Sektor als Motor für Wachstum und Beschäftigung unerlässlich,. *Handelsblatt.*

Hemmert, M., Cross, A. R., Cheng, Y., Kim, J.-J., Kohlbacher, F., Kotosaka, M., Waldenberger, F., & Zheng, L. J. (2019). The distinctiveness and diversity of entrepreneurial ecosystems in China, Japan, and South Korea: an exploratory analysis. *Asian Business & Management, 18*, 211–247.

Hofstede, G. (1984a). Culture's consequences: International differences in work-related values. *Cross Cultural Research and Methodology.*

Hofstede, G. (1980). Culture and organizations. *International Studies of Management & Organization, 10*, 15–41.

Hofstede, G. (1984b). Cultural dimensions in management and planning. *Asia Pacific Journal of Management, 1*, 81–99.

Hofstede, G. (1991). Empirical models of cultural differences. In N. Bleichrodt & P. J. D. Renth (Eds.), *Contemporary issues in cross-cultural psychology*. Swets & Zeitlinger Publisher.

Holt, D. H. (1997). A comparative study of values among Chinese and U.S. entrepreneurs: Pragmatic convergence between contrasting cultures. *Journal of Business Venturing, 12*, 483–505.

House, R. J., Hanges, P. J., Javidan, M., Dorfman, P. W., & Gupta, V. (2004). *Culture, leadership, and organizations: The GLOBE study of 62 societies*. Sage Publications.

Hunt, S., & Levie, J. (2002). Culture as a predictor of entrepreneurial activity. In Babson college, B*abson Kauffmann Entrepreneurship Research Conference (BKERC)*, 2006.

Kalden, J. N., Cunningham, J., & Anderson, A. R. (2017). The social status of entrepreneurs. *The International Journal of Entrepreneurship and Innovation, 18*, 91–104.

Kidd, J. B., & Richter, F. J. (2003). *Corruption and governance in Asia*. Palgrave Macmillan.

Kretschmer, F. (2021). Deutschland als Vorbild für China–der Mittelstand als Weg,. *Frankfurter Rundschau.*

Liu, Y., Dai, W., Liao, M., & Wei, J. (2021). Social status and corporate social responsibility: Evidence from Chinese privately owned firms. *Journal of Business Ethics, 169*, 651–672.

Ma, C., Liu, H., Gu, J., & Dou, J. (2018). How entrepreneurs' Zhong-yong thinking improves new venture performance. *Chinese Management Studies, 12*, 323–345.

Mattheis, P. (2014). *Start-ups in China*. Reich werden im Kommunismus.

Moriano, J. A., Gorgievski, M., Laguna, M., Stephan, U., & Zarafshani, K. (2012). A cross-cultural approach to understanding entrepreneurial intention. *Journal of Career Development, 39*, 162–185.

Müller, G. F., & Gappisch, C. (2005). Personality types of entrepreneurs. *Psychological Reports, 96*, 737–746.

Obschonka, M. (2017). The quest for the entrepreneurial culture: Psychological big data in entrepreneurship research. *Current Opinion in Behavioral Sciences, 18*, 69–74.

Obschonka, M., Zhou, M., Zhou, Y., Zhang, J., & Silbereisen, R. K. (2019). "Confucian" traits, entrepreneurial personality, and entrepreneurship in China: A regional analysis. *Small Business Economics, 53*, 961–979.

Pahnke, A., & Welter, F. (2019). The German Mittelstand: Antithesis to Silicon Valley entrepreneurship? *Small Business Economics, 52*, 345–358.

Radziszewska, A. (2014). Intercultural dimensions of entrepreneurship. *Journal of Intercultural Management, 6*, 35–47.

Richter, N., Jackson, P., & Schildhauer, T. (2018). Entrepreneurial behavior and startups: The case of Germany and the USA. In *In entrepreneurial innovation and leadership, 1–14*. Palgrave Pivot.

Schumpeter, J. (1934). *The theory of economic development*. Harvard University Press.

Shaiq, H. M. A., Khalid, H. M. S., Akram, A., & Ali, B. (2011). Why not everybody loves Hofstede? What are the alternative approaches to study of culture. *European Journal of Business and Management, 3*, 101–111.

Stephan, U., & Pathak, S. (2016). Beyond cultural values? Cultural leadership ideals and entrepreneurship. *Journal of Business Venturing, 31*, 505–523.

Tan, J. (2002). Culture, nation, and entrepreneurial strategic orientations: Implications for an emerging economy. *Entrepreneurship Theory and Practice, 26*, 95–111.

Thomas, A. (2003). *Psychologie Interkulturelles Handeln*. Hogrefe.

Thomas, A., Kinast, E.-U., & Sylvia, S.-M. (2010). *Handbook of intercultural communication and cooperation: Basics and areas of application*. Vandenhoeck & Ruprecht.

Triandis, H. C. (1998). Intercultural education and training. In P. Funke (Ed.), *Understanding the US–across culture prospective, 305–322*. Tübingen.

Weber, M. (2001). *The Protestant ethic and the Spirit of capitalism*. Routledge.

Xie, X., Xie, X., & Martínez-Climent, C. (2019). Identifying the factors determining the entrepreneurial ecosystem of internet cultural industries in emerging economies. *International Entrepreneurship and Management Journal, 15*, 503–522.

Yoo, B., Donthu, N., & Lenartowicz, T. (2011). Measuring Hofstede's five dimensions of cultural values at the individual level: Development and validation of CVSCALE. *Journal of International Consumer Marketing, 23*.

Yue, Z. (2021). *Registration, management regulation of market entities unveiled* [Internet document] [created 25 August 2021; cited 29 August 2021]. Available from https://www.chinadaily.com.cn/a/202108/25/WS61262e4ba310efa1bd66b1e0.html.

Joerg Bueechl received his master's degree in international business and cultural studies and his research doctorate degree in international business, which centers around the investigation of trust and fairness in Sino-German supervisor-employee settings. After having worked for several small and medium-sized companies as well as in the corporate sector with focus on internationalization, human resources and organizational development, he transitioned back to academia. Mr. Büechl currently works as a professor and study dean of management of small and medium-sized enterprises at Aalen University. His recent research interests focus on entrepreneurship and intrapreneurship in international settings.

Felix Haefner is a master's graduate in business administration from Aalen University of Applied Sciences with a focus on small and medium-sized enterprises. His interest in international business strategies and the related different cultures started in an internship 2011 in Canada. He got to know different cultures and their behavior in a business context which has inspired him ever since. In the course of his studies, he developed a more profound knowledge, which he also presented in scientific papers. Felix Häfner currently works as a consultant for a software startup that is active worldwide.

South Korea's Startup Ecosystem

Gi Min Kim

Abstract Many Western companies are interested in the Asian market, which has great growth potential. Entering the Asian market is no longer a risk-taking venture and is considered the standard for many multinational companies. However, the Korean market in particular is still largely unknown compared to its importance.

Recently, the proliferation of startups has become common to promote innovation, create jobs, and stimulate economic growth. The Korean government has also provided support for entrepreneurs to actively engage in startup activities. Korea has a startup environment that provides business opportunities for Westerners as well. This makes Korea a promising emerging market for startups.

The purpose of this study is to study whether Korea actually has a business-friendly environment and whether entrepreneurs have the potential to develop entrepreneurship. Therefore, we study the social and Korean cultural aspects of Korea for the development of startups. This article helps decision makers in the public sector as well as businesses preparing to enter the Korean market.

In fact, various government support programs and policies operating in Korea support various companies. Nevertheless, risk-averse tendencies and a culture of networking importance are factors that need to be improved for a healthy startup ecosystem.

Keywords Korean Startup ecosystem · Social/financial factors · Cultural factor · Risk aversion · Networking-oriented culture · Startup mentoring

1 Introduction

Startups encourage innovation and promote the development of new products and services. Entrepreneurship is more active and thriving when startups are properly supported at the ecosystem level. Therefore, it is very important to understand the startup ecosystem (Kong, 2019). A well-established startup ecosystem not only

G. M. Kim (✉)
University of Regensburg, Regensburg, Germany

H. Pechlaner et al. (eds.), *The Clash of Entrepreneurial Cultures?*, FGF Studies in Small Business and Entrepreneurship, https://doi.org/10.1007/978-3-030-97050-5_7

forms a positive attitude toward entrepreneurial activity, but also enables the expression of entrepreneurship. Thus, it ultimately promotes job creation and overcomes low-growth economic conditions (Kuckertz et al., 2015). Therefore, it is very important to establish a sustainable startup ecosystem in which entrepreneurs are willing to take risks and take on challenges.

Compared to other developed countries and regions, the Korean startup ecosystem has a high positive evaluation of government support (Kong, 2019). This is a result of the active support of the government and local governments to revitalize startups (Kong, 2019). Nevertheless, Korean cultural characteristics are acting as an obstacle to startups.

The purpose of this study is to study the potential aspects of entrepreneurship and entrepreneurship development in Korea. So far, the Korean startup scene has been the subject of various case studies. Nevertheless, studies on the specific financial support status, the Korean government's startup support policies, and the Korean startup ecosystem from a cultural context are still lacking. Therefore, this study focuses on the Korean startup ecosystem by dividing the social and cultural aspects.

2 Status of Startups in South Korea

The Korean startup ecosystem has achieved quantitative growth in recent years by reason of continued support from the government. As of 2018, the number of new startups is 37,000, and the number of startups with sales of about $ 86 million or more is 572 (Hyun, 2020). In addition, in 2019, about $ 4.27 billion of domestic venture investment was invested in 1608 companies, and the amount of angel investment was $ 469 million (Hyun, 2020). These investments reached an all-time high (Hyun, 2020).

In 2018, the exit size was $ 2 billion, and out of a total of nine cases, three IPOs and six M & As were recorded (Hyun, 2020). In the case of the domestic venture investment recovery market, the exit through M & A is quite weak as it is only 0.5% of the 2019 amount, and the proportion of recovery through IPO is 36.7% (Hyun, 2020).

As such, the current Korean startup ecosystem is showing dynamic changes. Coupang, an e-commerce startup, received an investment of $ 86 million from Sequoia Capital in the U.S. in 2014, the fourth year after its establishment. In 2015, it was recognized with a corporate value of $ 4 billion from SoftBank and attracted an investment of $ 951 million (Hyun, 2020). It was then listed on the US NASDAQ in 2021.

In addition, companies such as "Yello Mobile," "Wemakeprice," and "MUSINSA" are all attracting attention as unicorn companies with a corporate value of more than $ 865 million. These are all startups founded after 2009 and are representative examples of predicting the growth of the Korean startup ecosystem (Kong, 2019). As of June 2020, the cumulative number of unicorns in Korea is 11, ranking sixth in the world. In particular, Korean unicorns consist of e-commerce,

Table 1 Korea unicorn corporate value ranking and major industries (source: Kim, 2020)

Ranking	Company	Transfer Period	Evaluation Amount ($B)	Business Field
1	Coupnag	May 2014	$9.00	E-commerce & direct-to-consumer
2	Krafton Game Union	August 2018	$5.00	Game
3	Yello Mobile	November 2014	$4.00	Mobile & telecommunications
4	Wemakeprice	April 2019	$2.33	E-commerce & direct-to-consumer
5	Viva Republica	December 2018	$2.20	Fintech
6	MUSINSA	November 2019	$1.89	E-commerce & direct-to-consumer
7	L & P Cosmetic	April 2017	$18	Consumer & retail
8	GPClub	June 2019	$16	Consumer & retail
9	Aprogen	December 2019	$1.04	Health
10	Yanolja	February 2019	$1.00	Travel

O2O, and fintech companies that have grown rapidly based on the mobile environment, game, fashion, and beauty companies that are in the spotlight in overseas markets (Hyun, 2020) (Table 1).

3 Social Characteristics of the Korean Startup Ecosystem

As startups have recently been attracting attention as a new growth engine to break through the stagnant economy after the financial crisis, countries around the world are making various efforts to foster startups. Accordingly, in Korea, various support policies for startups have emerged, and investment in startups is also on the rise (Hyun, 2020). Currently, Korea is providing strong government-led support for startups. Various ministries and affiliated organizations such as the Ministry of Science, ICT and Future Planning, the Ministry of Trade, Industry and Energy, the Ministry of Culture, Sports and Tourism, the Ministry of Strategy and Finance, and the Ministry of Education are implementing startup support policies. In addition, local governments such as the Seoul Metropolitan Government and Gyeonggi Provincial Government are also establishing business startup support centers.

3.1 Cluster in South Korea

In order to maintain competitiveness in a knowledge-based society, efficient diffusion and sharing of knowledge, information, and technology are required, and for this, the establishment and operation of a regional network are the most effective (Nam, 2004; Cooke, 2002). An integrated space based on this specialized local industry and infrastructure is called an "innovation cluster." Companies coexist with each other through role sharing and networking among individual actors within the innovation cluster (Park et al., 2020).

Pangyo Techno Valley, Korea's representative innovation cluster, has designated Seongnam, Gyeonggi-do as a "global R & D hub" to intensively foster IT and R & D convergence technology by cause of the development of Gyeonggi-do's knowledge-based industry (Kim & Jung, 2014). The physical infrastructure construction of Pangyo Techno Valley was completed in 2015, and as of 2016, 1306 companies have moved in. In addition, as of 2018, cumulative sales reach $ 74 billion, achieving growth in scale. Pangyo Techno Valley was built under the leadership of the local government (Gyeonggi-do), and its representation is growing as it is called "Korea's Silicon Valley" and "Asian Silicon Valley" (Park et al., 2020).

3.2 Government Support

The government promotes startup activities through the creation of policies that inspire entrepreneurship. In 2020, 90 projects were carried out in 16 government ministries, and the total budget was $ 1 billion (Hyun, 2020). This is a 29.8% increase from the previous year and the largest ever (Hyun, 2020).

The types of support include startup commercialization, R & D, startup facilities/space, education, and mentoring/consulting. The Ministry of SMEs and Startup, the ministries for startups account for the highest proportion of the budget by ministries at $ 1 billion (87%) (Hyun, 2020). As for the budget by type of support, the startup commercialization type has the highest amount at $ 632 million (50.4%) (Hyun, 2020). The three representative programs are the following.

First, there is a preliminary startup, early startup, and *'startup leap forward package'* (startup commercialization). Commercialization services such as commercialization funds, mentoring, and education are provided for prospective entrepreneurs, companies within 3 years of business, and companies within 3–7 years of business (Hyun, 2020). The budget for 20 years is $ 96 million for the preliminary startup package, $ 92 million for the initial startup package, and $ 110 million for the startup package (Hyun, 2020).

Second, there is a *'startup growth technology development (R & D)'* program. The startup growth technology development project is a project that supports technology development funds for startup companies that have growth potential but are having difficulties due to lack of technology development funds. The target

Table 2 Contents of the Korean government support programs (source: own table)

Program	Contents	Institution	Support type
Startup leap Forward package	Commercialization funds, mentoring, and education within 3–7 years of business	Ministry of SMEs and Startup/Korea Institute of Startup and Entrepreneurship Development	Commercialization
Startup growth technology R & D	Support for technology development funds	Ministry of SMEs and Startup/Technology & Information Promotion Agency for SMEs	R & D
Creative economy innovation center	Commercialization of creative ideas of local talent and vitalization of the local startup ecosystem through creative innovation centers	Ministry of SMEs and Startup/Creative Economy Innovation Center	Facility/space

of support is those that meet the qualification criteria for each task among startup companies that have been in business for less than 7 years and have sales of less than $ 1.7 million in their previous year (Hyun, 2020). Selected companies can receive support up to $ 432,619 for up to 2 years (Hyun, 2020).

The third program is the *'Creative Economy Innovation Center'* (startup facilities, space). It supports the commercialization of creative ideas of local talent and vitalization of the local startup ecosystem through creative innovation centers across the country. It provides business support services such as on/offline counseling, mentoring, commercialization/market support, investment attraction, and global expansion for prospective entrepreneurs and companies within 3 years of starting a business (Hyun, 2020). It helps to establish an innovative startup ecosystem through collaboration with local partner companies and related organizations. Such government support programs play a key role in revitalizing early-stage startup investment (Kim, 2019) (Table 2).

3.3 Policy Support

Currently, the Korean government is putting all-out efforts in place to revitalize startups across ministries to alleviate job problems, increase growth rates in a low-growth era, and solve social and economic problems (Hyun, 2020). As a result, support for fostering domestic startups has been continuously expanded, and the government's startup support policies have been consistent. To this end, efforts are being made to create jobs and create a virtuous cycle startup ecosystem. In other words, it has strived to strengthen support for technology startups and idea startups, expand the base of startups, create a virtuous cycle fund ecosystem, strengthen access to support policies, and create a private-centered ecosystem. The three representative policies are as follows.

First, there is the *'Measures to Create an Innovative Startup Ecosystem'* which was announced in 2017 (Hyun, 2020). The plan to create an innovative startup ecosystem aims to realize an innovative startup nation that grows through venture investment. It is a policy for innovative startups, creating a friendly environment, dramatically increasing venture investment funds, and establishing a virtuous cycle of startup/investment (Hyun, 2020).

Second, there is the *'Private-centered Venture Ecosystem Innovation Measures'* announced in 2018 (Hyun, 2020). Venture ecosystem innovation measures aim to create a vital venture ecosystem that grows led by the private sector. This promotes venture capital's self-sufficiency and investment expansion. As a result, it has the driving principles of private leadership, market-friendliness, autonomy, and responsibility.

Third, the *'Second Venture Boom Expansion Strategy'* announced in 2019 is a strategy to achieve an innovative and inclusive nation through the second venture boom. To strengthen the startup growth stage (startup → investment → growth → recovery/reinvestment) and create a startup ecosystem, it has a specific goal of $ 4 billion in new venture investment per year, the creation of 20 unicorns, and creation of a recovery market with active M & A by 2022 (Hyun, 2020).

3.4 Funding

In order to promote startup activities, financing in addition to policy support is essential. VC funds created over the past decade have grown steadily despite slight fluctuations (Schüler et al., 2020). In particular, the largest contributors to the creation of new funds in 2018 were financial institutions (30.3%) and policy financial institutions (25.7%) among fund of funds, activities of central government agencies, local governments, and Korea Development Bank financing (Schüler et al., 2020). The contribution of venture capitalists and general companies to new fund creation is about 12% on average (Schüler et al., 2020). Although the figure fluctuates somewhat from year to year. It is fairly stable, with financial institutions related to recent policies accounting for about a quarter or more (Schüler et al., 2020).

In terms of investment, the amount of venture capital investment increased by 371% from 2008 to 2018 (Schüler et al., 2020). In 2011, for the first time, the amount of investment exceeds USD 1 billion, and in 2017, it exceeds $ 2 billion (Schüler et al., 2020). The absolute number of simultaneous investments increased steadily with a positive growth rate from less than 500 in 2008 to about 1400 in 2018 (Schüler et al., 2020). In an international comparison, Korea ranked fourth in the OECD Venture Capital Investment Trend Statistics, with an increase of 130% between 2010 and 2016, followed by Poland (361%), Ireland (269%), and the United States (132%) (OECD, 2017).

As for the regional distribution of venture capital, 53% of new venture capital in 2017 are from companies located in Seoul and 23% from Gyeonggi and Incheon

(Schüler et al., 2020). This means that only a quarter of new venture capital is invested in non-metropolitan areas.

4 Cultural Characteristics

4.1 Risk Aversion

One of the main factors hindering entrepreneurial activity is risk aversion. This is related to the rapid growth of Korea's economic development from one of the world's poorest countries around 1960 to today's advanced and important OECD member country. Because of these experiences of poverty and economic instability, the preference for a stable job and high income is deeply ingrained in society. Moreover, the 1997 Asian financial crisis has a great impact on the Korean economy and society. This has served as an opportunity to drive all generations into stable public sector jobs, preferred by many in the face of unstable economic conditions (Schüler et al., 2020).

Risk aversion and preference for secure employment influence Korean entrepreneurship in two ways. First, interest in starting a business is generally low among Korean young people when they have an opportunity to get a job at a major conglomerate (Schüler et al., 2020). According to the 2019 Global Entrepreneurship Monitor (GEM) of Youth Entrepreneurship in Asia Pacific, only 3.6% of the Korean population aged 18–34 were engaged in early-stage startups (Guelich & Bosma, 2019).

Korean students compete fiercely for admission to prestigious universities. This comes from the expectation that employment will be guaranteed in large companies (Connell, 2014). According to a 2016 survey of university students, only 5% of respondents prefer to work in small- and medium-sized enterprises (SMEs), while 32% and 25%, respectively, want to work in large companies or state-owned institutions (Jones & Lee, 2018). In addition, young Koreans prefer stable positions in the form of full-time jobs over other types of employment. Therefore, competition for jobs in large corporations is getting fiercer. On the other hand, small- and medium-sized enterprises (SMEs), which lack the reputation, salaries, and benefits enjoyed by large corporations' employees, have difficulty filling jobs (Connell, 2014).

Second, the preference for stable employment makes it difficult for startups to find particularly skilled workers. Since startups are unstable despite offering high salaries, it is difficult for startup representatives to hire skilled employees. In addition, Korea has entrepreneurial potential because there are many highly educated young people, but it can be difficult for young people to become entrepreneurs and start a business. This is because older generations often project their experiences of poverty and economic shock on their children, driving them to the aforementioned stable jobs (Schüler, 2020).

According to GEM, 30.8% of young Koreans cited fear of failure as the reason for not starting a business (Guelich & Bosma, 2019), and 38% of students cited economic burden as the biggest obstacle when starting a business. Fear of business failure has to do with the way startups raise money in South Korea. As the VC market is still developing, many tech-focused companies are turning to debt financing, which has been the subject of so-called joint guarantee schemes in the past. This provision means that in the event of a business failure, the entrepreneur and his guarantor, a member of the family, are jointly liable for the debts of the business. Although technology-oriented startups have recently been exempted from this joint endorsement system, some companies are still following those rules. Moreover, the collective experience related to the joint guarantee system still remains in Korean society, shaping people's risk perception of corporate failure (Schüler, 2020).

4.2 Networking-Oriented Culture

The second factor that hinders entrepreneurship in Korean society is the strong network (Hoang & Antoncic, 2003). Korea was a traditional agricultural society, and as a result, voluntary associations in the modern sense are activated. In addition, there is a tradition of forming groups around the same region under the strong influence of blood-related communities and local communities.

However, due to rapid industrialization, the traditional community is rapidly disintegrating, while the formation of a social organization suitable for an urban society has not been properly achieved. In Western countries, traditional communities have been transformed into civil society-type participatory associations in the long-term industrialization process. On the other hand, in Korea, as a result of time compression due to the very rapid industrialization process, the traditional community was transformed into kinshipism. At the same time, individualism, competition, and a sense of alienation have spread, and civic awareness and culture have not been activated (Lee, 2006). In other words, it is a relationship-oriented society, a traditional Korean network based on education (hak-yeon), family (hyul-yeon), and regional origin (ji-yeon), that is, "belonging to an informally organized group" (Horak, 2014).

This phenomenon has a negative impact on the establishment and success of technology-oriented startups. Recruitment based on human resources rather than ability-based recruitment is a long-standing ill for companies. This leads to an outflow of talented people abroad. In a society with strong family values, it is difficult to build broad forms of social trust, and without social trust, it is difficult to form cooperation on a large scale (Fukuyama, 2002). From a long-term perspective, it causes national damage that kills valuable human resources and lowers national competitiveness. The importance of such networking is more evident in the metropolitan areas and Gyeonggi-do than in other regions. This is due to the concentration of the economy, high population density, VC investors, networking events and universities, and private institutions (Schüler et al., 2020).

4.3 Startup Mentoring

Mentors are people who break away from the stereotype of age, convey knowledge about the organization and job, increase the confidence of others through psychological support, and influence the mentee to succeed. A person who receives help from a mentor is called a mentee, and the mutual relationship between them for the purpose of developing their competency and career can be referred to as mentoring. Recently, many examples of startup support programs through mentoring have appeared and are being actively accepted by various institutions.

In addition to the existing investment institutions such as venture capital, there are various support policies at the government level to supplement this, but those involved in the startup ecosystem still feel that there is a lack of appropriate investment or support, especially for "early" startups (Yoo et al., 2018). Above all, since the history of Korean startups is still short, early mentoring is essential.

Among these, startup mentoring is being operated in combination with the accelerator model. Unlike existing investment types, accelerators provide additional support for mentoring, education, and networking to support the growth of early venture companies (Kong, 2019).

Incubating and accelerating[1] have something in common to support startups, but if incubation is hardware-oriented, such as space and facility support, accelerating is a software type that shares knowledge and experience related to startups. Representative programs operating in Korea include Primer, Fast Track Asia, Future Play, and The Ventures, which appeared in 2010. In addition, since Korea is one of the countries where various government ministries and affiliated organizations provide various support related to startups, government-led entrepreneurship mentoring is being operated in various ways (Yoo et al., 2018).

5 Conclusion

5.1 Summary

Entrepreneurs create many jobs and contribute to economic growth by continuously challenging entrepreneurship. Entrepreneurship is activated only when continuous support is provided to the startup ecosystem, which has a positive effect on startups.

[1] Accelerating can be traced back to Y Combinator in Silicon Valley, USA. In 2005, Y Combinator launched an accelerating program that aims to launch products and services through short-term mentoring and training within 6 months with a small equity investment. As successful cases of global success such as Airbnb and Dropbox appeared, similar programs began to appear rapidly around the world. Y Combinator, which discovered Airbnb and Dropbox, is called the guarantee of startup success by supporting a strong alumni network and know-how.

Therefore, it is essential to make efforts at the national level to create an environment in which entrepreneurship can be revitalized.

Korea's startup ecosystem is growing significantly in quantity thanks to support from the national level. As of 2020, the cumulative number of unicorns remains the sixth largest in the world, and the exit scale is also at an all-time high. This is due to strong government-led support for startups. The government promotes entrepreneurship and startup activities through various policies. In Korea, various startup support projects are being conducted by the central government and each local government, and the support is gradually increasing.

The financial support sector has also shown continuous growth in quantitative terms over the past decade. In particular, a significant amount of VC is being raised by financial institutions and policy financial institutions, among others. In other words, it can be seen that a fairly stable capital inflow is possible for startups.

Despite the government's continued support and smooth funding for startups, there are factors that hinder startup activities. This is due to Korean cultural factors. First, it is risk averse. Because of the economic crises, poverty and economic instability experienced in the past, the younger generation is very interested in stable employment. This risk aversion has a negative impact on Korean entrepreneurship.

Second, it is the culture that values human connections. Korea is a society that unites around informal networks based on education, community, and family. Since this prevents the recruitment of talents based on ability, it lowers the competitiveness of companies in the long term and further negatively affects the competitiveness of the country.

Third, the history of startups in Korea is also relatively short. Therefore, in Korea, startup mentoring and accelerator are combined to support mentoring, education, and networking for early startups.

5.2 Contribution

The Korean startup ecosystem is largely divided into social and cultural perspectives, and as a result, the purpose of this study is to determine whether Korea has an appropriate environment for starting a business.

In fact, there are various government support programs and policies operating in Korea, which include various support targets. In addition, it can be said that Korea is business-friendly and has great potential for future development through gradually increasing financial support. Nevertheless, pursuing only stability is an obstacle to business activities. If it breaks away from the informal network and strives to build a broader network, it will have a positive effect on the vitalization of startups. If we focus on creating a virtuous cycle startup ecosystem through this, more entrepreneurs will be able to actively start their own business.

References

Connell, P. S. (2014). Creating Korea's future economy: Innovation, growth, and Korea-US economic relations. *Asia Pacific Issues, 111*, January.

Cooke, P. (2002). *Knowledge economies: Clusters, learning and cooperative advantage.* Routledge.

Fukuyama, F. (2002). Social capital and development. *SAIS Review (1989–2003), 22*(1), 23–37.

Guelich, U., & Bosma, N. (2019). *Youth entrepreneurship in Asia and the Pacific 2018–19.* GEM-UNDP Repot.

Hoang, H., & Antoncic, B. (2003). Network-based research in entrepreneurship: A critical review. *Journal of Business Venturing, 18*(2), 165–187.

Horak, S. (2014). Antecedents and characteristics of informal relation-based networks in Korea: Yongo, Yonjul and Inmaek. *Asia Pacific Business Review, 20*(1), 78–108.

Hyun, J. G. (2020). Startup promotion policy. *National Assembly Library, 4*(80).

Jones, S. R., & Lee, J. W. (2018). *Enhancing dynamism in SMEs and entrepreneurship in Korea.* OECD Economics Department Working Papers, OECD.

Kim, B. G. (2019). Comparison of Korea, US, and China startup investment ecosystems. *Korea International Trade Association, 2019*(19).

Kim, G. M. (2020). *The contribution of HR activities to the success of startups.* Master Thesis. University of Regensburg.

Kim, M. J., & Jung, E.-j. (2014). A comparative study regarding provincially promoted innovation clusters in Korea and abroad -the case of research Triangle Park and Gyeonggi innovation clusters. *The Geographical Journal of Korea, 48*(4), 409–423.

Kong, H. (2019). Korean start-up ecosystem based on comparison of global countries - quantitative and qualitative research. *Asia-Pacific Journal of Business Venturing and Entrepreneurship, 14*(1), 101–116.

Kuckertz, A., Berger, E. S., & Allmendinger, M. (2015). What drives entrepreneurship? A configurational analysis of the determinants of entrepreneurship in innovation-driven economies. *A configurational analysis of the determinants of entrepreneurship in innovation-driven economies*, 273–288.

Lee, J. Y. (2006). Community community and social capital. *Proceedings of the Korean Sociological Association Symposium*, 23–49.

Nam, K. B. (2004). The role of innovation clusters and university research: Theory and reality. *Industrial location, 15*, 2–9.

OECD (Organisation for Economic Co-operation and Development). (2017). *Entrepreneurship at a glance 2017.* OECD Publishing.

Park, J. S., Park, S. H., & Hong, S. S. (2020). Integrated study on the factors influencing sustainable innovation cluster of Pangyo Techno Valley. *Asia-Pacific Journal of Business Venturing and Entrepreneurship, 15*(1), 71–94.

Schüler, D. (2020). *The influence of institutions on entrepreneurship as occupational choice: A study about the emergence of young entrepreneurs in South Korea.* Doctoral Dissertation. University of Duisburg-Essen.

Schüler, D., Suhalitca, M., Pascha, W., & Oh, K-Y. (2020). *Government policies for start-ups in Korea and its regions: Motives, mechanisms and major obstacles, Working Papers on East Asian Studies, No. 127/2020, University of Duisburg- Essen*, Institute of East Asian Studies (IN-EAST), Duisburg.

Yoo, B. J., Jeon, S. M., & Seok, M. S. (2018). A study on the effect of mentoring skills and mentoring functions on start-up mentoring satisfaction: Focused on the moderating effects of the characteristics of entrepreneurs. *Asia-Pacific Journal of Business Venturing and Entrepreneurship, 13*(6), 15–25.

Gi Min Kim majored in International Trade at Kyonggi University in South Korea. He received his master's degree from the Chair of Leadership & Organization (Prof. Dr. Thomas Steger) at the University of Regensburg, Germany. He currently works for Hwaseung Automotive Europe GmbH in Frankfurt, Germany, as Sales and Project Support. His research interests are in the startup ecosystem and human resource management in startups.

Peculiarities of Entrepreneurial Ecosystems in the Caucasus Countries: The Case of Georgia

Lela Grießbach

Abstract This chapter deals with the entrepreneurial ecosystem (EE) of post-Soviet Georgia, which has undertaken tremendous endeavours since the peaceful Rose Revolution, bringing about a democratic institutional design and improving institutional quality. Located in the Caucasus region, providing a transit corridor between Europe and Asia, Georgia offers a unique context for the examination of EEs, as it is affected by both the Soviet legacy and Western-style liberal market dynamics.

A bottom-up approach to analysis, supported by initial key insights from expert interviews, has been applied to determine the peculiarities of the EE in Georgia. Government regulations, the taxation system and corruption have been used as indicators for the institutional framework, whereas access to finance, R&D, infrastructure and a skilled workforce were considered physical conditions crucial for entrepreneurial activity.

Despite the global recognition of Georgia having transformed from a failed to a neoliberal modern state, its EE seems to be in its infancy. As many endeavours have been tactical rather than strategic, several constraints on systemic, institutional and social levels still hamper the development of local entrepreneurial activity. Although the successful removal of entry barriers at an administrative level has encouraged entrepreneurial activity, the ease of doing business is not directly related to productive entrepreneurship.

Keywords Entrepreneurship · Entrepreneurial ecosystem · Institution building · Transition economies · Post-Soviet context · Caucasus · Georgia

L. Grießbach (✉)
University of Siegen, Department III, Business Administration, Siegen, Germany

H. Pechlaner et al. (eds.), *The Clash of Entrepreneurial Cultures?*, FGF Studies in Small Business and Entrepreneurship, https://doi.org/10.1007/978-3-030-97050-5_8

1 The Importance of an Entrepreneurial Ecosystem Approach

The entrepreneurial ecosystem (EE) approach has gained increasing attention among scholars and policy makers, emphasizing the importance of the institutions, culture and networks that build up within a region and have a significant impact on local entrepreneurship development (Stam & Spigel, 2017). Entrepreneurial ecosystems (EEs) are considered a structure of different key actors around entrepreneurs, who interact with each other in order to enhance entrepreneurial thinking and enable successful entrepreneurship (Isenberg, 2011).

Different theoretical frameworks have been used to describe and examine EEs from a systemic view, focusing on an interactive relationship between entrepreneurs and key actors or other elements of the EE (Isenberg, 2011; Stam & Spigel, 2017). These studies have outlined the importance of ecosystem support in the creation of new businesses and market entry, a firm's survival and growth in a region (Stam, 2014), the effects of performance for small- and medium-sized enterprises (SMEs) (Ullah, 2019) and particular support for women entrepreneurs (Manolova et al., 2017). Accordingly, different studies have focused on different actors and factors of the ecosystem, concluding that the success of an entrepreneurial ecosystem is context-dependent (Isenberg, 2011; Smallbone & Welter, 2010).

The majority of studies on entrepreneurial ecosystems have focused on developed countries, where the EEs are seen as a driver of entrepreneurial activities with growth potential, and high rates of productive entrepreneurs and SMEs (Stam, 2014). By contrast, in post-Soviet countries affected by deep-rooted informality, corruption, high rates of unemployment and social insecurity, the economic and market conditions are entirely different (Sauka & Chepurenko, 2017). In many post-Soviet countries, all types of entrepreneurship are considered what Baumol (1990) calls "productive entrepreneurship", with an emphasis on any economic activity that would contribute to economic development and social advancement (Ullah, 2019). Consequently, this shifts the understanding of the EE approach to different dimensions and makes it necessary to explore the structure of EEs in a post-Soviet context.

Another reason for examining EEs from the perspective of a post-Soviet context is to find out how rigorous institutional reforms of some post-Soviet countries, aimed towards a Western-style liberal market economy, influence local EE development. Institutional reforms aimed at modernizing and strengthening democratic institutions positively influence the development of entrepreneurship and enable new opportunities for entrepreneurs (Welter & Smallbone, 2011). Accordingly, it can be argued that institutional reforms would impact entrepreneurial ecosystem positively and enhance its development in a specific context.

This chapter deals with the EE in post-Soviet Georgia, which has undertaken tremendous endeavours since the Rose Revolution in November 2003, focusing on simplifying institutional design and improving institutional quality (Aliyev, 2014; Papava, 2006). In its Ease of Doing Business Report 2018, the World Bank ranked Georgia 9th (World Bank Group, 2018), and the country's Corruption Perception

Index decreased from 64th out of 183 countries to 44th (Transparency International Georgia, 2019). In a post-Soviet context, Georgia is a specific case in terms of implementing radical institutional reforms and achieving relative reductions in reliance on informality (Aliyev, 2017). What is more, due to its central location in the Caucasus region—a transit corridor between Europe and Asia—and its political and economic openness towards both European and Asian economies (Pechlaner et al., 2021; Tsuladze, 2017), Georgia offers a unique context for the examination of EEs, as it is affected by both its Soviet legacy and Western-style liberal market dynamics. However, despite tremendous progress since the Rose Revolution, scholars still struggle with several aspects of new-institutional reforms, which seem to have loopholes in terms of a more inclusive market economy, thus questioning existing SME and entrepreneurship policies (Rekhviashvili, 2016; Rudaz, 2015).

Against this background, this chapter aims to outline and discuss the shortcomings of market-enhancing reforms since the Rose Revolution in Georgia and their effects on the development of the Georgian entrepreneurial ecosystem. Accordingly, this work contributes to a better understanding of peculiarities in entrepreneurship development in the post-Soviet Caucasus region, and explains why institutional remedies do not always lead to a Western-style liberal market, despite tremendous institutional efforts. With this in mind, the following research question is raised:

> How have institutional reforms since Rose Revolution affected the development of a local entrepreneurial ecosystem in Georgia, and what does this mean for the region and the future of local entrepreneurial activities?

In order to determine the existence and composition of the EE in Georgia, a bottom-up approach to analysis (Isenberg, 2011; Ullah, 2019) has been applied, using relevant studies and statistical data. In addition, initial key insights from expert interviews are included, assessing and discussing the different elements of the Georgian entrepreneurial ecosystem that could be crucial for successful entrepreneurial activity in the country.

2 Institution Building and the Business Environment Since the Rose Revolution

The peaceful Rose Revolution in 2003 was a result of growing discontent among the population, supported by a circle of young, mostly Western-educated politicians, about the continuing corruption practiced by the government elite (Aliyev, 2014). At that time, more than 70% of the Georgian economy was informal, and about 51.8% of the population lived below the poverty line (UN Georgia, 2001).

The primary goals of the new government were to build a functional institutional framework based on democratization and to tackle the core obstacles to Georgia's economic development (Livny, 2016). The reforms started with the cleansing of the system, ranging from the communist era's criminal elements to radically changing police structures. In addition, entrance examinations for universities (which were previously affected by nepotism and corrupt practices) were centralized and a new accreditation system for higher education institutions was implemented. Extensive reforms were established in the health sector, judicial sector, civil service area and tax services. By 2003, only 80,000 taxpayers were officially registered in Georgia and tax evasion by bribing officials or via interpersonal networks was a common practice among entrepreneurs (Aliyev, 2017). From 2005, the GDP rates grew by about 10% and the number of foreign investments and registered firms increased considerably. For continuous improvement of its entrepreneurial environment, Georgia was considered a top reformer for 2005-2010 (Timm, 2013). Scholars argue that the key success of the Rose Revolution government was its strategy of "zero tolerance" in handling crime, corruption and other informal practices. At the same time, the "zero tolerance" strategy was criticized for its lack of humane, inclusive institutions, which led to the political downfall of the "Revolutionaries" in 2012 (Livny, 2016).

The newly elected government started immediately with reforms aimed primarily at social inclusivity. Despite some fragmented achievements, generous social outlays and rushed measures, the new government has not yet improved general inclusivity. Nevertheless, the new government has managed to advance the European integration agenda of Georgia, resulting in an agreement with the EU on the Deep and Comprehensive Free Trade Agreement (DCFTA) in 2014. Accordingly, Georgia committed to significant economic and institutional reforms in exchange for greater access to the European market (Livny, 2016). At the same time, the Georgian government advanced its economic collaboration with Asian countries. For example, Georgia and China successfully signed a Free Trade Agreement in 2016. This increased exports from Georgia to China, as well as direct Chinese investment into the Georgian economy. With its desire to become a part of the recent Belt and Road Initiative (BRI) project, Georgia aims to facilitate trade relations between China and Europe as a transit hub (Pechlaner et al., 2021). Furthermore, Georgia is a member of different international organizations facilitating its economic, social and cultural advancement (IMUNA, 2021).

The geographical location of Georgia means that it has the opportunity to play an important role in the region, especially in trade and the international shipping of goods. Compared to others, the Georgian route from Europe to Asia and back is shorter. However, although Georgia's transit capacity has been steadily increasing, much of its potential remains untapped. For example, the current capacity of the transport infrastructure fails to provide increased cargo service, there are only a few logistics centres that meet modern requirements and the competitiveness of the route through Georgia is reduced by different procedures for crossing the borders of neighbouring countries (Government of Georgia, 2014).

Participation in huge infrastructure projects connecting Europe and Asia would allow the Georgian government to increase the competitiveness of its local business environment and support infrastructure development and trade facilitation in both the European and Asian regions, thus contributing to regional (service) development and integration (Pechlaner et al., 2021). Pechlaner et al. (2021) outline the importance of developing the service ecosystem, with a focus on distributive, productive, social and personal services. Accordingly, transit traffic would enable participation through cooperation and support, thus enabling entrepreneurship development in trade and services (Pechlaner et al., 2021). In addition, researchers and policy makers agree about the huge benefits for the development of local and regional tourism through transport infrastructure building and development (Government of Georgia, 2014). The above makes Georgia an important player in building and maintaining multi-stakeholder relations, in increasing regional value chains, in promoting sustainable development and strengthening cooperation with independent (economic) actors (Invest in Georgia, 2020; Pechlaner et al., 2021). Reforms after the Rose Revolution changed the economic environment in the country, which led to the simplification of starting and doing business in Georgia. The new neoliberal policy, which aimed to change government interference in the economic sphere, subjected SME activities to two different laws: The Law on the Georgian National Investment Agency and the Tax Code (Rudaz, 2012, 2015). Accordingly, both laws used different descriptions of SMEs based on company's turnover and number of employees, which ultimately led to frustration for entrepreneurs and small business owners (Machavariani et al., 2015). According to Machavariani et al. (2015), SMEs in Georgia count for 21.8% of value added, providing jobs for 45.6% of the population. By contrast, only 8% of the registered enterprises are large companies, providing around 80% of the production in the country (Machavariani et al., 2015). The majority of Georgia's employed population are self-employed. It is especially challenging for young people in rural regions to find a job: about 35% of the unemployed are 20-29 years old (Kuriakose, 2013).

As previous studies have shown, entrepreneurs in Georgia are driven by necessity rather than opportunity (Rudaz, 2012). Most founders have a bachelor's degree, followed by technical education. It is noticeable that entrepreneurs mostly found a company in the industry they have worked in for a long time. The majority of entrepreneurs are over 40 years (Kuriakose, 2013), implying that most of them are motivated to run their own business since they had already been in the workforce or earned a wage for a long time. Not finding a suitable job is often mentioned by entrepreneurs as the main reason for starting a business (Bzhalava, Jvarsheishvili, et al., 2017, b), along with the motivation to become one's own boss and to make more money (Kuriakose, 2013).

3 The Dynamics of the Georgian Entrepreneurial Ecosystem

In the following, the institutional framework and physical conditions of the EE in Georgia are described, based on identified data and expert interviews. Following Ullah (2019), government regulations, the taxation system and corruption have been used as indicators for the institutional framework. These three elements have been described in this chapter, as they seem appropriate to the Georgian context. Furthermore, different elements of the physical condition of the EE have been suggested in the literature (Isenberg, 2011; Stam & Spigel, 2017). However, the following elements of physical conditions have mostly been mentioned in expert interviews as characteristics of the EE in Georgia: access to finance, research and development (R&D), infrastructure and a skilled workforce. Therefore, these elements will be considered in this chapter.

3.1 Institutional Framework

Governmental policy and regulations are rated most positively in the Georgian context (Bzhalava, Lezhava, et al., 2017, b). It is possible to register a business in only one day (World Bank Group, 2018). However, although the authorities have managed to combat corruption and establish a seemingly neoliberal economic policy, it is argued that in Georgia in addition to an "observed" economy, which is regulated by statistics and official authorities, a "non-observed" economy still exists (Rudaz, 2015).

Since adopting a new Tax Code in 2004, rates for different taxes decreased considerably and more than twenty taxes used under several old laws were reduced to only seven (Papava, 2006). However, continually changing taxation regulations and high tax rates have been cited as one of the biggest obstacles by entrepreneurs in Georgia, as in neighbouring countries Armenia and Azerbaijan (Kuriakose, 2013). By contrast, the 2016-2017 Georgia GEM report names taxes as one of the positive conditions of the entrepreneurial ecosystem in Georgia (Bzhalava, Lezhava, et al., 2017, b), which might be related to the favourable conditions for foreign direct investment. This is in accordance with the argument that in knowledge-based economies, changes in tax policies support the promotion of innovation and the creation of entrepreneurship, whereas in newly industrialized low-middle-income countries like Georgia, governments change corporate taxes, for example, to attract foreign investors (Ullah, 2019). In fact, according to the program "Invest in Georgia", FDI in Georgia amounted to 6.8 billion US dollars from 2016 to 2020 (Invest in Georgia, 2020). Despite a positive inflow of FDI, the experts interviewed argue that existing efforts are insufficient and specific programs for investing in small businesses should be created and promoted.

Corruption has been widely shown to be detrimental to economic growth. The drastic reforms in Georgia that followed the Rose Revolution were able to combat corruption in the country. However, scholars and experts notice that, despite the previous reforms, many deep-rooted informal practices have only been undermined to some extent (Aliyev, 2017; Rekhviashvili, 2016). This seems unsurprising in terms of interrelation between formal and informal institutions, especially in a transition country context (Smallbone & Welter, 2010). In fact, scholars argue that formal institutional reforms in Georgia were too fast, not adjusted to local specifics and did not involve the entire population in institutional transition (Aliyev, 2017;

Rekhviashvili, 2016; Rudaz, 2015). Furthermore, unlike formal institutions, informal institutions do not change quickly (Smallbone & Welter, 2010). Although accepting bribes and gift-giving practices were a norm in Soviet time and early 1990's Georgia, they are not tolerated anymore. "Informal kinship and friendship networks continue to serve as important coping mechanisms in areas neglected by the government's reforms" (Aliyev, 2014, p. 30), for example, for obtaining jobs. This, in fact, leads to a mismatch of employees' skills with the industry's needs, and thus hinders the development of local industry (Chakhaia, 2013). The experts interviewed agreed on such existing practices and outlined that this is characteristic for the entire Caucasus region. In Armenia, for example, entrepreneurs felt that government officials favour well-connected individuals (Kuriakose, 2013).

3.2 Physical Conditions

The existence and interrelation of the elements of physical conditions largely determine the success of entrepreneurial ecosystems (Isenberg, 2011). As mentioned above, the following elements of physical conditions of the Georgian EE are analysed in this chapter: access to finance, R&D, infrastructure and a skilled workforce.

Financial systems in Georgia do not seem conducive to business development. High interest rates and risk-averse lending policies require high levels of collateral, hindering entrepreneurs in starting or expanding a firm (Kuriakose, 2013). In transition countries, nascent entrepreneurs rely mostly on families and friends when borrowing money for their entrepreneurial activities (Grigore & Dragan, 2020; Ullah, 2019). Experts contradict this view in the Georgian case, arguing that it is difficult to borrow money from family members, relatives or friends because most of them do not have a stable income or savings. Like in many other post-Soviet societies, financial sources other than bank loans are limited. To find the necessary funding is one of the main obstacles for entrepreneurs in other Caucasian countries as well (Kuriakose, 2013).

The lack of financial opportunities influences R&D activities in Georgia. Studies show that the vast majority of products are modifications of existing ones, mostly oriented on local, standardized markets. Furthermore, most entrepreneurs in Georgia neglect the importance of achieving a market advantage based on R&D. As a result, most products are only slightly distinguishable from those of competitors (Kuriakose, 2013). The experts interviewed agree that universities and research institutes are less associated with important sources of knowledge for new business opportunities and innovative business activities by entrepreneurs in Georgia. By contrast, Armenian firms spend more on R&D and thus offer more innovative products, and are also more competitive in international markets (Kuriakose, 2013).

Infrastructural support plays a pivotal role in attracting new entrepreneurs and improving the efficiency of existing firms (Ullah, 2019). Although commercial and legal infrastructure is available in Georgia, it might be difficult for new firms to find adequate services or afford them (Bzhalava, et al., 2017, b). Despite high rates in the recent GEM Georgia 2016 report on physical infrastructure development, entrepreneurs in Georgia find technological risk and uncertainty to be one of the most common obstacles (Kuriakose, 2013). This can be traced back to limited R&D and a lack of industry-relevant information. According to the experts interviewed, although the necessary infrastructure is available in Georgia, its function is still episodic and not goal driven. Furthermore, they emphasize that skilled staff for the management of infrastructure and the useful allocation of resources is one of the main obstacles. This contradicts the recent investment paper from the Georgian government, which makes a bold statement about a "Competitively priced, skilled and productive workforce" (Invest in Georgia, 2020), although it is argued that there is no database or statistics for graduates and their employment information (Bregvadze, 2013).

To find skilled workforce in general is a big problem in Georgia. Several studies have outlined that the professions, people are trained in, do not match with the local market needs (Bzhalava, et al., 2017, b; Kuriakose, 2013). In addition, no systemic approach has been implemented to analyse this relationship and identify gaps (Bregvadze, 2013). Despite 64 higher education institutions in a country of 3.7 million people (Invest in Georgia, 2020), it is impossible to estimate the benefits of higher education on individual and economic development. Some research has shown that the majority of students in Georgia seem to go to university because of enhancing or maintaining their social status, impressing their parents, peers and the community rather than on the basis of their own skills, the market needs and employment or increased income in the future (Chakhaia, 2013). Given that entrepreneurship is a desired career choice and established entrepreneurs gain a high status in Georgian society (Bzhalava, et al., 2017, b), it can be argued that entrepreneurship training could attract more students and encourage them in their entrepreneurial activities. However, like in many other post-Soviet countries, the role and activities of universities in promoting entrepreneurial mindsets and involvement in academic research on entrepreneurship are relatively low in Georgia (Griessbach & Ettl, 2020).

4 Conclusion

In light of the institutional framework and physical conditions presented above, it can be argued that the EE in Georgia is in its infancy. While some important EE elements are available to some extent, a tight interrelationship between them is lacking.

Unlike most post-Soviet countries, where the state is less of an agent of change (Smallbone & Welter, 2010), the post-Rose Revolution government in Georgia can be characterized as an agent of change, as it had recognized the (potential) role of entrepreneurship in fostering economic development and institutional change, and certain measures in this regard have been implemented successfully. However, many endeavours seem to be tactical rather than strategic, thus several constrains at systemic, institutional and social levels still hamper the development of local entrepreneurial activity. Though administrative barriers and access to finance have been simplified, the progress is barely visible for SMEs. Nascent entrepreneurs and small business owners feel alone on the "playing field", which seems to favour big companies and high-tech start-ups. This deepens entrepreneur and small business owner distrust of the state (programs) and other key entrepreneurial ecosystem actors (Rudaz, 2015). Furthermore, scholars pay attention to destructive actors of the EEs, especially in transition societies, the so-called "political entrepreneurs" who run their businesses by favouring the government and might influence state officials to subsidize their venture or industry, or to establish regulations that impact competitors (Grigore & Dragan, 2020).

By analysing the Georgian case, it becomes clear that the successful removal of entry barriers at an administrative level in Georgia encourages entrepreneurial activity, but if we define entrepreneurship as a "process of discovering and exploiting profitable opportunities" (Rudaz, 2015, p. 11), we see that the ease of registering a business is not directly related to productive entrepreneurship. Registering a business with the authorities is certainly one of the steps for formalizing entrepreneurial activity, but business registration alone does not make people entrepreneurs. Self-employed and micro business owners in Georgia, for example, do what they do by default and often lack the motivation to seize opportunities, start new activities or propose new services or products, enrol in training courses or take more financial risks in developing their business activities (Kuriakose, 2013; Rudaz, 2015). This transformation of "quasi-entrepreneurial" activity, which rather reflects survival motivation or episodic business deals, into "enterprise" activity, which according to Western concepts is stable and repetitive, should be supported by entrepreneurship and business training (Rudaz, 2015). We have seen that existing nepotism and the use of informal networks worsen the deep lack of a skilled local workforce, and this will be prevalent until ingrained informal practices in this regard are entirely undermined.

Although many endeavours have been undertaken since the Rose Revolution at an administrative level, and thus global recognition of the transformation of Georgia from a failed state to a neoliberal modern state has been successful, much work is still needed to develop the local entrepreneurial ecosystem from the top-down. However, a bottom-up approach—whether entrepreneurs are part of the observed economy with growth intentions and overall economic development motivations, and how other EE actors participate in this development—should be considered by future studies and related policy papers.

In addition, future studies should focus on the importance of Georgia as a central transit corridor in contributing to the development of more inclusive and sustainable international ecosystems. Empirical data, policy recommendations and action plans would enable the Georgian government to use this great opportunity to accelerate proceedings in this regard, establishing effective measures in order to build both material and immaterial networks for infrastructure building and facilitating international trade and services at the crossroads of Europe and Asia.

In summary, the understanding of the EE in a transition country context provided in this chapter can be utilized as a starting knowledge base for future research in countries with similar levels of economic and social development. This chapter thus allows researchers and policy makers to consider transition country perspectives in cross-country comparisons, and to identify effective aspects in different environments that may promote entrepreneurship.

References

Aliyev, H. (2014). The effects of the Saakashvili era reforms on informal practices in the republic of Georgia. *Studies of Transition States and Societies, 6*(1), 19–33.

Aliyev, H. (2017). When informal institutions change: Institutional reforms and informal practices in the former Soviet Union. *University of Michigan Press.* https://doi.org/10.3998/mpub.8772004

Baumol, W. J. (1990). Entrepreneurship: Productive, unproductive, and destructive. *Journal of Political Economy, 98*(5, Part 1), 893–921. https://doi.org/10.1086/261712

Bregvadze, T. (2013). *Strategic development of higher education and science in Georgia: V–Higher education and employment.* Tbilisi. The International Institute for education policy, planning and management. Retrieved July 7, 2021, from http://eprints.iliauni.edu.ge/1983/

Bzhalava, L., Jvarsheishvili, G., Brekashvili, P., & Lezhava, B. (2017). Entrepreneurial intentions and initiatives in Georgia. In A. Sauka & A. Chepurenko (Eds.), *Entrepreneurship in transition economies* (pp. 261–279). Springer International Publishing. https://doi.org/10.1007/978-3-319-57342-7_15

Bzhalava, L., Lezhava, B., Brekashvili, P., & Melua, I. (2017). *Global entrepreneurship monitor: 2016-2017 Georgia report.* Caucasus University.

Chakhaia, L. (2013). *Strategic development of higher education and science in Georgia: II–funding research and higher education financial governance.* The International Institute for education policy, planning and management. https://doi.org/10.13140/RG.2.1.1076.7123

Government of Georgia (2014): *Social-economic development strategy of Georgia "GEORGIA 2020".* Retrieved July 6, 2018, from https://policy.asiapacificenergy.org/sites/default/files/Georgia%202020_ENG.pdf

Griessbach, L., & Ettl, K. (2020). The entrepreneurial ecosystem and its impact on female managers in transition economies: The case of Georgia. In I. Rybnikova, A. Soulsby, & S. Blazejewski (Eds.), *Journal of east European management studies. Women in management in central and eastern European countries* (pp. 150–171). https://doi.org/10.5771/9783748907190-7

Grigore, A.-M., & Dragan, I.-M. (2020). Towards sustainable entrepreneurial ecosystems in a transitional economy: An analysis of two Romanian city-regions through the lens of entrepreneurs. *Sustainability, 12*(15), 6061. https://doi.org/10.3390/su12156061

IMUNA. (2021). Country profile Georgia. IMUNA education through simulation. Retrieved October 20, 2021, from https://www.imuna.org/resources/country-profiles/georgia/

Invest in Georgia. (2020). *Georgia: A pleasure doing business.* Tbilisi. Ministry of economy and sustainable development Georgia. Retrieved July 8, 2021, from https://investingeorgia.org/en/downloads/brochures

Isenberg, D. (2011). *The entrepreneurship ecosystem strategy as a new paradigm for economic policy: Principles for cultivating entrepreneurship* [The Babson Entrepreneurship Ecosystem Project]. Babson Global.

Kuriakose, S. (2013). Fostering entrepreneurship in Georgia: directions in development; private sector development. Retrieved May 5, 2021, from http://hdl.handle.net/10986/15786

Livny, E. (2016). Georgia's revolutions and economic development. In G. Nodia (Ed.), *25 years of independent Georgia: achievements and unfinished projects (pp. 162–207)*. Retrieved June 6, 2021, from http://www.kas.de/wf/doc/kas_45857-1522-1-30.pdf?160714115123

Machavariani, S., Shatberashvili, O., Tavartkiladze, S., & Ghaghanidze, G. (2015). *saqarTveloSi mcire da saSualo biznesis ganviTarebis perspeqtivebi: [Perspectives for the development of small and medium business in Georgia]*. Caucasus University and Friedrich-Ebert-Stiftung.

Manolova, T. S., Brush, C. G., Edelman, L. F., Robb, A. M., & Welter, F. (2017). *Entrepreneurial ecosystems and growth of women's entrepreneurship: A comparative analysis*. Edward Elgar.

Papava, V. (2006). The political economy of Georgia's rose revolution. *Orbis, 50*(4), 657–667. https://doi.org/10.1016/j.orbis.2006.07.006

Pechlaner, H., Thees, H., Manske-Wang, W., & Scuttari, A. (2021). Local service industry and tourism development through the global trade and infrastructure project of the new silk road–the example of Georgia. *The Service Industries Journal, 41*(7-8), 553–579. https://doi.org/10.1080/02642069.2019.1623204

Rekhviashvili, L. (2016). Counterbalancing marketization informally: Georgia's new-institutionalist reform and its discontents. *Journal of Contemporary Central and Eastern Europe, 24*(3), 255–272. https://doi.org/10.1080/0965156X.2016.1260657

Rudaz, P. (2012). Entrepreneurship in Georgia. *Caucasus Analytical Digest, 45*, 2–8. Retrieved April 20, 2019, from https://www.laender-analysen.de/cad/pdf/CAD-45.pdf

Rudaz, P. (2015). Institutional trust and the informal sector of Georgia. *Caucasus Analytical Digest* (75). Retrieved April 20, 2019, https://www.files.ethz.ch/isn/192445/CaucasusAnalyticalDigest75.pdf

Sauka, A., & Chepurenko, A. (Eds.). (2017). *Entrepreneurship in transition economies*. Springer International Publishing. https://doi.org/10.1007/978-3-319-57342-7

Smallbone, D., & Welter, F. (2010). *Entrepreneurship, institutions and institutional change in transition economies*. Conference Paper. www.gsom.spbu.ru/files/upload/niim/seminar/smallbone_discussion_paper.pdf

Stam, E. (2014). The Dutch entrepreneurial ecosystem. *SSRN Electronic Journal*. https://doi.org/10.2139/ssrn.2473475

Stam, E., & Spigel, B. (2017). Entrepreneurial ecosystems. In *Handbook for Entrepreneurship and Small Business* (pp. 1–15). https://dspace.library.uu.nl/handle/1874/347982

Timm, C. (2013). *Economic regulation and state interventions. Georgia's move from neoliberalism to state managed capitalism* (2013/03). Göttingen. PFH Private Hochschule. Retrieved June 25, 2021, from http://hdl.handle.net/10419/75297

Transparency International Georgia. (2019). *Transparency international Georgia reports*. Retrieved May 29, 2021, from https://www.transparency.ge/en/post/results-2019-corruption-perceptions-index-point-stagnation-anti-corruption-reforms-georgia

Tsuladze, L. (2017). On Europeanisation, national sentiments and confused identities in Georgia. *Communist and Post-Communist Studies, 50*(2), 125–133. https://doi.org/10.1016/j.postcomstud.2017.05.003

Ullah, S. (2019). *The effect of entrepreneurial ecosystems on performance of SMEs in low middle income countries with a particular focus on Pakistan* [PhD Thesis]. Lancaster University. Retrieved June 15, 2021, from https://eprints.lancs.ac.uk/id/eprint/135130/

UN Georgia. (2001). *Georgia–common country assessment: United Nations development assistance framework*. United Nations.

Welter, F., & Smallbone, D. (2011). Institutional perspectives on entrepreneurial behaviour in challenging environments. *Journal of Small Business Management, 49*(1), 107–125. https://doi.org/10.1111/j.1540-627X.2010.00317.x

World Bank Group. (2018). Doing business 2018: Reforming to create jobs. Retrieved June 6, 2021, from https://openknowledge.worldbank.org/handle/10986/28608

Lela Grießbach is a doctoral candidate at the University of Siegen. Her research interest focuses on entrepreneurial ecosystems and women's entrepreneurship in transition economies. Lela Grießbach was born and grew up in Georgia, where she also studied and worked. She completed her master's degree in marketing and sales in Germany. At present Lela Grießbach works as a lecturer of Marketing and Business Management and as a freelance entrepreneurship consultant in Berlin.

Connecting Asia and Europe: Opportunities and Barriers for Knowledge-Oriented Regional Development in Central Asia

Justine Markisch

Abstract Central Asia is geographically located at the center of the Eurasian continent in between strong and dynamic economies such as Russia, China, India, and the European Union. Despite being abundant on natural resources, Central Asia is not greatly integrated into the world economy due to several reasons, such as being landlocked and rural, depending on the primary sector and suffering from an insufficient absorptive capacity regarding knowledge and technology transfer.

In the past decade, connecting Asia and Europe got increasingly important with the launch of China's Belt and Road Initiative and the EU Connectivity Strategy, offering Central Asia the opportunity to become the continental land bridge and therefore integrate into global value chains and achieve knowledge-oriented regional development. The Belt and Road Initiative and the EU Connectivity Strategy can be distinguished in their political nature, objectives, and values, thus offering different potentials for Central Asia. However, knowledge-oriented regional development in Central Asia will be a lengthy process, which can only be successful if the region increases its capabilities to substantially benefit from knowledge transfer.

Keywords Central Asia · Regionalism · Belt and Road Initiative · EU Connectivity Strategy · Knowledge transfer · Regional development

1 Introduction

Central Asia is geographically located at the center of the Eurasian continent in between strong and dynamic economies such as Russia in the North, China in the East, India in the South, and the European Union (EU) in the West. Even though the Central Asian countries are abundant on natural resources, they are not greatly integrated into the world economy. Categorized as Landlocked Developing Countries by the United Nations, they are economically hindered by not having direct

J. Markisch (✉)
Chamber of Industry and Commerce for the Palatinate, Ludwigshafen, Germany
e-mail: justine.markisch@pfalz.ihk24.de

H. Pechlaner et al. (eds.), *The Clash of Entrepreneurial Cultures?*, FGF Studies in Small Business and Entrepreneurship, https://doi.org/10.1007/978-3-030-97050-5_9

Fig. 1 Central Asian region consisting of Kazakhstan, Kyrgyzstan, Tajikistan, and Uzbekistan. Cartography: A. Kaiser 2021

access to the sea and being dependent on export of primary resources such as fossil fuels, minerals, and agricultural outputs. Despite increasing investments in Central Asian infrastructure, the region has only access to 45 to 60 percent of the global gross domestic product (GDP), a situation which it shares with many African and South Asian countries (ITF, 2019). Bound by history and geography, Central Asia is considered a region consisting of the five post-Soviet countries Kazakhstan, Kyrgyzstan, Tajikistan, Turkmenistan, and Uzbekistan (Fig. 1).

Some scholars even view the region as a natural grouping since they are contiguous, share the languages (except for Tajikistan) as well as cultural and economic ties. Moreover, all Central Asian countries are (semi-)authoritarian and rely on clan politics (Hancock & Libman, 2016).

Since knowledge is, today, perceived as the crucial resource for long-term economic growth (Liefner & Schätzl, 2017), its potential role for regional development of yet underdeveloped regions such as Central Asia is not to be underestimated. In the past two decades, Central Asia is becoming increasingly important for China for geostrategic reasons, commercial and resource interests, and foreign relations. Also, China is now Central Asia's biggest trade partner (Ghiasy & Zhou, 2017). The intensified interactions between Central Asia and strong economies such as China deliver a chance for Central Asian countries to benefit from knowledge transfer and accomplish regional development. Central Asia can potentially access new markets, sources of finance, and knowledge, thereby integrating into global value chains (GVC) (Linn, 2011). In 2013, China announced the Belt and Road Initiative (BRI) which, today, is one of the most ambitious globalization projects, offering Central Asia the chance to become the continental land bridge between Asia and Europe. The EU followed 5 years later with its Connectivity Strategy (EUCS), likewise aiming at connecting the Eurasian continent. On these grounds, while certainly being a global objective, connecting Asia and Europe can be perceived as an outcome of intensified regionalism and a "world of regions" (Katzenstein, 2015).

2 The Role of Knowledge Transfer for Regional Development

In the past decades, the world experienced a transition from the industrial to a knowledge age with knowledge becoming the crucial resource for long-term economic growth. In contrast to the mass production of the industrial age, the knowledge age is characterized by flexible production and specialization reflected in vertical disintegration along value chains. Thus, the knowledge age led to spatial distribution of production. For innovation and technological progress, continuing personal share of knowledge, information and experiences between production, Research and Development (R&D), marketing, etc., is essential (Liefner & Schätzl, 2017).

Developing countries are mostly behind in the global technological progress. Thus, they can access advanced technologies and knowhow through joining GVCs while implementing information and communications technology (ICT) into their production processes and upgrading their industries to remain competitive on the international market (Jenish, 2018). Through intensive contact with sophisticated firms in terms of trade, investment, and movement of human capital, weaker firms are exposed to knowledge that can be used for improving productivity. With the capacity to upgrade and learn, firms can also increase their productivity through more intense competition or specialization (Gould, 2018). However, transferring knowledge from developed to developing countries is difficult due to several factors such as spatial, technological, or psychological distance. This phenomenon is closely linked to the term absorptive capacity (Liefner & Schätzl, 2017), which is described as the "capacity to assess the value of external knowledge and technology, and make necessary investments and organizational changes to absorb and apply this in its productive activities" (Goldberg et al., 2011). Therefore, absorptive capacity defines the ability of a country to absorb knowledge and technology of other (usually developed) countries. Assumedly, the BRI and the EUCS offer potential to increase knowledge transfer between regions through enhanced infrastructure, increased trade and investments, and intensified cooperation between economies.

3 Belt and Road Initiative and EU Connectivity Strategy in the Context of Regionalism

In the literature, regionalism is highly studied theoretically but not consistently defined. Söderbaum (2015) states that "regionalism means different things to different people in different contexts and time-periods," therewith stressing the dynamics of this research field. Likewise, Börzel (2011) names various forms of regionalism such as economic, monetary, security and cultural regionalism, cross-, inter-, trans-, and multiregionalism, open or closed regionalism, and informal or institutional regionalism, to name a few. For this chapter, the following definition of regionalism will be used: "'Regionalism' represents the policy and project, whereby state and non-state actors cooperate and coordinate strategy within a particular region or as a type of world order. It is usually associated with a formal programme, and often leads to institution building" (Söderbaum, 2009).

The current phase of regionalism, so-called Comparative Regionalism, is characterized by the involvement of almost all governments in the world and various non-state actors. This results in pluralism and multidimensionality (Söderbaum, 2009). With today's comparative regionalism, a regional world order evolved as described by Katzenstein (2015). Comparative Regionalism is also defined by various trends such as war on terror, rising protectionism, a multiplex world order (with state as well as non-state actors), financial crises, overlapping regional projects and institutions, and finally, the rise of BRICS and other emerging countries. Generally, regionalism today is getting more complex with multifold interactions between actors and institutions on a bilateral, regional, interregional, and multilateral or global level (Söderbaum, 2015).

Regionalism is not only reflected in interactions within a region but also between regions. In the case of interregionalism, two formal regional organizations interact with each other (e.g., EU and ASEAN). Some scholars even accept relations between a regional organization and a state as interregionalism (Baert et al., 2014). Transregionalism, on the other hand, refers to less formalized relations as well as relations between non-state actors (Hoffmann, 2016). For this reason, transregionalism is a more flexible approach to understand and conceptualize regional organization and to apprehend different levels of cooperation, such as transregional cooperation, bilateralism, and multilateralism (Baert et al., 2014).

Theorization of regionalism is typically dominated by the European case leading to a bias toward Western approaches and the EU being the benchmark for comparison (Closa, 2015). However, the rise of China might challenge the concepts and frameworks to study inter- and transregionalism due to its engagement with many regions and regional organizations (Hoffmann, 2016). This also reflects in the strategies of China and the EU to connect Asia and Europe. Generally, it is difficult to fit the BRI into the currently existing frameworks of regionalism. Due to the loose definition of the BRI, the initiative offers great flexibility and thus the chance to learn, evolve, and adapt (Ghiasy & Zhou, 2017). Garlick (2020) refers to the BRI as an "all-inclusive framework" since its flexibility gives China the option to alter its measures as the partner countries' needs require. The EUCS, however, is an outcome of the Asia-Europe Meeting, an interregional forum between ASEAN and the EU (Holzer, 2020). Since the 1990s, the EU has been focused on region-to-region relations, which is by some scholars defined as "complex interregionalism" (Hardacre & Smith, 2009) as the EU interacts with other regional organizations, other types of regional groupings, and third countries (Hoffmann, 2016). Despite not mentioning it in the official document (European Commission, 2018), the EUCS is seen as an answer to the BRI (e.g. Holzer, 2020).

4 Connecting Asia and Europe as a Chance for Regional Development in Central Asia?

Generally, the approaches of China and the EU differ in their political nature. The EU emphasizes progress in governance, the judicial system, the civil society, and the relationship between state and citizens with focusing on democracy and human rights. China, on the other hand, acts on the principle of non-interference in politics and domestic affairs (Bayok, 2020). These visions are visible in the official documents of the EUCS and the BRI, respectively (Table 1).

Table 1 Comparison of the BRI and the EUCS (European Commission, 2018, 2019; NDRC, 2015)

	Belt and Road Initiative	EU Connectivity Strategy
Launch	2013	2018
Language	Symbolic, positive	Mostly neutral
Vision	"Win-Win cooperation that promotes common development and prosperity and a road towards peace and friendship"	"Enhancing connectivity on a global scale, with emphasis on people's rights and benefits"
Principles	Open, harmonious, and inclusive, market-based, mutual benefit	Sustainable, comprehensive, and rules-based
Main objectives	Policy coordination, facilities connectivity, unimpeded trade, financial integration, people-to-people bonds	Sustainable development, decarbonization, digitalization, investment, innovation, global leadership
Types of investment	Conditional loans	Developmental aid
Role of Central Asia	Continental land bridge between Asia and Europe	Continental land bridge between Asia and Europe, energy supply, market potential, regional security
Objectives for Central Asia	Connecting Central Asia with regions along the Belt and Road	Regional cooperation, resilience, prosperity, connectivity
Projects	China as implementor, high recognition	EU as donor, low recognition

The EUCS aims at enhancing rules-based connectivity "with emphasis on people's rights and benefits" (European Commission, 2018), while the BRI stresses "mutual respect for each other's sovereignty and territorial integrity" and "mutual non-interference in each other's internal affairs." China even uses symbolic phrases such as "instill[ing] vigor and vitality into the ancient Silk Road" that was historically explored by "the diligent and courageous people of Eurasia" and "will inject new positive energy into world peace and development." Also, China stresses the existence of a "Silk Road Spirit," which refers to the principles of an open, harmonious, and inclusive, market-based initiative with mutual benefit, according to the Chinese government (NDRC, 2015). The EU, on the other hand, focuses on sustainable development and current trends in Asia and Europe such as digitalization, decarbonization, and innovation to answer the challenges of rapid technological change, climate change, and environmental degradation. They further emphasize that "investments need to ensure market efficiency and be fiscally viable" (European Commission, 2018).

China's overall interest is to widen and deepen overland trade and economic ties to mainly Asian and European countries with Central Asia being the key geoeconomics area (Chen & Fazilov, 2018). Both, the BRI and the EUCS aim at connectivity of transport (including rail, road, sea, and air), ICT, energy, and people. They consider Central Asia the continental land bridge between Asia and Europe, thereby integrating the region into GVCs and benefitting from its energy resources.

Aside from transport infrastructure, connecting Asia and Europe delivers potential for knowledge-oriented development in the Central Asian region. Since the Central Asian countries are landlocked, they are dependent on their neighboring countries in terms of digital connectivity, leading to inadequate international bandwidth and high transit costs to access international links (Kunavut et al., 2018). With the BRI, China also supports the development of ICT, such as high-speed internet, mobile network, and satellite services, among others (Kolosov et al., 2017). Enhancing the ICT infrastructure together with transport infrastructure offers potential synergies due to the "dig once" principle, lowering necessary investment costs (World Bank, 2019).

The BRI further provides potential for Central Asian countries to upgrade and diversify their economies since China is aiming at the relocation of its labor-intensive industries. Most nations along the Belt and Road are perceived as ideal destinations for this relocation (Grimmel & Li, 2018). For example, China wants to transfer several industrial production sites from China to Kazakhstan, e.g., aluminium production (Garlick, 2020). When it comes to agriculture, Central Asia mostly suffers from low efficiency, poor technical equipment and experience, and a lack of investment. In this regard, cooperation with China offers potential for upgrading the agricultural sector, integration into agricultural GVCs, and import of knowhow and inputs (Kolosov et al., 2017). To achieve regional development, China offers to provide partners with money and institutional assistance (such as development planning, management training, consulting, etc.), but host countries must grant benefits for Chinese companies in return (Kolosov et al., 2017). This is an example for China's conditional loans, they mainly use to invest in underdeveloped regions such as Central Asia while fulfilling their own national interests. In this context, China often refers to the term win-win cooperation. The EU's investments, on the other hand, can be described as developmental and are often conditioned to progress in democracy and human rights (Tian, 2018).

Looking at the potential increase of knowledge transfer, both strategies aim at scientific exchange, exchange of students, and, as mentioned before, enhancing the ICT infrastructure. Additionally, China emphasizes the role of cooperation in science and technology, technology transfer, and innovation. They want to establish R&D and foster youth employment, entrepreneurship training, and vocational skill, among others (European Commission, 2018; NDRC, 2015). In Central Asia, Chinese communication companies, such as Huawei Technologies and ZTE, supported the modernization of the communication sector through hiring local staff or implementing social and educational programs (e.g., equipping schools with computers) (Sadovskaya & Utyasheva, 2018).

The EU, on the other hand, functions mostly as a donor instead of implementing projects. Yet, the Central Asian population grant recognition mostly to implementers of projects, not funders. For this reason, the EU is less visible in Central Asia (Peyrouse, 2014). According to the European Commission (2021), the EU programs aim at promoting regional cooperation in topics such as environment, education, trade, and the rule of law (referring to human rights and democracy). The programs align with the Central Asia strategy, lastly updated in 2019. The measures range from enhancing border management through training of border guards, customs officers and other officials, exchanging knowledge on water management and climate issues, funding research projects, and conducting studies in the region.

5 Central Asia's Lacking Capability to Absorb Knowledge

The literature on knowledge transfer in Central Asia is scarce. The region is often studied as "Central Asia and the Caucasus" (e.g., Linn, 2011), "Eurasia" (e.g., Hancock & Libman, 2016), or "Europe and Central Asia" (e.g., Goldberg et al., 2011; Gould, 2018). According to a few studies published before the launch of the BRI, Central Asia lagged in aspects such as knowledge management, licensing, incentive structures, and staffing (Goldberg et al., 2011). Interaction between R&D and industry sectors was low. While foreign direct investment (FDI) and trade are perceived as contributor to knowledge transfer and growth, positive effects on Central Asia could not be proved (Lau et al., 2015). Presumably, the absorptive capacity of some Central Asian states is still not sufficient to benefit significantly from knowledge transfer. Several reasons contribute to this statement. Central Asia's economy is dominated by the primary sector, including the extraction and export of natural resources (e.g., fossil fuels and minerals) and agriculture. This applies to Kazakhstan, Kyrgyzstan, and Turkmenistan (ADBI, 2014). Furthermore, the region has a poorly developed transport infrastructure both across land borders and internally. Due to the lack of quality roads and railways, trade is inefficient (Garlick, 2020).

While China claims to work on a principle of win-win cooperation, their partners need to ensure benefits for their own country when signing agreements with China (Dadabaev, 2019). Yet, commitment is often tied to specific reasons, commonly energy and security, thus, Central Asia is treated instrumentally (Chen & Fazilov, 2018). However, China is accused of leading countries into debt traps and favoring Chinese companies (Holzer, 2020). Agreements are often not transparent concerning its terms and conditions, possibly leading to an overdependence on exporting goods to China or a general overconnectivity with China (Tian, 2018). Schmidt (2020) states that Chinese investments do not leave the Chinese system. Rather, they flow into Chinese companies in Central Asia bringing Chinese equipment and workforce into the region to implement the project. The local population is usually left with about 30 percent of available jobs. Additionally, Chinese infrastructure projects mostly do not promote transfer of infrastructure construction knowhow into local countries (Dadabaev, 2019).

The lack of absorptive capacity in Central Asia can also be explained by the identified gaps in ICT (Kunavut et al., 2018) and the institutional disparities or lack of information within the Central Asian region. For example, Tajikistan and Kyrgyzstan are perceived to have an underdeveloped institutional structure and low levels of administrative competence. Moreover, some countries within the region barely understand how the EU is managed and how cooperation could be forged (Peyrouse, 2014). Another widely recognized issue within Central Asia is corruption, which further hinders regional development. Corruption reduces the willingness of an investor to engage in projects, increases transaction costs, and limits entrepreneurship (Lau et al., 2015). Linn (2011) further states that a bad investment climate in a country also negatively impacts neighboring states, thus reducing regional development in the whole region.

6 Suggestions to Improve Regional Development in Central Asia

To substantially benefit from knowledge transfer, several improvements within the region are necessary. First, further improvements of infrastructure and border management are needed to lower costs of ICT and transport, facilitating or initiating trade relations that have not been beneficial before due to high transport and transactions costs. Nevertheless, the impact is manifested individually among countries. While Kyrgyzstan can gain real income by above 8 percent, Tajikistan can even experience negative welfare effects since gains from integration might be lower than infrastructure costs (World Bank, 2019). The International Transport Forum (2019) considers increased connectivity to positively impact transport, consequently offering businesses the opportunity to access higher quality or lower cost inputs, which could foster the integration of domestic companies into GVCs. This potential varies among different regions.

Yet, Central Asia must diversify their economy, e.g., by finding niches in GVCs. This would further increase trade and expand the region's market destinations (ADBI, 2014). In this regard, China is potentially capable of reshaping Central Asia's economy through its initiative (Chen & Fazilov, 2018). ICT and the Internet can improve production efficiency as well as optimize and upgrade the industrial structure. The expansion of internet-related industries can further drive diversification and promote economic growth (Li, 2019). Moreover, Kunavut et al. (2018) perceive enhanced broadband services to attract international companies and investment on a medium- and long-term perspective. To improve the absorption capacity, it is also necessary for Central Asia to foster education and invest in R&D, so the human capital is able to use external knowledge. Additionally, knowledge transfer can be improved through tariff protection, subsidies, tax benefits, training, and technical assistance (Jenish, 2018).

The regional development of the whole Central Asian region is hindered by disparities between countries on the one hand, and between urban and rural regions on the other hand. Especially small and rural countries such as Kyrgyzstan and Tajikistan lag behind in economic development. For this reason, those disparities must be addressed for Central Asia to become an overall developed region. With China and the EU focusing on bilateral and multilateral cooperation, the Central Asian region should aim for Central Asian regional cooperation, so they can build up efficient infrastructure region-wide, thereby improving their attractiveness for transport, trade, and FDI. Lastly, Central Asia should enhance institutional structure and fight corruption to increase their diplomatic capabilities, avoid debt traps and dependencies, and to ensure benefits for their own regional development when cooperating with China and the EU. In the end, the potential positive impacts of the BRI and EUCS depend on the quality of the strategies' implementation and the degree to which Central Asian governments will prioritize good governance and long-term development (Ghiasy & Zhou, 2017).

7 Conclusion

As landlocked countries, the Central Asian countries are not greatly integrated into the world economy, despite being abundant on natural resources. The poor quality of the region's transport infrastructure hinders efficient trade. Due to its dependency on the primary sector, Central Asia's economy is barely diversified and offers little opportunities do develop.

Therefore, the objective of connecting Asia and Europe offers great potential for Central Asia since the region is perceived to function as continental land bridge. The region gets the opportunity to integrate into GVCs. Due to increased knowledge transfer, trade, and FDI through cooperation with China and the EU, Central Asia could assumedly achieve regional development and growth. In this context, the two strategies partly differ in their political nature. Both, China and the EU perceive Central Asia as the continental land bridge between Asia and Europe, but while China is aiming for win-win cooperation with conditional loans, the EU focuses on sustainable development. However, the potential positive effects for regional development in Central Asia are not visible yet, which can to an extent be explained by the low absorptive capacity of Central Asian states. Thus, impacts of the BRI and the EUCS cannot yet fully unfold in the region.

Indeed, the BRI and EUCS, with the goal of connecting Asia and Europe, can diversify and upgrade Central Asia's economy by relocating labor-intensive industries to the region. The BRI offers mainly short-term impacts due to its strong investments, in contrast to the EUCS that mainly aims for long-term development. For this reason, the strategies can be perceived as complementary rather than competitive. Thus, Central Asia can benefit from cooperating with both China and the EU. However, restructuring a country's economy is a lengthy process, not showing immediate positive results. Therefore, Central Asian countries must improve their infrastructure, border management, and education, train their human capital, and strengthen R&D to achieve long-term regional development through knowledge transfer. Additionally, impediments such as corruption, institutional disparities, and lack of information must be reduced, so the countries can ensure cooperation with China and the EU beneficial for their own development and pursue their own national interests.

References

ADBI (Asian Development Bank Institute). (2014). *Connecting Central Asia with economic centers*. Asian Development Bank Institute. Retrieved August 14, 2021, from https://www.adb.org/publications/connecting-central-asia-ecnomic-centers

Baert, F., Scaramagli, T., & Söderbaum, F.(2014). *United Nations university series on regionalism: Vol. 7. Intersecting Interregionalism. Regions, Global Governance and the EU*. Springer Netherlands. https://doi.org/10.1007/978-94-007-7566-4.

Bayok, A. (2020). Challenges and threat perceptions regarding central Asia in China and the EU. In Institute for Peace Research and Security Policy (Ed.), *OSCE Yearbook 2019: Yearbook on the Organization for Security and Co-operation in Europe (OSCE)* (pp. 273–286). Nomos. https://doi.org/10.5771/9783748906421-273.

Börzel, T. A. (2011). *Comparative regionalism: A new research agenda* (KFG Working Paper Series No. 28). Berlin. Kolleg-Forschergruppe "The Transformative Power of Europe", Freie Universität Berlin. Retrieved August 14, from https://nbn-resolving.org/urn:nbn:de:0168-ssoar-374751

Chen, X., & Fazilov, F. (2018). Re-centering Central Asia: China's "new great game" in the old Eurasian heartland. *Palgrave Communications, 4*(71), 1–12. https://doi.org/10.1057/s41599-018-0125-5

Closa, C. (2015). *Mainstreaming regionalism* (EUI Working Paper RSCAS No. 12). Fiesole. Robert Schuman Centre for Advanced Studies. Retrieved August 14, from https://doi.org/10.2139/ssrn.2559777.

Dadabaev, T. (2019). Transcontinental silk road strategies: Comparing China, Japan and South Korea in Uzbekistan. In *Routledge Contemporary Asia Series* (Vol. 67). Routledge.

European Commission. (2018). *Joint Communication to the European Parliament, the council, the European economic and social committee, the committee of the regions and the European investment bank: Connecting Europe and Asia–Building Blocks for an EU Strategy.* Retrieved August 14, from https://eeas.europa.eu/headquarters/headquarters-homepage/50699/connecting-europe-asia-eu-strategy_en

European Commission. (2019). *Joint communication to the European parliament and the council: The EU and Central Asia: New opportunities for a stronger partnership.* Retrieved August 14, from https://eeas.europa.eu/headquarters/headquarters-homepage/62411/european-union-and-central-asia-new-opportunities-stronger-partnership_en.

European Commission. (2021). *Central Asia.* European Union. Retrieved August 14, from https://ec.europa.eu/international-partnerships/where-we-work/central-asia_en

Garlick, J. (2020). The impact of China's belt and road initiative: From Asia to Europe. In *Rethinking Asia and International Relations.* Routledge.

Ghiasy, R., & Zhou, J. (2017). *The silk road economic belt: Considering security implications and EU-China cooperation prospects.* Solna. Stockholm International Peace Research Institute. Retrieved August 14, from https://www.sipri.org/publications/2017/other-publications/silk-road-economic-belt

Goldberg, I., Goddard, J. G., Kuriakose, S., & Racine, J.-L. (2011). *Igniting innovation: Rethinking the role of government in emerging Europe and Central Asia.* World Bank. doi:https://doi.org/10.1596/978-0-8213-8740-5.

Gould, D. M. (2018). *Critical connections: Promoting economic growth and resilience in Europe and Central Asia. Overview booklet (Europe and Central Asia Studies).* World Bank. https://doi.org/10.1596/978-1-4648-1157-9

Grimmel, A., & Li, Y. (2018). *The belt and road initiative: A hybrid model of regionalism* (Working Papers on East Asian Studies No. 122). Duisburg. University of Duisburg-Essen, Institute of East Asian Studies. Retrieved August 14, from http://hdl.handle.net/10419/179974

Hancock, K. J., & Libman, A. (2016). Regional orders around the world: Eurasia. In T. A. Börzel & T. Risse (Eds.), *The Oxford handbook of comparative regionalism* (pp. 202–224). Oxford University Press.

Hardacre, A., & Smith, M. (2009). The EU and the diplomacy of complex Interregionalism. *The Hague Journal of Diplomacy, 4*(2), 167–188. https://doi.org/10.1163/187119109X440898

Hoffmann, A. R. (2016). Inter- and Transregionalism. In T. A. Börzel & T. Risse (Eds.), *The Oxford handbook of comparative regionalism* (pp. 600–618). Oxford University Press.

Holzer, C. (2020). Identity narratives in China and the EU's economic diplomacy: Comparing the BRI and the EU connectivity strategy for Asia. In Z. Lu (Ed.), *Chinese National Identity in the age of globalisation* (pp. 183–202). Springer. https://doi.org/10.1007/978-981-15-4538-2_8

ITF (International Transport Forum). (2019). *Enhancing connectivity and freight in central Asia: Case-specific policy analysis* (International Transport Forum Policy Papers No. 71). OECD Publishing. Retrieved August 14, from https://www.itf-oecd.org/enhancing-connectivity-and-freight-central-asia

Jenish, N. (2018). *ICT-driven technological and industrial upgrading in Afghanistan, Kyrgyzstan and Tajikistan: Current realities and opportunities* (IPPA Working Paper Series No. 47). Bishkek. University of Central Asia. Retrieved August 14, from https://www.ucentralasia.org/Resources/Item/1905/EN

Katzenstein, P. J. (2015). *A world of regions: Asia and Europe in the American imperium. Cornell studies in Political economy.* Cornell University Press. https://doi.org/10.7591/9781501700385

Kolosov, V. A., Suocheng, D., Portyakov, V. Y., Chubarov, I. G., Tarkhov, S. A., & Shuper, V. A. (2017). The Chinese initiative "the belt and road". *A Geographical Perspective. Geography, Environment, Sustainability (GES Journal), 10*(1), 5–20. https://doi.org/10.24057/2071-9388-2017-10-1-5-20

Kunavut, K., Okuda, A., & Lee, D. (2018). Belt and road initiative (BRI): Enhancing ICT connectivity in China-Central Asia corridor. *Journal of Infrastructure, Policy and Development, 2*(1), 116–141. https://doi.org/10.24294/jipd.v2i1.164

Lau, C. K. M., Yang, F. S., Zang, Z., & Leung, V. K. K. (2015). Determinants of innovative activities: Evidence from Europe and Central Asia region. *The Singapore Economic Review, 60*(1), 1–18. https://doi.org/10.1142/S0217590815500046

Li, Y. (2019). Influence of the internet on the economic growth of the belt and road region. *Global Journal of Emerging Market Economies, 11*(3), 248–259. https://doi.org/10.1177/0974910119887054

Liefner, I., & Schätzl, L. (2017). *Theorien der Wirtschaftsgeographie* (11th ed.). *UTB: Vol. 782.* Ferdinand Schöningh.

Linn, J. F. (2011). Connecting Central Asia and the Caucasus with the world. In W. Hermann & J. F. Linn (Eds.), *Central Asia and the Caucasus: At the crossroads of Eurasia in the 21st century* (pp. 1–16). Sage.

NDRC (National Development and Reform Commission). (2015). Vision and actions on jointly building silk road economic belt and 21st-century maritime silk road. National Development and Reform Commission. Retrieved August 14, from http://de.china-embassy.org/det/zt/yidaiyilude/t1250293.htm

Peyrouse, S. (2014). *How does Central Asia view the EU?* (EUCAM Working Paper No. 18). Madrid. Foundation for International Relations and Foreign Dialogue. Retrieved August 14, from https://eucentralasia.eu/how-does-central-asia-view-the-eu/

Sadovskaya, Y., & Utyasheva, L. (2018). "Human silk road": The people-to-people aspect of the belt and road initiative. In M. Laruelle (Ed.), *China's belt and road initiative and its impact in Central Asia* (pp. 109–125). The George Washington University.

Schmidt, M. (2020). Reconfigurations in Central Asia: Challenges, opportunities and risks of China's belt and road initiative. In H. Pechlaner, G. Erschbamer, H. Thees, & M. Gruber (Eds.), *China and the new silk road: Challenges and impacts on the regional and local level* (pp. 77–86). Springer International Publishing.

Söderbaum, F. (2009). Comparative Regional Integration and Regionalism. In T. Landman & N. Robinson (Eds.), *The SAGE handbook of comparative politics* (pp. 477–496). Sage. https://doi.org/10.4135/9780857021083.n27

Söderbaum, F. (2015). *Early, old, new and comparing regionalism: The scholarly development of the field* (KFG Working Paper Series No. 64). Berlin. Kolleg-Forschergruppe "The Transformative Power of Europe", Freie Universität Berlin. Retrieved August 14, from https://refubium.fu-berlin.de/bitstream/handle/fub188/18003/WP-64-Soederbaum_WEB.pdf?sequence=1&isAllowed=y

Tian, H. (2018). China's conditional aid and its impact in Central Asia. In M. Laruelle (Ed.), *China's belt and road initiative and its impact in Central Asia* (pp. 21–33). The George Washington University.

World Bank. (2019). Belt and road economics: Opportunities and risks of transport corridors. *World Bank.* https://doi.org/10.1596/978-1-4648-1392-4

Justine Markisch is currently working at the Chamber of Industry and Commerce for the Palatinate, responsible for spatial planning, location development and tourism. She holds an M. Sc. in Tourism and Regional Planning from the Catholic University of Eichstätt, Germany, and an Ing. in Economics and Management of Tourism from the Matej Bel University in Banská Bystrica, Slovakia. Her research interests include economic geography, geopolitics, regional development and tourism with focus on the regions of Central and East Asia.

Vietnam and Thailand: Southeast Asian Prospects for Corporate Cultures and Ecosystems in an Asian Century

Gerhard Leypoldt

Abstract The aim of this chapter is to describe, compare and analyse the different features of corporate cultures and ecosystems in both countries. Vietnam has pursued political capitalism since the "Doi Moi" opening policy (1986) and Thailand traditionally has more liberal capitalism. This case study focuses on analysing the developments resulting from this and possible prospects for the future. Factors such as digitalisation, startup cultures, the role of women that have an impact on business ecosystems in both countries will be examined, as will the effects of the COVID-19 pandemic.

Keywords Vietnam · Thailand · Corporate Cultures and Ecosystems · Asian Century · Southeast Asia

1 Southeast Asia: Thailand and Vietnam: An Introduction

"ASEAN (Association of Southeast Asian Nations), the overlooked giant" is the title of an essay published by the Asia-Pacific correspondent of the Frankfurter Allgemeine Zeitung, Dr. Christoph Hein, at the German Federal Agency for Civic Education 2014 (bpb, 2014). In fact, Europe and North America have so far not recognised Southeast Asia's real economic and geostrategic importance. This is beginning to change with China's increasing influence, trade disputes and the pandemic.

ASEAN has a population of 650 million, making it the third-largest economic area and sales market in Asia. The Southeast Asian countries are strategically located between China and India at the "seam" between East Asia and South Asia. In terms of gross domestic product, ASEAN is already the equivalent to being the world's fifth-largest economy (AHK, 2021). In 2050, four ASEAN countries are expected to

G. Leypoldt (✉)
Entrepreneur and Investor in Asia, Hanoi, Vietnam

H. Pechlaner et al. (eds.), *The Clash of Entrepreneurial Cultures?*, FGF Studies in Small Business and Entrepreneurship, https://doi.org/10.1007/978-3-030-97050-5_10

be among the 25 largest economies in the world, including Thailand and Vietnam (PWC, 2017).

So far, there have been three waves of economic growth and development in Asia: the first wave in Japan and South Korea since the 1960s, the second wave in Taiwan, Hong Kong and China since the 1980s, and the current third wave from South Asia, but mainly from Southeast Asia (Khanna, 2019).

An essential feature of Southeast Asia is also its cultural, political, religious and economic heterogeneity. As examples, Thailand and Vietnam are good illustrations of this heterogeneity. Both countries have developed from completely different historical and political backgrounds. Both countries have different economic systems.

Thailand and Vietnam have similar roots as agricultural countries. Vietnam was colonised from the middle of the nineteenth century, and in 1887 it became the most important part of the General Government of French Indochina. Thailand was able to impede colonisation through clever tactics by its monarchs and governments, and due to its geographical location between the British and French colonies.

Vietnam's history since the Second World War has been shaped by successful resistance against the French as colonial rulers, the division of the country driven by the USA, the Vietnam War and finally reunification by victorious communist North Vietnam. Vietnam suffered a long time from the huge consequences of the war and an embargo by the USA that prevented international aid from coming. Thailand, in turn, became the USA's most important partner in the Vietnam War and has been industrialised since the 1960s. The country received support on a massive scale during the Vietnam War through Western aid funds and export guarantees. The numerous US soldiers in the country ultimately brought about the Thai tourism industry, which is still one of the country's most important business sectors today.

After reunification, Vietnam initially established a planned economy based on the Soviet model. With the economic reforms "Doi Moi", however, the economic system was converted into a socialist market economy just over 10 years later. Vietnam was definitely influenced by Singapore, the developments in China on the one hand and the USSR on the other hand. Thailand follows liberal capitalism, but for a long time was dependent on Western aid funds. Furthermore, numerous private and state oligopolies emerged. Vietnam has successfully integrated itself into the global economy since the end of the US embargo in 1994 and has seen a remarkable economic rise since then, although Vietnam continues to be classified as an authoritarian regime. Thailand experienced a boom until the Asian crisis in 1997, and for many years the country had belonged to the second generation of "Asian tiger states". However, the country has been struggling with political conflicts since the 2000s (military coups in 2006 and 2014). Economically, the country has been in a "middle-income trap" since then. Politically, the country is seen as being one of the incomplete democracies (The Economist, 2020).

2 Features of Corporate Cultures and Ecosystems in Thailand and Vietnam

2.1 *Working Hypothesis*

In the following, the working hypothesis that the different forms of capitalism in the two countries reflect different developments in corporate cultures and ecosystems will be examined. The sources for studying this turned out to be poor, but due to the considerable development potential of Southeast Asia, it seems imperative that the social interest groups in business, science, politics and media in Europe will pay much more attention to this region in the future.

2.2 *Framework Conditions Based on SWOT*

2.2.1 Thailand

Thailand is one of the emerging markets with slightly better than average income. The country has 69.8 million inhabitants and the per capita income (GDP/Atlas method) was 7260 US dollars in 2019 (WKO/TH, 2021).

S-Strength: Thailand, as the second-largest economy in Southeast Asia, is listed 21st in the World Bank's "Doing Business Index", ahead of the DACH region. The country has well-developed industries with suppliers (automotive, electronics and food). Due to its high consumption and tech-savvy population, Thailand is an interesting sales market (GTAI/TH, 2021). Thailand has a well-developed service sector, especially its tourism industry.

W-Weaknesses: There are clear weaknesses in its state education and training system. It lacks qualified employees in the labour market. Thailand has an ageing population (the second oldest in Southeast Asia) and very high household debt (GTAI/TH, 2021).

O-Opportunities: The population's high affinity for digital technology is definitely one of the country's great opportunities and the basis for a startup ecosystem (see Sect. 2.6.1.). Thailand is a world leader in terms of mobile internet usage (Statista, 2021). The coronavirus pandemic acts as an accelerator and booster for the (already extremely popular) e-commerce sector (Bangkok Post, 21st May, 2021a, b). There are other options in the area of environmental protection and infrastructure (GTAI/TH, 2021).

T-Threads: The political division in the country that has existed for over a decade and a half has had an adverse effect on foreign direct investment (AHK, 2021). Even Thai companies prefer investing in other countries or shifting capacities abroad (e.g. Vietnam). Tourism, which is so important for the country, has proven to be particularly vulnerable during the pandemic (GTAI/TH, 2021).

2.2.2 Vietnam

The Vietnamese per capita income is currently 3499 US dollars (GDP). The country belongs to the middle-income countries and has a population of 97.4 million (WKO/VN, 2021).

S-Strength: One of Vietnam's greatest strengths is undoubtedly its very young, motivated, promotion-oriented population that is hungry for education and willing to work (Focus Money 25/2020). The population sees new technologies and digitalisation in a positive light. The wage level is reasonable and significantly lower than China's. Vietnam is well integrated into the global economy and pursues a robust free trade policy. Vietnam has the lowest market barriers in Asia (AHK, 2021) and provides stable political conditions. The government is vigorously pushing forward with the country's modernisation (e.g. 5G network) (GTAI/VN, 2021). By comparison, the Vietnamese are well educated, and the country is a leader in Southeast Asia as far as gender equality is concerned (see Sect. 2.6.1.).

W-Weaknesses: Since "Doi Moi", the development of the Vietnamese economy has been largely financed by foreign capital. Industrial companies that are financed from abroad usually lack qualified suppliers. The productivity of local companies is often low, work processes or production processes are often outdated and their products are therefore not competitive internationally. Vietnamese SMEs often suffer from undercapitalisation (GTAI, 2021). Overall, it is too much dependent on foreign investments.

O-Opportunities: Urbanisation is driving the country's development. Millions of people are moving to the big cities of Hanoi, Ho Chi Minh City and Danang. Higher wages and qualifications allow for more consumption, better medical care and education. The government is, to a considerable extent, investing in the infrastructure of urban centres (Focus Money 26/2020). Due to its neutrality and good framework conditions, the country offers itself as an alternative or addition to existing production sites or supply chains in the USA/China trade conflict. As early as 2018, 22% of Chinese companies said they had lost market shares to Vietnamese competitors (Focus Money 25/2020).

T-Threads: In addition to the strongly required development of local companies, the government urgently needs to increase power generation to meet the needs of manufacturing companies that are financed from abroad and its own companies. Real wages are also currently rising faster than productivity (GTAI, 2021).

2.3 *Features of Corporate Cultures and Entrepreneurial Ecosystems in Thailand and Vietnam*

2.3.1 Features of Thailand's Corporate Culture and Ecosystem

Thailand's economy is shaped by the service sector. Service providers contributed 58.3% to its gross value added in 2020 and 45.7% of Thais were employed by a service provider in 2019. Industrial companies contribute 33.1% to Thailand's gross value added with 22.8% of Thailand's employees (WKO/TH, 2021).

In numerical terms, Thai SMEs seem to be the backbone of the Thai economy, with just over three million companies accounting for more than 99% of all Thai companies, but only generating around 42% of Thailand's GDP. In contrast, private and state-owned corporations only account for 0.3% of companies but generate a large part of Thailand's GDP (OECD Scoreboard, 2020). The corporations' dominance has contributed to the emergence of oligopolies, in which a few family-run and state-owned conglomerates and corporations dominate entire industries. Due to the close interlinking of the leading entrepreneurial families with the heads of the Thai state and Thai society, it is much easier for corporations to lobby and assert their interests as it is for SMEs to do so.

Thailand's economy is heavily dependent on exports, and mainly industrial products (70%) are exported. Thailand's medium-sized companies often lack basic knowledge of modern corporate management or foreign language skills. Due to a shortage of skilled workers (see Sect. 2.4.1.). SMEs have hardly any qualified applicants at their disposal, who usually prefer working for corporations. Companies often do not have the know-how and budget to be able to educate or train staff themselves (Sumipol, 2018). Furthermore, Thailand's SMEs mostly have problems with their capital resources—they are too weakly capitalised and therefore particularly vulnerable to crises (see Sect. 2.6.1.). 50.4% of all national loans from private banks were taken out by SMEs (OECD Scoreboard, 2020).

For economic promotion by the state to be able to effectively support the emergence of a strengthened medium-sized ecosystem, the following fields of action must be considered:

1. Reducing bureaucracy, relaxing legal regulations, training government personnel.
2. Making financing programmes and subsidy programmes more effective and facilitating access to them.
3. Training in corporate management and internationalisation.
4. Reforming the education system and aligning it with market requirements.
5. Increasing training in and research on new technologies.
6. Special programmes for founders and startups.

(GEM Monitor 2019/2020)

With the Thailand 4.0 programme having been launched in 2017, the government has announced a comprehensive reform programme. The areas of innovation, technology and creativity are to act as drivers for the country. Services, industry and agriculture are to be upgraded to Level 4.0. The aim is to turn traditional SMEs into innovative startups (OSEMP, 2021).

Conclusion

Thailand's corporate culture, like its society, is hierarchically structured and based on networks. The majority of Thailand's SMEs neither have sufficient access to qualified staff or financing nor do they have strong networks. Unfortunately, the owners often lack basic knowledge of business management. And the opportunities for internationalisation, which are so important for the nation's exports, i.e., for the ASEAN domestic market and the "Asianisation of Asia" (Khanna, 2019) have not been able to be seized by a large part of Thailand's SME ecosystem so far. In the startup area, there are some promising approaches (see Sect. 2.5.1.) but it remains incomprehensible why in a country in which the latest digital technologies are used as a matter of course and on a daily basis, founders and young entrepreneurs are predominantly active in the low-tech sector (GEM Monitor 2019/2020).

For the country not to fall behind in Asia, the fields of action mentioned above must be taken up urgently.

2.3.2 Features of Vietnam's Corporate Culture and Ecosystem

Vietnam's economy is dominated by industry. Fifty-five percent of employees worked in an industrial company in 2016 and generated 62% of its gross value added, while the average employment rate of OECD countries is 23% and 33% for industrial value added (OECD, 2021). The production companies that are financed from abroad are the main drivers of Vietnam's economic development. So far, however, no medium-sized ecosystem, in particular suppliers, has been able to be developed to meet the needs of the industry that is financed from abroad. This fact and the strong focus on export explain the unusually committed free trade policy of the Vietnamese government.

The country's economic development has three epicentres: Ho Chi Minh City, Hanoi, Danang and their surrounding provinces. A new global business culture has emerged here, which is made up of international investors, ex-pats and new Vietnamese private corporations (e.g. Vingroup, FPT, Hoa Phat, etc.), state-owned flagship companies (Viettel, Vietcombank, etc.), the second-largest startup ecosystem in Southeast Asia (see Sect. 2.6.2.), and, above all, urbanisation. In the rest of the country, local industry and local SMEs still dominate the scene. Work is often still done by hand, mostly with outdated methods and mostly with low productivity and poor capital resources. Furthermore, agriculture still plays an important role in large parts of the country and contributed 16.5% to value creation in 2010 (WKO/VN, 2021).

A peculiarity of Vietnam's corporate culture and/or ecosystem is the huge informal sector. In other emerging countries, e.g., Thailand (in developing countries in general), there are informal sectors. But the fact that there are 500,000 registered companies in comparison to more than five million non-registered companies is remarkable (OECD, 2021). Collaborating with non-registered companies cannot always be avoided as they are ubiquitous in Vietnam's business life. Most of them are self-employed and small businesses. Due to its lack of transparency, the informal sector causes some problems with taxes, social security contributions and the accounting of benefits. Of the 500,000 registered companies, 45% are local SMEs and the rest are made up of state-owned companies, companies that are financed from abroad and local industries.

Vietnam has a strong corporate culture: 56.5% of employees are self-employed (OECD, 2021). On the other hand, this picture is significantly distorted by the huge informal sector. For many workers and employees, it is also quite common to be self-employed at the same time.

The Vietnamese government has recognised the necessity to strengthen its SME ecosystem and has made this one of the main goals of its economic policy. Seventy-five percent of all export goods are manufactured by companies that are financed from abroad. Vietnam's medium-sized companies not only lack capital and entrepreneurial know-how, but they also lack internationalisation competencies and foreign language skills. Local SMEs and industrial companies are also at a disadvantage on the labour market. Vietnamese prefer working for foreign-controlled companies, listed Vietnamese corporations or renowned state-owned companies (GTAI/VN, 2021).

Vietnam's corporate culture and ecosystem are very heterogeneous. On the one hand, the privatisation and transfer of state-owned companies into modern companies are making slow progress, and local industries and SMEs have not yet been internationally competitive. On the other hand, there are state-run model companies and private corporations that, together with foreign investors, are the drivers of Vietnam's dynamic development. In the urban centres, ecosystems are being created for startups and founders, many of whom have already completed their training abroad. There are state subsidy programmes for SMEs and startups, but they are often thwarted by non-transparent and lengthy awarding at the local level. Since the Vietnamese government is pursuing its goals vigorously and has a great deal of power, it can be safely assumed that it will be successful in its plan to strengthen the middle class and to create a supplier structure for the industry.

2.4 *Future Prospects: Startup Ecosystems in Thailand and Vietnam*

2.4.1 Thailand's Startup Ecosystem

In Thailand, there are currently only about 540 tech startups and thus significantly fewer than in Singapore (approx. 10,000) or in Vietnam (approx. 3000). But the kingdom is a world leader when it comes to mobile internet and social media usage (Jumpstart, 2020). It therefore already has an affinity for technology as a prerequisite for a modern and strong startup ecosystem. Furthermore, the country has well-developed industries and is relatively cosmopolitan thanks to tourism and many ex-pats living in the country.

Thailand's startup ecosystem is struggling with the same challenges as all Thai SMEs do (see Sect. 2.5.1.). In addition, the authorities there often lack the technical know-how and understanding of SMEs' mindset and needs. Nevertheless, new trends are emerging in Thailand's startup scene: Thai corporations are no longer joining in as pure financial investors but are accompanying and also stimulating operational business from the start. Partnerships between local founders, who are familiar with the situation and founders from abroad who contribute with their global know-how, seem to work particularly well (Startup Universal, 2021). It is also fitting that Bangkok was named the best city for digital nomads in Asia (fourth place worldwide) (Bangkok Post, 3rd May, 2021a, b). The Thai government has also recognised this potential and is supporting this development with special "smart visas". Digital media are not only creating new business options (e.g. for booming coworking spaces) but also potential partners for Thai startups and digital know-how are being brought into the country. If Thailand succeeds in implementing the technical affinity of its population more strongly into entrepreneurial initiatives and at the same time developing its image as a metropolis for digital nomads, then the country has many options as a startup hub.

2.4.2 Vietnam's Startup Ecosystem

After Singapore, Vietnam's startup ecosystem with 3000 companies is the second largest in Southeast Asia. This may come as a surprise at first, but it is a logical consequence of two factors: firstly, the Vietnamese population is on average very young (see Sect. 2.4.2.). And secondly, in large parts of the country 15 years ago people switched directly from using public telephone booths to smartphones. The Vietnamese government (like the government of Thailand) no longer relied on intermediate technologies such as fixed network expansion, ISDN, etc., but instead switched to a powerful nationwide mobile network (Researchgate, 2019). This is also called the "advantage" of late development (Khanna, 2019).

In Vietnam, digital technology is viewed very positively—with the advent of smartphones, many millions of people also got better jobs in the city, their own motorcycles, more affluence and improved medical care. In addition, it was and is a dream for many Vietnamese to work for one of the major technology investors such as Samsung, LG or now Apple or Foxconn. This breeding ground is ideal for creating a startup ecosystem. Currently, Vietnamese startups are active in the fields of information and communication technology (41%), agricultural technology (20%), EdTech/education (16%), Internet of Things (IoT) (9%) and Foodtech (7%). A special feature of Vietnam is that the FinTech and e-commerce sectors are still completely underdeveloped. Many Vietnamese have neither a bank account nor a credit card. Social media and apps are used for orders, but payments are done through cash on delivery.

On the one hand, the Vietnamese startup ecosystem is facing similar problems like the one in Thailand (see Sect. 2.6.1.) On the other hand, the pressure for development is much higher. The Vietnamese education market alone will be worth 240 billion US dollars in a few years, and a young urban population would like to be offered digital education. The vast majority of Vietnamese will be living in cities as early as 2035. Urbanisation is one of the main drivers of digitalisation and leads to a demand for local digital services and apps. The advantage of "late development" again applies here. The Vietnamese government wants to make

Vietnam an international innovation hub for artificial intelligence, robotics, EdTech and agricultural technology. To this end, it has set up numerous funding programmes—but here, too, allocation at the regional level needs to be significantly improved in terms of transparency, target accuracy and made less bureaucratic. Vietnam's startup scene also offers many opportunities and options for foreign participation and cooperation (East Asian countries, but also Singapore are already very active here) (Australia Trade and Investment Commission, 2019). Due to the factors described, the high level of motivation and positive attitude towards entrepreneurship, the prognosis for the startup ecosystem is good.

2.5 Women in the Entrepreneurial Ecosystems of Thailand and Vietnam

2.5.1 Thailand

Thailand achieved an excellent eleventh place in this year's Master Card Index for female entrepreneurship (Germany: 28th) (Vietnam Express, 2020).

More than 33% of management positions in Thai companies are held by women (15% worldwide). Thailand has the highest quota of female students worldwide. In order to avoid the middle-income trap, to reduce the shortage of skilled workers and to train more qualified managers and entrepreneurs, Thailand urgently depends on the female population contributing to this. On the other hand, there is a lack of special support programmes for female managers and entrepreneurs. Studies show that women tend to spend more of their income on children's education and health care than men. This also speaks in favour of the better promotion of female employment. In any case, the Japanese-Thai bank Krungsri has recognised the signs of the times and has issued a special bond for female entrepreneurs (Bangkok Post 16th October, 2019). In many companies, the majority of middle management and an increasing proportion of the management level are occupied by women. Even if they are not yet in a majority at the executive level of companies, they give the Thai economy an increasingly "feminine look", and they often appear more ambitious and more target-oriented than their male counterparts. However, the role of women correlates with education and background. In rural regions, patriarchy is still dominant.

2.5.2 Vietnam

In Vietnam, 73% of women are employed and 31.3% of Vietnamese companies were owned by women in 2018 (Thailand 25.2%) (The ASEAN Post, 2019). There is a conflict between economic modernity and the image of women in a socialist state, on the one hand, and the traditional female role model of a Confucian society. Just a few years ago, many families preferred sons because they traditionally stay with their parents, continue farming and business and, together with their wives, care for the elderly. This role model is increasingly changing by the exorbitantly high employment rate of women and increasing urbanisation. Thirty-six percent of managers in Vietnamese companies are female (Vietnam Express, 2020).

2.6 Effects of the COVID-19 Pandemic on Business Ecosystems in Thailand and Vietnam

2.6.1 Thailand

The pandemic hit Thailand's SMEs particularly hard. The SMEs' capital weakness described above (see Sect. 2.5.1.) is proving to be fatal in the crisis, and numerous SMEs are active in the tourism industry. The Thai tourism industry accounts for 20% of Thailand's gross domestic product, which is around twice as much as the world average. While 40 million tourists visited the kingdom in 2019, only 700,000 visitors are expected for 2021 (Bloomberg, 2021). The government is trying to stimulate domestic tourism, but this has repeatedly come to a standstill through measures to combat the pandemic. Sangchai Theerakulwanich, Chairman of the Federation of Thai SMEs, expects that 80% of Thailand's SMEs will have to file for bankruptcy if the situation of the pandemic does not improve by the end of 2021 (Bloomberg, 2021). This would be a disaster for the job market.

Nonetheless, it is good for Thailand's economy that it is being supported by growth in the export sector. This growth was made possible because the global economy was able to recover faster than initially assumed. However, due to the ongoing crisis, the forecast for economic growth was recently lowered from 2.1 to 1.8% (Kasikorn, 2021).

It is to be expected that the Thai economy will not be able to return to pre-pandemic levels until 2022 or even 2023. Between the fourth quarter of 2020 and the first quarter of 2021 alone, 720,000 jobs were lost, but unemployment still doubled between early 2020 and early 2021 (The Worldbank, 2021). In Thailand, too, everything ultimately depends on the progress of people getting their vaccinations—this will be the deciding factor as to when the country can be reopened.

2.6.2 Vietnam

Vietnam was considered a model country for fighting pandemics for almost 18 months. Its economic growth of 2.91% in 2020 made Vietnam one of the leading countries in this respect in Asia and the world, and 6.7% growth was initially expected for 2021 (Asia Nikkei, 2021). In the meantime, the Asia Development Bank has lowered its forecast to 5.8% (Xinhua, 2021). Vietnam's growth is primarily driven by exports. Exports to the USA and the EU have also increased significantly, which is partly explained by the new free trade agreement with the EU and, on the other hand, through the US-China trade conflict. In addition, the country is significantly less dependent on contact-intensive services (e.g. tourism) than Thailand, for example.

Nevertheless, due to the recent outbreak of the delta variant, since July 2021, many SMEs in the tourism or catering and retail sectors are facing bank loan foreclosures. The companies lack income to pay back the loans. A huge wave of insolvencies is looming, the extent of which is hard to predict due to the huge informal sector in Vietnam (Vietnam News, 2021). As in Thailand, SMEs need grants rather than loans. Loans provide short-term liquidity but will lead to companies being unable to pay if there continue to be lockdowns. Vietnam is also trying to get more and more people vaccinated so that the production plants can remain open.

3 Analysis and Conclusion

But how can the working hypothesis, that the different forms of capitalism in Thailand and Vietnam also have different effects on the respective entrepreneurial ecosystems and corporate cultures, be answered?

Both countries have their roots in agricultural societies, but Thailand was never colonised. Since the beginning of the colonial era, Vietnam has lived through an extremely difficult one-and-a-half century, when the country was at times one of the poorest in the world; Colonisation by France (simultaneously with the Japanese occupation during the Second World War), a decades-long partisan war to liberate the country, the division, the Vietnam War and ultimately the establishment of a communist planned economic system after reunification. Thailand, on the other hand, was seen as a bulwark against spreading communism within the framework of the prevailing domino theory and was supported by massive military and economic aid from the west. It became dependent on capital from abroad through its tourism industry that developed during the Vietnam War. This slowed down or even prevented the development of self-initiative and the creation of sustainable, innovative SMEs. Thailand traditionally follows liberal capitalism, but at the same time, suffers from political instability. In recent decades, the monarchy and bureaucracy acted as a stabiliser to curb the centrifugal forces of the diverging interests of the army, elites and people. These institutions ensured order and reform more than the government (Khanna, 2019). However, in the last one-and-a-half decade, the social divide has become much stronger and deeper.

On the one hand, Thailand's ecosystem is very liberal; in principle, it is easy to set up and operate a company (see Sect. 2.4.1.). The Thai economy is largely dominated by oligopolies of a few private corporations and state-owned companies. Although there are millions of medium-sized companies, most of them and the few startups lack capital, access to important networks, skilled workers and entrepreneurial skills. Thailand has for five decades remained in the group of middle-income countries and is in the "middle-income trap". So far, the country has not managed to catch up with high-income countries such as South Korea through innovation and productivity. On the other hand, other middle-income countries in the region offer significant cost advantages (wages) or lower market barriers, such as Vietnam. And above all, the sword of Damocles hovers above political and social conflicts. Liberal capitalism alone obviously does not guarantee economic prosperity. The problems of Thailand's entrepreneurial ecosystems lie in contextual conditions such as a shortage of skilled workers, a lack of entrepreneurial skills, a lack of access to important networks and the instability described. Furthermore, entrepreneurial initiatives are not sufficiently developed in Thailand and the population is the second oldest in Southeast Asia (see Sect. 2.4.1).

Vietnam has had much bigger problems to deal with in the past few decades, which makes the development since the country's economic liberalisation in 1986 all the more astonishing. After choosing a socialist market economy or political capitalism, Vietnam began its advancement, one which is likely to be one of the greatest economic success stories alongside China in the annals of the twentieth and twenty-first centuries. At the end of the Vietnam War in 1975, Vietnam had a per-capita income of just 80 US dollars (Countryeconomy, 2021) and was one of the poorest countries in the world. In 2020, Vietnam's per capita income was almost 44 times higher than 45 years ago (see Sect. 2.4.1.). Vietnam is also referred to as "Little China" (Khanna, 2019) (in terms of work ethic) or the "better China" (Focus Money 25/2020) (in terms of low market barriers, wage levels and being neutral in trade disputes). Vietnam has been able to integrate itself successfully into the world economy since the end of the US embargo in 1994. The country (after Singapore as the financial centre) is now the second-highest country with foreign direct investments in Southeast Asia. The rise of Vietnam was made possible most of all by foreign investments from East Asia (especially South Korea and Japan). Vietnam's entrepreneurial ecosystem is very heterogeneous—the companies financed from abroad, the new private corporations (e.g. Vingroup) and modern state-owned corporations (e.g. Viettel) are on a global and sometimes even 4.0. level. On the other hand, there are, however, 500,000 local industrial companies and SMEs, a gigantic informal sector and "lead-footed" state-owned companies that have not yet been privatised and which mostly work with outdated structures and processes and lack capital and/or know-how.

Nonetheless, the prognosis for Vietnam's entrepreneurial ecosystems appears to be significantly more favourable, and moving up to the group of high-income countries is very likely by 2050 (PWC, 2017). The country can take full advantage of its late development (Khanna, 2019). The population of Vietnam is young, motivated, disciplined and enthusiastic about new technologies. In 2016, 55.2 billion high-tech products were exported from Vietnam (Thailand: 8.8 billion) (Bangkok Post, 2020). This number already shows that foreign investors not only contribute to urbanisation and development but above all to training the labour market. The Vietnamese education system appears to be more efficient than, for example, the Thai one, which can be seen in the top positions in science and its good position in mathematics in the PISA studies (OECD PISA, 2018). The large number of female entrepreneurs and managers also contribute to Vietnam's development, as they use a large part of their income for educating their children well (see Sect. 2.5.2.). And overall, entrepreneurial initiatives are highly developed, although they often do not correspond with the skills of actual company management (see Sect. 2.5.2.).

At a first glance, the problems of the SME ecosystems in Thailand and Vietnam appear similar. Foreign investors are also putting more pressure on Vietnam to better develop the local ecosystems. The Vietnamese government has made the promotion of SMEs one of the main goals of its policy. The country urgently needs to become more independent of foreign capital and know-how. In addition, a decisive factor in the medium term will be to acquire suppliers for foreign production companies in order to bind them. Due to its abundance of power, the government will be able to do this itself against resistance. This blend of political stability, moderate wages, free trade, low market barriers and a young, technology-enthusiastic and advancement-oriented population will continue to attract investors and thus keep the Vietnamese success story alive. Current global political events such as trade conflicts seem to be developing to the advantage of Vietnam.

In many countries in Southeast Asia and East Asia, order is seen as being at least as important as freedom. The people in Vietnam do not want to experiment with thing. Other countries' experience with democracy in the region tends to put them off. And in Thailand, too, large parts of society have already called on the army to end political blockades in the country by divided parties, which is often difficult for people in the USA or Europe to understand or accept. Liberal capitalism only seems to flourish when it is embedded in a context of a functioning education system, possible social advancement and, above all, political and social stability and the rule of law. In this respect, it requires a high level of complexity as a basic requirement. This is why political capitalism will presumably for the time being be considered a more promising model because of it being steered strongly by the state, especially in the rapidly developing Asian countries.

If you look more closely, the hasty equation of political capitalism with the socialist systems of Vietnam or China turns out to be wrong; the roots seem to be more in the pragmatic, technocratic connection of capitalist success factors with traditional Asian values and structures (Khanna, 2019). And geographically, these roots most likely originate from Lee Kuan Yew's Singapore, where quite a few officials from China and later Vietnam have been trained since the late 1970s. Capitalism with a pronounced control from the state, e.g., industrial policy, export policy or the promotion of future technology can be found (with all other differences) not only in authoritarian states such as China or Vietnam but also in hybrid regimes such as Singapore or Malaysia to democracies such as South Korea or Japan. In any case, capitalism influenced by the west (be it as a free or social market economy) sees itself challenged today by technocratic, pragmatic capitalism in Asia in which states take on a more active role of guide, promoter, coordinator and moderator. Without the active role of the Asian governments, East Asia's and Southeast Asia's advancement in its various waves would be unthinkable.

References

AHK: ASEAN Snapshot 2021. (2021). Accessed on 21st July 2020 from https://vietnam.ahk.de/infothek/publikationen/ahk-broschuere

Asia-Nikkei: Economy/Vietnam's GDP grows 6.6% in April–June despite COVID outbreaks. (2021, Jun 29). Accessed on 30th August 2021 from https://asia.nikkei.com/Economy/Vietnam-s-GDP-grows-6.6-in-April-June-despite-COVID-outbreaks

Australia Unlimited: Vietnam's Innovation Ecosystem 2019 Australian Government/Australia Trade and Investment Commission. (2019). (pp. 4–20).

Bangkok Post: Woman entrepreneurs key to Thai growth story. Bangkok Post. (2019, October 16). Accessed on 22nd August 2021 from: https://www.bangkokpost.com/opinion/opinion/1772999/women-entrepreneurs-key-to-thai-growth-story

Bangkok Post: Path to economic progress: A tale of two nations. Bangkok Post. (2020, April 17). Accessed on 3rd September 2021 from: https://www.bangkokpost.com/opinion/opinion/1901645/path-to-economic-progress-a-tale-of-two-nations

Bangkok Post: Bangkok ranks top in Asia for Digital Nomads. Bangkok Post. (2021a, May 03). Accessed on 17th August 2021 from: https://www.bangkokpost.com/tech/2109479/bangkok-ranks-top-in-asia-for-digital-nomads

Bangkok Post: The Changes brought by COVID might have an upside for Thai Consumers, Businesses and Economy. (2021b, May 21). Accessed on 13th August 2021 from: https://www.bangkokpost.com/thailand/pr/2119527/the-changes-brought-by-covid-might-have-an-upside-for-thai-consumers-businesses-and-economy

Bloomberg: Business/Pandemic Pushes Millions of Small Thai Companies Into Crisis. (2021, July 06). Accessed on 28th August 2021 from: https://www.bloomberg.com/news/articles/2021-07-05/pandemic-pushes-millions-of-small-thai-businesses-into-crisis

bpb: Aus Politik und Zeitgeschichte (APUZ 40–41/2014). (2014, September 22). ASEAN, der übersehene Riese. Bundeszentrale für politische Bildung. Accessed on 15th July 2021 from https://bpb.de/apuz/191924/asean-der-uebersehene-riese

Countryeconomy: Vietnam GDP-Gross Domestic Product. Accessed on 4th September 2021 from: https://countryeconomy.com/gdp/vietnam?year

Focus Money 25/2020: Vietnam das bessere China/Focus Money 25/2020. (2020, July 10). (pp. 56–57) Focus Magazin Verlag München 2020.

Focus Money 26/2020: Aufstrebendes Asien-Chancen im Fernost/Focus Money 26/2020. (2020, Jun 17). (pp. 34–36) Focus Magazin Verlag 202.

GEM: Global Entrepreneurship Monitor Thailand, Report. (2019/2020). Bangkok University (pp. 6–21)-Bangkok University School of Entrepreneurship and Management (BUSEM).

GTAI/TH: German Trade And Investment SWOT- Analyse Thailand -Corona legt Stärken und Schwächen schonungslos offen. (2021, Jun 07). Accessed on 10th August 2021 from https://www.gtai.de/gtai-de/trade/wirtschaftsumfeld/swot-analyse/thailand/corona-legt-staerken-und-schwaechen-schonungslos-offen-243534

GTAI/VN: German Trade And Investment SWOT- Analyse Vietnam hofft auf Wachstum wie vor der Krise. (2021, Jun 03). Accessed on 18th August 2021 from https://www.gtai.de/gtai-de/trade/wirtschaftsumfeld/swot-analyse/vietnam/vietnam-hofft-auf-wachstum-wie-vor-der-krise%2D%2D248630

Jumpstart: Introduction to the Thai Startup Ecosystem. (2020, October 13). Accessed on 14th August 2021 from https://www.jumpstartmag.com/introduction-to-the-thai-startup-ecosystem/

Kasikorn: Thailand's 2021 GDP Growth Projected to Slip to 1.8% due to the Latest Wave of COVID-19 (Business Brief No. 3923). (2021, April 20). Accessed on 27th August 2021 from: https://kasikornresearch.com/en/analysis/k-econ/economy/Pages/Thai-GDP-y3923

Khanna P. (2019). *Unsere Asiatische Zukunft* (p. 10, p. 159, pp. 188–191, p. 232, pp. 347–350 und p. 374) Hamburg, Rowohlt.

OECD: OECD studies on SME's and Entrepreneurship/SME and Entrepreneurship Policy in Vietnam. (2021). (pp. 3–18).

OECD PISA: OECD PISA 2015 Results in Focus. (2018). (p. 5, p. 7).
OECD Scoreboard: Financing SME and Entrepreneurs 2020- OECD Scoreboard 46. Thailand. (2020). Accessed on 7th August 2021 from https://www.oecd-ilibrary.org/sites/2c7b8253-en/index.html?itemId=/content/component/2c7b8253-en
OSMEP: Office of the Small and Medium Enterprise at the Ministry of Industry Thailand/Economy Overview/Accessed on 21st August 2021 from https://www.sme.go.th/en/page.php?modulekey=373
PWC: The Long View- How will the global economy order change by 2050. (2017). *Price Waterhouse Cooper LLP* (pp. 2–4, und p. 23) Accessed on 31st July 2021 from https://www.pwc.com/gx/en/world-2050/assets/pwc-world-in-2050-summary-report-feb-2017.pdf
Researchgate: When Vietnam Awakes–A Review of the Vietnamese Startup Ecosystem. (2019). Accessed on 2nd August 2021 from: https://www.researchgate.net/profile/Denis-Lambert/publication/331989053_When_Vietnam_awakes_-_A_review_of_the_Vietnamese_Startup_Ecosystem/
Startup Universal: Country Guide Thailand. (2021). Accessed on 10th August 2021 from: https://startupuniversal.com/country/thailand/
Statista: Tägliche Dauer der mobilen Internetnutzung nach Ländern weltweit. (2021, Jun 09). Accessed on 16th August 2021 from: https://de.statista.com/statistik/daten/studie/809553/umfrage/taegliche-dauer-der-mobilen-internetnutzung-nach-laendern-weltweit/
Sumipol: SME‘s the real backbone of Thai Economy–Sumipol. (2018, May). Accessed on 1st August 2021 from: https://www.sumipol.com/knowledge/smes
The ASEAN Post: Women-led businesses on the rise in Vietnam. The ASEAN Post. (2019, August 28). Accessed on 19th August 2021 from: https://theaseanpost.com/article/women-led-businesses-rise-vietnam
The Economist Intelligence Unit, Democracy Index 2020. (2020). Accessed on 3rd August 2021 from: www.eiu.com/n/campaigns/democracy-index-2020/
The Worldbank: Thailand Economic Monitor July 2021: The Road to Recovery. (2021, July 15). Accessed on 30th August 2021 from: https://www.worldbank.org/en/country/thailand/publication/thailand-economic-monitor-july-2021-the-road-to-recovery
Vietnam Express: Vietnam 25th best place to be woman entrepreneur. Vietnam Express. (2020, November 24). Accessed on 20th August 2021 from: https://e.vnexpress.net/news/news/vietnam-25th-best-place-to-be-woman-entrepreneur-report-4195867.html
Vietnam News: Tourism-related firms face bankruptcy due to pandemic. (2021, May 20). Accessed on 31st August 2021 from: https://vietnamnews.vn/economy/952125/tourism-related-firms-face-bankruptcy-due-to-pandemic.html
WKO/TH: Wirtschaftskammer Österreich, Länderprofil Thailand. (2021, August). Accessed on 15th August 2021 from: https://wko.at/statistik/laenderprofile/lp-thailand.pdf
WKO/VN: Wirtschaftskammer Österreich, Länderprofil Vietnam. (2021, August). Accessed on 19th August 2021 from: https://wko.at/statistik/laenderprofile/lp-vietnam.pdf
Xinhua: Economic Watch/Vietnam's GDP outlook in jeopardy as COVID-19 wave rages. (2021, August 09). Accessed on 30th August 2021 from: http://www.xinhuanet.com/english/asiapacific/2021-08/09/c_1310117611

Gerhard Leypoldt born 1971. Managing Partner and General Director of the Drossapharm Group in Asia (Hong Kong, Thailand and Vietnam). He has 22 years of expertise as an executive and entrepreneur in China and Southeast Asia. As a consultant, he has advised many companies (corporations and SMEs) but also Thai governments and government organizations. From 2010 to 2012, he established a multi-award-winning manufacturing business in Vietnam, which he still manages today. As an investor and entrepreneur, he is involved in several Asian companies, including trading companies and training companies. He lives year-round in Hanoi and Bangkok.

The Role of Strategic Alliances in Developing the Entrepreneurial Ecosystem of ICV Industry: The Case of NIO Inc.

Xiao Han

Abstract The emergence of the knowledge economy and information technology has increased the value of strategic alliances in a wide range of industries. In recent years, strategic alliances have also developed rapidly in China. The strategic alliance can create an innovative "entrepreneurial ecosystem" by condensing the scientific and technological resources, talents, and excellent platform of scientific research institutes, uniting various professional institutions and innovation systems and mechanisms, establishing a mechanism and environment for the linkage and integration of science and technology, industry, and capital. In this chapter, we analyze and discuss the entrepreneurial ecosystem in the Intelligent Connected Vehicle (ICV) industry through a case study of Chinese ICV firms (NIO Inc.). Results show that, first, strategic alliances play an essential role in the entrepreneurial ecosystem (EE) given the advantage of accessing valuable and complementary external resources that firms do not already possess; second, the strategic alliances as elements of external accumulation sub-ecosystem of the entrepreneurial ecosystem are mutually interdependent and co-evolved with internal accumulation sub-ecosystem.

Keywords Strategic alliance · Entrepreneurial ecosystem · Sub-ecosystem · ICV industry · NIO Inc.

X. Han (✉)
College of Business Administration, Ningbo University of Finance & Economics, Ningbo, China
e-mail: hanxiao@nbufe.edu.cn

H. Pechlaner et al. (eds.), *The Clash of Entrepreneurial Cultures?*, FGF Studies in Small Business and Entrepreneurship, https://doi.org/10.1007/978-3-030-97050-5_11

1 Introduction

The sustainable development of the Intelligent Connected Vehicle (ICV) industry is receiving increasing global attention. According to the "Made in China 2025" strategy,[1] ICV is defined as a new generation of a vehicle equipped with advanced sensors, controllers, and actuators in combination with modern network communication technologies. ICV enables functions including information sharing, complex environment sensing, intelligent decision-making, and automated cooperation, which is able to realize highly effective, safe, comfortable, and energy-efficient driving (Kuang et al., 2018). With the support of national policies, new ventures in the new energy automobile industry continue to emerge and develop (Cai et al., 2018). However, a complete entrepreneurial ecosystem has not yet been found to boost the development of the ICV industry, especially for high-tech start-ups that are targeting the high-end consumer groups.

Borrowing from biology, the metaphor of an entrepreneurial "ecosystem" (EE) is increasingly used by scholars (Acs et al., 2017; Spigel, 2017; Stam & van de Ven, 2021) and practitioners (Feld, 2012; Isenberg, 2010) for understanding the context for entrepreneurship in particular territories (countries, regions, cities). The entrepreneurial ecosystem comprises a set of interdependent elements that are governed in such a way that they enable productive entrepreneurship (Stam, 2015). According to Mason and Brown (2014), the EE is made up of entrepreneurial actors, entrepreneurial organizations (e.g., firms, venture capitalists, business angels, banks), institutions (universities, public sector agencies, financial bodies), and entrepreneurial processes.

The emergence of the knowledge economy and information technology has increased the value of strategic alliances in a wide range of industries. In recent years, strategic alliances have also developed rapidly in the ICV industry (Kuang et al., 2018). A strategic alliance is defined as a cooperative arrangement between two or more independent organizations that exchange or share resources for achieving certain strategic objectives (Zhao et al., 2015). In 2015, the Chinese Academy of Sciences launched the "Innovation and Entrepreneurship" alliance to create a high-end entrepreneurial ecosystem[2] and assert that the strategic alliance could help to create an innovative "entrepreneurial ecosystem" by condensing the scientific and technological resources, talents, and excellent platform of scientific research institutes, uniting various professional institutions and innovation systems and mechanisms, establishing a mechanism and environment for the linkage and integration of science and technology, industry, and capital. Therefore, in this chapter, we focus on the strategic alliance and regard it as an element of entrepreneurial ecosystem to find out its role in developing ICV industry EE.

---

[1]"Made in China 2025" is a national strategic plan and industrial policy of the Chinese Communist Party (CCP) to further develop the manufacturing sector of the People's Republic of China, issued by Premier Li Keqiang and his cabinet in May 2015.

[2]http://scitech.people.com.cn/n1/2015/1220/c1007-27951824.html

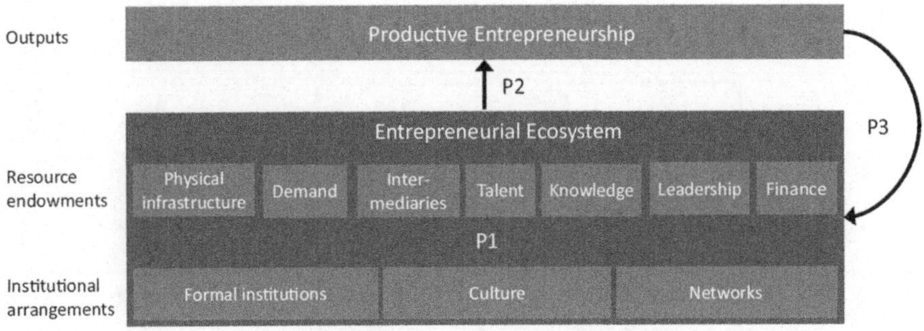

Fig. 1 Elements and outputs of the entrepreneurial ecosystem proposed by Stam and van de Ven (2021)

Question: What role do various strategic alliances play in creating and promoting an entrepreneurial ecosystem, thereby enabling the development of entrepreneurial ventures in the ICV industry?

2 Literature Review

An entrepreneurial ecosystem consists of all the elements that are required to sustain entrepreneurship in a particular territory. Van De Ven (1993) was one of the first to propose four broad components of an ecosystem for entrepreneurship, including institutional arrangements, public resource endowments, market demand, proprietary business activities. Isenberg (2010) formulated six distinct domains of an ecosystem: policy, finance, culture, support, human capital, and markets. Feld (2012) emphasized the interaction between the players in the ecosystem and access to all kinds of relevant resources, with an enabling role of government in the background. Woolley (2017) discusses how scholars have subsequently elaborated and expanded on these elements of an entrepreneurial ecosystem, which largely elaborates Van De Ven (1993) infrastructure components. Stam and van de Ven (2021) proposed an integrative model of entrepreneurial ecosystems consisting of ten elements and entrepreneurial outputs (see Fig. 1).

Building on these studies and prior academic studies (e.g., Feld, 2012; Isenberg, 2010; Stam & van de Ven, 2021; Van De Ven, 1993; Woolley, 2017), this chapter proposes a model of entrepreneurial ecosystems in the ICV industry consisting of three sub-ecosystems (see Fig. 2). The three sub-ecosystems are operational constructs of the broader concepts of institutions and resources of an entrepreneurial ecosystem.

In the previous EE models, for example, Stam and van de Ven (2021) defined the element, networks, as the social context of actors, especially the degree to which they are socially connected, and assert that networks of entrepreneurs provide information flow, enabling an effective distribution of knowledge, labor, and capital.

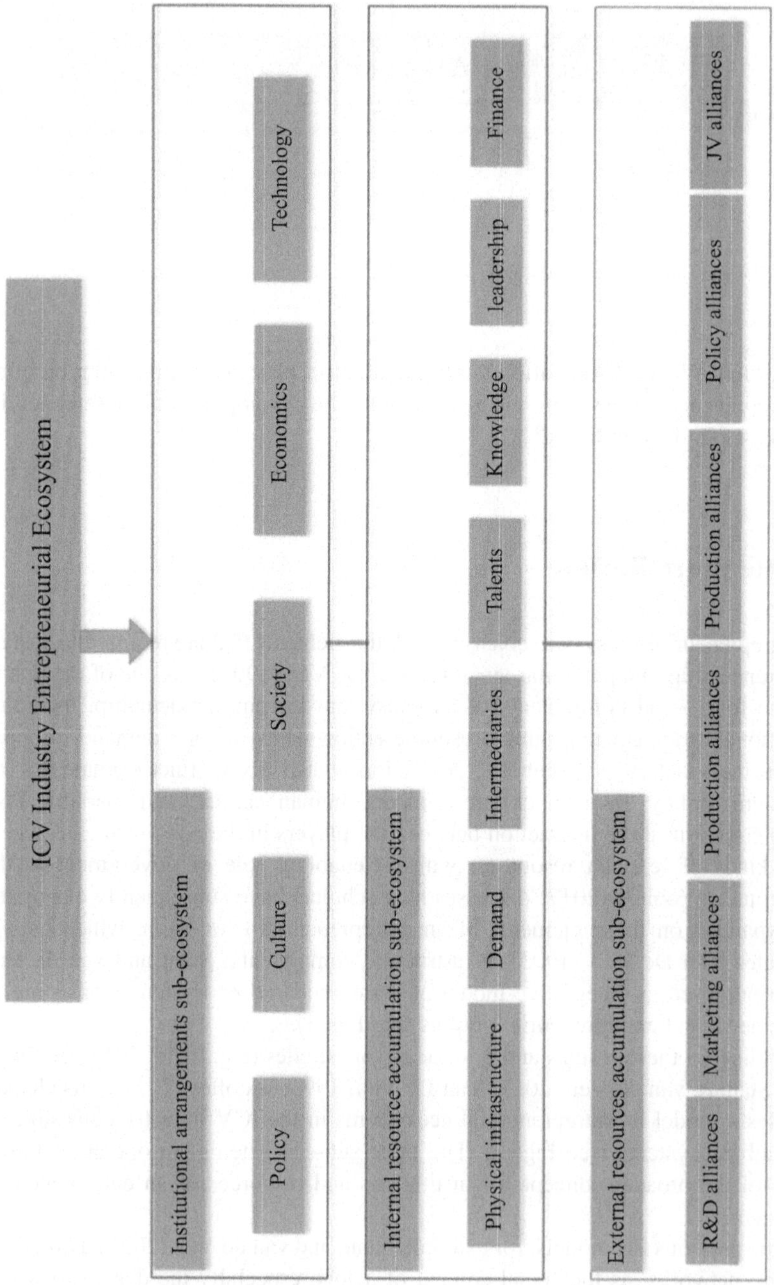

Fig. 2 Entrepreneurial ecosystem of the ICV industry

However, previous research (e.g., Stam & van de Ven, 2021) has tended to neglect the role of inter-organizational networks (strategic alliances or alliance networks) that might influence entrepreneurial efficiency.

However, in this chapter, the entrepreneurial ecosystem of the ICV industry includes institution arrangement sub-ecosystem, internal resources accumulation sub-ecosystem, and external resources accumulation sub-ecosystem. The institutional arrangements sub-ecosystem is captured by the policy, culture, society, economics, and technology elements. The internal resources accumulation sub-ecosystem is captured by the physical infrastructure, finance, leadership, talents, knowledge, intermediaries, and demand elements. The third sub-ecosystems, external resources accumulation, consists of the R & D alliances, marketing alliances, production alliances, policy alliances, and JV alliances, which are regarded to be the key part of the entrepreneurial ecosystem in the ICV industry. Aiming to timely gain a foothold, start-ups, especially the company targeting high-end markets, carrying out strategic alliances is a fast way to obtain the valuable and core resources (Chan et al., 1997). Alliances allow access to complementary resources for value creation (Bouncken & Fredrich, 2016). Table 1 summarizes and relates these concepts, constructs, and elements of the ICV industry entrepreneurial ecosystem.

3 Research Design

3.1 Case Study Approach

The case study method is best suited for constructing theory (Eisenhardt, 1989). An exploratory case study approach with a single case (Rashid et al., 2019) was considered for this study as it enabled the researchers to look at "how" the strategic alliance facilitated the EE development in the ICV industry. According to Yin (2009), the case study design is best suited when one can observe the behavior of those involved in the process without manipulation, as well as the contextual conditions where there are no clear boundaries between the phenomenon and context.

3.2 Data Collecting

In this chapter, we only collect data relating to external resources accumulation sub-ecosystem to explore the development path of the alliance and how it plays a role in the entrepreneurial ecosystem. Alliance samples were collected by going

Table 1 Constructs of entrepreneurial ecosystem elements in the ICV industry

Sub-ecosystem	Construct	Definition	Elements	References
Institutional arrangements	Formal institution	The rules that government formulate	Policy	Author added
	Informal institution	Cultural context	Culture	Stam and van de Ven (2021)
		Society context	Society	Author added
		Economics context	Economics	Author added
		Technology context	Technology	Author added
Internal resources accumulation	Physical resources	The physical context of actors enables them to meet other actors in physical proximity.	Physical infrastructure	Stam, (2015); Stam and van de Ven, (2021); Van De Ven, (1993)
	Means of consumption	The presence of financial means in the population to purchase goods and services	Demand	
	Producer services	The intermediate service inputs into the proprietary function.	Intermediate	
	Financial resources	The presence of financial means to invest in activities that do not yet deliver financial means.	Finance	
	Leadership	Leadership that provides guidance for, and direction of, collective action.	Leadership	
	Human capital	The skills, knowledge, and experience possessed by individuals.	Talents	
	Knowledge resources	Investments in (scientific and technological) knowledge creation.	Knowledge	
External resources accumulation	R & D corporation	Cooperation between enterprises to develop new products or new technologies.	R & D alliance	Lin et al., (2012); Sampson, (2007); Zhao et al., (2021)
	Marketing corporation	Cooperation between enterprises to open up new markets or promote new products.	Marketing alliance	Li et al., (2010)
	Production corporation	Cooperation among enterprises to produce new products.	Production alliance	Yamamura et al., (1997)
	Corporation with government	The cooperation between the enterprise and the government in product	Policy alliance	Named by author

(continued)

Table 1 (continued)

Sub-ecosystem	Construct	Definition	Elements	References
		promotion, plant construction, site selection, etc.		
	JV corporation	Enterprises establish new companies through joint ventures, cooperate in the production of new products, develop new brands or develop new technologies, etc.	JV alliance	Sillars and Kangari, (2004)

through company annual reports, Baidu News,[3] corporate websites, and Industry Association Official websites using reptile software (Octoparse, website: https://www.octoparse.com). After data cleaning, sorting, the basic research data includes 24 alliance samples from 2016 to 2021. Table 2 presents the composition of our samples.

4 Case Study

4.1 The Origin of NIO Inc.

NIO Inc. is a Chinese multinational automobile manufacturer headquartered in Shanghai, specializing in designing and developing electric vehicles. NIO Inc. was founded in November 2014 by William Li, as Nextev Inc., which was changed to the current name NIO Inc. in July 2017. After launch, several companies invested in NIO Inc., including Tencent, Temasek, Sequoia, Lenovo Inc., and Texas Pacific Group.

In this chapter, we chose NIO Inc. as the case to explore its external resources accumulation sub-ecosystem. Because unlike previous Chinese auto companies, NIO Inc.'s market positioning at the beginning of its establishment was up-market. NIO Inc. is a pioneer in China's premium electric vehicle market. It designs, jointly manufactures, and sells smart and connected premium electric vehicles, driving innovations in next-generation technologies in connectivity, autonomous driving, and artificial intelligence.[4] Redefining user experience, they provide users with comprehensive, convenient, and innovative charging solutions and other

[3]Baidu News is a Chinese news search platform launched by Baidu Inc. Unlike other news services, it collects and screens news reports from thousands of news sources, provides the latest and most timely news to users, and highlights the objectivity and integrity of the news, which truly reflects the hot news of every moment.

[4]Company Profile I NIO Inc., https://ir.nio.com/governance/company-profile/

Table 2 The strategic alliances of NIO Inc. from 2016 to 2021

Year	Time	Alliances	Corporation content	Corporation type	Country/ Partners' types	Industry
2016	May 2016	NIO Inc., JAC co., ltd	Corporation for producing vehicles.	Production	China/state-owned company	Automobile
	Aug. 2016	NIO Inc., NavLnfo co., ltd	In-depth cooperation in navigation engine, internet of vehicles, autonomous driving, traffic big data online service system, global business, etc.	R & D	China/state-owned company	Internet
2017	May 2017	NIO Inc., CHANGAN co., ltd	The two parties have launched cooperation in the entire industry, including R & D, production, sales, and service, to achieve resource sharing and win-win cooperation.	R & D, production, marketing, and service	China/state-owned company	Automobile
	June 2017	NIO Inc., continental AG Inc.	The two parties will cooperate closely in the fields of pure electric vehicles, intelligent transportation, and automated driving.	R & D	Germany/Inc.	Automobile
	July 2017	NIO Inc., Lenovo Inc.	Jointly develop a smart car computing platform.	R & D	China/Inc.	Internet
	Oct. 2017	NIO Inc., Shouqi Limousine & Chauffeur co., ltd	NIO Inc. invested equity in Shouqi Limousine & Chauffeur's B+ round financing.	Minority equity investments	China/ co., ltd	Services
	Nov. 2017	NIO Inc., STATE GRID	The two parties will deepen cooperation in the construction and operation of electric vehicle charging and swapping networks, battery energy storage, and other energy fields.	Operation/ marketing	China/state-owned company	Electric power
	13 Dec. 2017	NIO Inc., Tencent cloud co., ltd	The two parties will use Tencent Cloud's data processing capabilities, artificial intelligence algorithms, and other capabilities to develop smart car networking.	R & D	China/co., ltd	Internet
	28 Dec. 2017	NIO Inc., TianJin motor dies Inc.	TianJin motor dies company produced some stamping products for NIO Inc.	Production	China/Inc.	Automobile

	28 Dec. 2017	NIO Inc., China Southern Power Grid	The two parties will be based on mobile internet smart technology, using interconnection standards for platform docking, and jointly building charging and replacement facilities.	Operation/ marketing	China/state-owned company	Electric power
2018	Mar. 2018	NIO Inc., Tata technologies co., ltd	The two groups work closely together throughout the entire development process of electric vehicle series products.	R & D	India/co., ltd	Technology
	July 2018	NIO Inc., Bosch group GmbH	The two parties will cooperate in key areas, such as sensor technology, autonomous driving, motor control, and intelligent transportation systems.	R & D	Germany/ GmbH	Automobile
	April 2018	NIO Inc., GAC Group Inc.	Co-founded HYCAN company for developing new models and brands.	JV/R & D	China/Inc.	Automobile
	July. 2018	NIO Inc., Changan co., ltd	Co-founded the establishment of Changan NIO Inc. new energy automobile technology co., ltd.	Joint venture	China/ CHANGAN co., ltd	Automobile
2019	May 2019	NIO Inc., SGL carbon GmbH	SGL carbon GmbH will develop a prototype of a carbon fiber reinforced plastic (CFRP) battery case for NIO Inc.	R & D	Germany/ GmbH	Materials
	Oct. 2019	NIO Inc., Mobileye	The two parties will build an L4-level autonomous driving model based on the second-generation vehicle platform of NIO Inc.	R & D	Israel/subsidiary of intel	Technology
	Dec. 2019	NIO Inc., Xiaopeng co., ltd	The two parties have reached cooperation in the charging network.	Operation/marketing	China/ co., ltd	Automobile
2020	Feb. 2020	NIO Inc., Hefei government	The two parties agreed to jointly plan and build the Xinqiao intelligent electric vehicle Industrial Park to build a world-class intelligent electric vehicle industrial cluster with a complete industrial chain.	Policy	China/ government	/
	Mar. 2020	NIO Inc., Xiaomi co., ltd	Xiaomi mi watch will launch an NIO Inc. app that can perform car control functions anytime and anywhere.	R & D/marketing	China/ co., ltd	Internet

(continued)

Table 2 (continued)

Year	Time	Alliances	Corporation content	Corporation type	Country/ Partners' types	Industry
	6 Aug. 2020	NIO Inc., SUNING co., ltd	The two parties have cooperated in the areas of store expansion, product sales, Suning commercial and hotel project charging pile construction, brand cooperation promotion, and other areas of NIO Inc.	Marketing	China/co., ltd	Retail
	13 Aug. 2020	NIO Inc., Dida co., ltd	NIO Inc. owners are encouraged to join the Dida lift car platform to share the empty seats on the car with passengers on the road, and Dida travel will provide a green review channel for all NIO Inc. owners.	Marketing	China/co., ltd	Services
2021	2 Feb. 2021	NIO Inc., red star Macalline group Inc.	Jointly build a car charging and swapping station.	Operation/marketing	China/Inc	Household
	April 2021	NIO Inc., Sinopec group	The two parties will also cooperate in all aspects of new materials and smart electric vehicles, battery rental services (BaaS), vehicle procurement, and leisure consumption scene construction.	Marketing	China/state-owned company	Energy
	3 May 2021	NIO Inc., University of Science and Technology of China	Joint technology research, talent training, and interaction, etc.	R & D	China/ university	/
	24 May 2021	NIO Inc., OPPO co., ltd	The two parties jointly developed and tested the digital car key based on the CCC 2.0 version.	R & D/marketing	China/co., ltd	Internet

Table 3 Financial Data of NIO Inc. from 2016 ~ 2020

	For the year ended December 31, 2020					
	2016	2017	2018	2019	2020	
	RMB	RMB	RMB	RMB	RMB	Us$
	In thousands, except for per share data					
Revenues						
Vehicle sales	/	/	4,852,470	7,367,113	15,182,522	2,326,823
Other sales	/	/	98,701	457,791	1,075,411	164,814
Total cost of sales	/	/	4,951,171	7,824,904	16,257,933	2,491,637

Sources: NIO annual report, 2020, https://ir.nio.com/static-files/cb42cc7f-6069-45a2-bbe4-21d4808609b8

user-centric service offerings. NIO Inc.'s total number of employees in 2020 was 7763, a 4.31% increase from 2019 (7442).[5] For the financial situation, NIO Inc. is not profitable from the beginning of its establishment. It began generating revenues in June 2018, when NIO Inc. began making deliveries and sales of the ES8. It currently generates revenues from vehicle sales and other sales (see Table 3).

4.2 *External Resources Accumulation Sub-Ecosystem of NIO Inc.*

In order to better observe the development status of NIO Inc's alliance, this chapter uses UCINET 12.0 software to visualize all NIO Inc's alliance partners. Fig. 3 shows the alliance network of NIO Inc., as shown in Fig. 3, we can see that NIO Inc.'s alliance network is already quite large, with diverse partners that come from different industries including automobile, internet, technology, materials, electric power, services, household, retail, etc. Besides, NIO Inc. has entered strategic alliances, including joint ventures, R & D, minority equity investments, marketing, production, services, policy, etc., with various third parties to further their business purpose from 2016.

The external resources accumulation sub-ecosystem is a critical and necessary part of NIO Inc.'s entrepreneurial ecosystem. In this way, NIO Inc. overcomes many problems in production, technology, marketing, big data, etc. with low economic cost. NIO Inc. deployed the alliance network in 2016. It initially corporated with traditional auto body and parts companies such as JAC Co., Ltd., CHANGAN, TianJin Motor Dies to solve the production problems of automotive vehicles and parts. And cooperation with internet companies such as NavLnfo Co., Ltd., Lenovo Inc., Tencent Cloud Co., Ltd. to solve software development issues and data issues, etc.

[5]NIO: Number of Employees 2019–2021 I NIO, https://www.macrotrends.net/stocks/charts/NIO/nio/number-of-employees

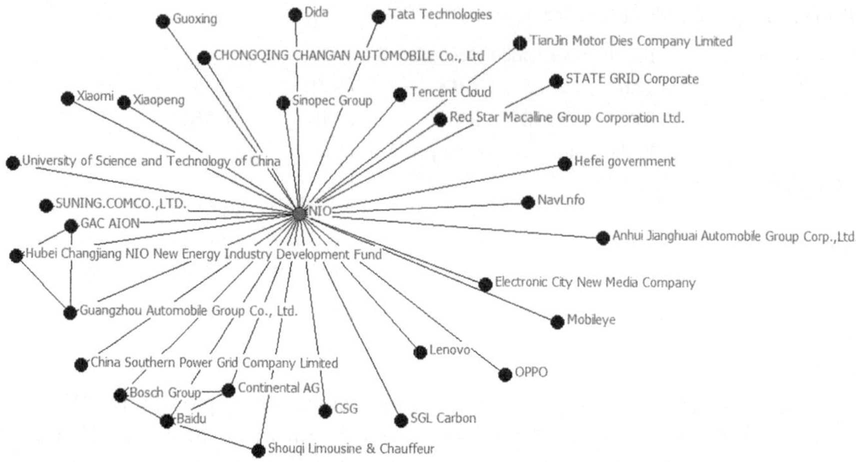

Fig. 3 The alliance networks of NIO Inc.

4.2.1 R & D Alliances and Knowledge

It is intelligent for a start-up enterprise to quickly obtain rich external resources and knowledge in the form of a strategic alliance. NIO Inc. has entered into an arrangement with various alliance partners, such as automobile enterprise (Changan Co., Ltd., Continental AG Inc., Bosh Group, GAC Group Inc.), internet enterprise (NavLnfo Co., Ltd., Lenovo Inc., Tencent Cloud Co., Ltd., Tata Technology Co., Ltd), materials enterprise (SGL carbon GmbH), and technology enterprise (Mobileye), etc. for the R & D corporation from 2016 to 2021. The cooperative projects involve various technological fields, including pure electric vehicles, smart car computing platforms, artificial intelligence algorithms, sensor technology, autonomous driving, motor control, intelligent transportation systems, digital car key, etc.

Correspondingly, by counting the number of patents granted by NIO Inc. from 2014 to 2021, we found that the number of patents granted by NIO Inc. has rapidly increased since 2016 (see Fig. 4). Therefore, to some extent, this shows that the heterogeneous knowledge resources brought by the R & D alliance might enrich NIO Inc.'s knowledge base and promote the combination of new knowledge elements and the generation of new products.

4.2.2 Marketing Alliances and Demand

NIO Inc. has entered into an arrangement with various alliance partners, such as automobile enterprise (Changan Co., Ltd., Xiaopeng Co., Ltd), energy enterprise (STATE GRID, China Southern Power Grid, Sinopec Group), internet enterprise (Xiaomi Co., Ltd., OPPO Co., Ltd), and service enterprise (Dida Co., Ltd), etc. for the marketing corporation from 2016 to 2021. The cooperative projects involve

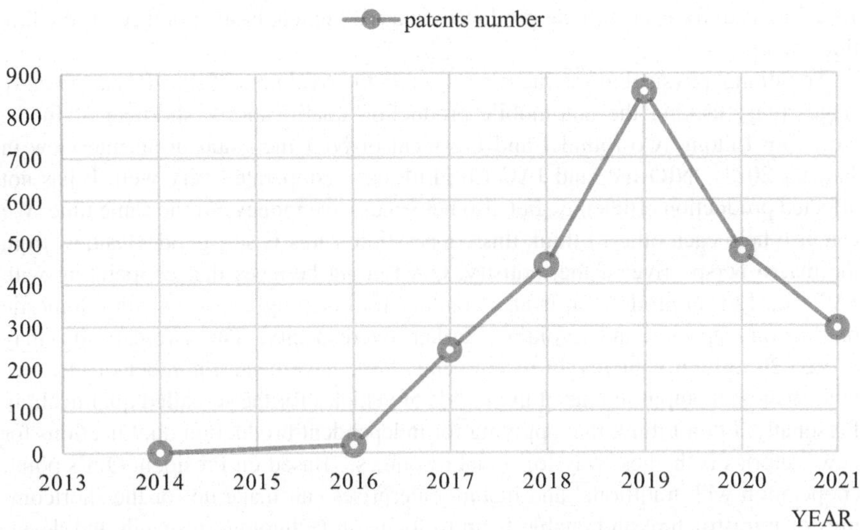

Fig. 4 Granted patent number of NIO Inc. from 2014 ~ 2021. Source: Innojoy patent database, http://www.innojoy.com

various marketing fields, including jointly construction and operation of electric vehicle charging and swapping networks, battery energy storage, platform docking, charging and replacement facilities, Xiaomi Mi Watch and OPPO app with digital car key function, lift car platform, battery rental services (BaaS), vehicle procurement and leisure consumption scene construction, etc.

Demand is measured as a potential market demand (Stam & van de Ven, 2021). Corporating with automobile enterprise, energy enterprise, internet enterprise, and service enterprise, NIO Inc. could integrate customer resources in various fields and expand multi-channel marketing methods.

4.2.3 Production Alliances and Physical Infrastructure

NIO Inc. has entered into an arrangement with Jianghuai Automobile Group Co., Ltd., or JAC, for the manufacturing of their vehicles, initially the ES8, for five years starting from May 2016. In April 2019 and March 2020, NIO Inc. entered into manufacturing cooperation agreements with JAC Co., Ltd. for the manufacturing of the ES6 and the EC6, respectively. The ES8, ES6, and EC6 are manufactured in partnership with JAC Co., Ltd. at its Hefei manufacturing plant. JAC Co., Ltd. is a major state-owned automobile manufacturer in China and is constructed such as the Hefei manufacturing plant for the production of the ES8 (with a modified production line for the ES6 and EC6) and potentially ET7 and other future vehicles. Under the arrangement with JAC Co., Ltd. concerning the ES8, ES6, and EC6, NIO Inc. pays

JAC Co., Ltd. for each vehicle produced on a per-vehicle basis monthly for the first three years.

Traditional physical infrastructure is usually the weakness of start-ups at the early stages (e.g., lacking the automobile production qualifications, shortage of funds, etc.). Qin Lihong (Co-founder and President of NIO Inc.) said in an interview in January 2021: "NIO Inc. and JAC Co., Ltd. have cooperated very well. It has not affected production efficiency, but also helped us save money. At the same time, We can also help each other. I think this cooperation status is still good. Besides, from the macro perspective of the industry, Qin Lihong believes that cooperating with JAC Co., Ltd. in production is also conducive to making use of existing domestic production capacity and avoiding further overcapacity. The overcapacity may exceed 20 million vehicles. In recent years, there have been a number of factories with an annual output of tens of thousands of vehicles for the so-called qualification. Personally, I don't think that applying for independent production qualifications for new factories is the best way for social resources." Based on President Qin's point, cooperation with traditional and mature enterprises can make up for the shortcomings of infrastructure and enable them to focus on technology research and development, reducing production costs, and marketing expansion.

4.2.4 Policy Alliances and Physical Infrastructure

Similarly, cooperation with the government provides a favorable system guarantee for the construction of enterprise infrastructure (Yang et al., 2016). In February 2020, NOI Inc. entered into a collaboration framework agreement with the municipal government of Hefei, Anhui province, where NOI Inc.'s main manufacturing hub is located. Subsequently, from April to June 2020, NOI Inc. entered into the Hefei Agreements with the Hefei Strategic Investors for investments in NIO Inc. China.

4.2.5 JV Alliances and Finance

In April 2018, NOI Inc. co-funded with GAC Group and established HYCAN company for developing new models and brands. And then, NOI Inc. co-funded with Changan and established Changan NIO Inc. New Energy Automobile Technology Co., Ltd. (rename: Avatar technology) for developing new products in July.

The supply and accessibility of finance for new and small firms are important conditions for their growth and survival (Shinozaki, 2012). JV alliances firm's financial performance is stronger in the joint venture than other alliances (Jiang & Li, 2008; Ryu et al., 2019). Conversely, in firms with abundant funds, more JV activities can be carried out.

4.3 The Entrepreneurial Ecosystem Model of NIO Inc.

Based on the model of the ICV industry entrepreneurial ecosystem (see Fig. 2) and the analysis of the external resources accumulation sub-ecosystem, the framework of NIO Inc.'s entrepreneurial ecosystem can be drawn into three overlapping layers in which all components can affect each other inter and/or intra-layers (see Fig. 5). In the most outer layer of the framework, the institutional arrangements are placed. In the second layer, the actions and resources brought by strategic alliances are essential for the creation and growth of start-up companies. In the core layer, these elements present NIO Inc.'s specific features and core competitiveness. Besides, as discussed in Sect. 4.2, the internal resources accumulation sub-ecosystem and external resources accumulation sub-ecosystem are interdependent, and resources complement each other, especially in knowledge integration, sharing, and accumulation.

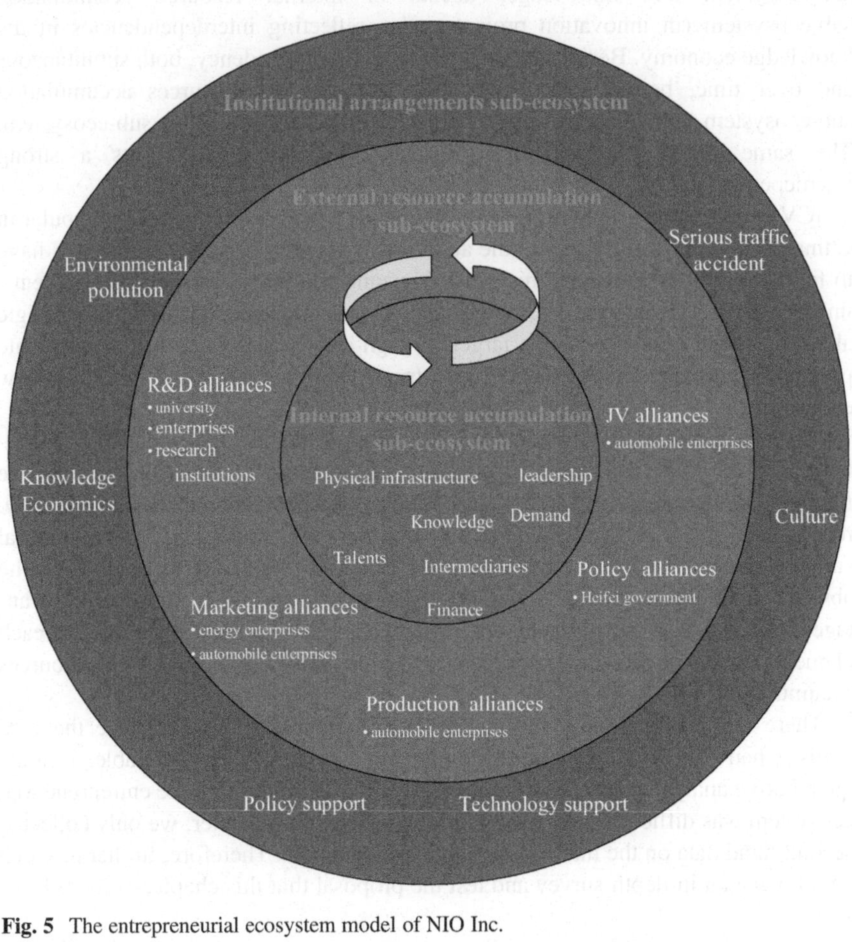

Fig. 5 The entrepreneurial ecosystem model of NIO Inc.

5 Discussion and Conclusion

This chapter aims to figure out what role do strategic alliances playing in creating and promoting an entrepreneurial ecosystem in the ICV industry. Through creating the ICV EE model and case study, we find that, first, strategic alliances play an essential role in EE since firms enter alliances could access valuable and complementary resources that they do not already possess, including the capital, technology, specialized knowledge, etc. (Tjemkes et al., 2017). Second, the strategic alliance as an element of the external accumulation sub-ecosystem of EE is mutually interdependent and co-evolved with the internal accumulation sub-ecosystem. Specifically, production alliances, policy alliances in external resources accumulation sub-ecosystem, and physical infrastructure in internal resource accumulation sub-ecosystem are strongly correlated, both simultaneously and over time. The same counts for R & D alliances in external resources accumulation sub-ecosystem and knowledge, talents in internal resource accumulation sub-ecosystem (in innovation projects), also reflecting interdependencies in the knowledge economy. Besides, there is a strong interdependency, both simultaneous and over time, between JV alliances in the external resources accumulation sub-ecosystem and finance in the internal resource accumulation sub-ecosystem. The same count for marketing alliances and demand presents a strong interdependence.

ICV is undergoing rapid progress in the whole world and is especially popular in China. However, as followers in the automotive industry, Chinese enterprises have to find an additional resource reserve for instant response to market requirements, finite capacities, and limited resources. Thus, a distinct understanding of strategic alliances is necessary for firms targeting high-end consumer groups to generate proper positioning strategies and reconstruct their core competitiveness in new environments.

Through a case study, this research has several practical and theoretical contributions to the ICV industry. First, based on an overview of the NIO Inc. case, we figure out and created the model of an entrepreneurial ecosystem in the ICV industry, recognizing the strategic alliance is one of the important entrepreneurial sub-ecosystems. To acquire more benefits, enterprises should focus more on the absorption of alliance resources and processing to gain sustained competitive advantages. Second, this chapter provides explanations for essential meanings of each element using specific cases, especially the elements in the external resources accumulation sub-ecosystem.

There are several limitations in this study admittedly. Firstly, since the ICV industry had a short history and relevant market data were hardly available, accurate quantitative analysis to describe the strategic alliance impacts on the entrepreneurial ecosystem was difficult at the moment. Secondly, in this chapter, we only collected second-hand data on the internet, lacking first-hand data. Therefore, further research could make an in-depth survey and test the proposal that this chapter proposed.

References

Acs, Z. J., Stam, E., Audretsch, D. B., & O'Connor, A. (2017). The lineages of the entrepreneurial ecosystem approach. *Small Business Economics, 49*(1), 1–10.

Bouncken, R. B., & Fredrich, V. (2016). Business model innovation in alliances: Successful configurations. *Journal of Business Research, 69*(9), 3584–3590.

Cai, L., Peng, X., & Wang, L. (2018). The characteristics and influencing factors of entrepreneurial behaviour: The case of new state-owned firms in the new energy automobile industry in an emerging economy. *Technological Forecasting and Social Change, 135*, 112–120.

Chan, S. H., Kensinger, J. W., Keown, A. J., & Martin, J. D. (1997). Do strategic alliances create value? *Journal of Financial Economics, 46*(2), 199–221.

Eisenhardt, K. M. (1989). Building theories from case study research. *Academy of Management Review, 14*(4), 532–550.

Feld, B. (2012). *Startup communities: Building an entrepreneurial ecosystem in your city*. John Wiley & Sons.

Isenberg, D. J. (2010). How to start an entrepreneurial revolution. *Harvard Business Review, 88*(6), 40–50.

Jiang, X., & Li, Y. (2008). The relationship between organizational learning and firms' financial performance in strategic alliances: A contingency approach. *Journal of World Business, 43*(3), 365–379.

Kuang, X., Zhao, F., Hao, H., & Liu, Z. (2018). Intelligent connected vehicles: The industrial practices and impacts on automotive value-chains in China. *Asia Pacific Business Review, 24*(1), 1–21.

Li, N., Boulding, W., & Staelin, R. (2010). General alliance experience, uncertainty, and marketing alliance governance mode choice. *Journal of the Academy of Marketing Science, 38*(2), 141–158.

Lin, C., Wu, Y.-J., Chang, C., Wang, W., & Lee, C.-Y. (2012). The alliance innovation performance of R & D alliances—The absorptive capacity perspective. *Technovation, 32*(5), 282–292.

Mason, C., & Brown, R. (2014). Entrepreneurial ecosystems and growth oriented entrepreneurship. *Final report to OECD, Paris, 30*(1), 77–102.

Rashid, Y., Rashid, A., Warraich, M. A., Sabir, S. S., & Waseem, A. (2019). Case study method: A step-by-step guide for business researchers. *International Journal of Qualitative Methods, 18*, 1609406919862424.

Ryu, D., Kim, M. H., & Ryu, D. (2019). The effect of international strategic alliances on firm performance before and after the global financial crisis. *Emerging Markets Finance and Trade, 55*(15), 3539–3552.

Sampson, R. C. (2007). R & D alliances and firm performance: The impact of technological diversity and alliance organization on innovation. *Academy of Management Journal, 50*(2), 364–386.

Shinozaki, S. (2012). *A new regime of SME finance in emerging Asia: Empowering growth-oriented SMEs to build resilient national economies: ADB Working Paper Series on Regional Economic Integration*.

Sillars, D. N., & Kangari, R. (2004). Predicting organizational success within a project-based joint venture alliance. *Journal of Construction Engineering and Management, 130*(4), 500–508.

Spigel, B. (2017). The relational organization of entrepreneurial ecosystems. *Entrepreneurship Theory and Practice, 41*(1), 49–72.

Stam, E. (2015). Entrepreneurial ecosystems and regional policy: A sympathetic critique. *European Planning Studies, 23*(9), 1759–1769.

Stam, E., & van de Ven, A. (2021). Entrepreneurial ecosystem elements. *Small Business Economics, 56*(2), 809–832.

Tjemkes, B., Vos, P., & Burgers, K. (2017). *Strategic alliance management*. Routledge.

Van De Ven, H. (1993). The development of an infrastructure for entrepreneurship. *Journal of Business Venturing, 8*(3), 211–230.

Woolley, J. (2017). *Infrastructure for entrepreneurship, Oxford research encyclopedia of business and management*. Oxford University Press.

Yamamura, K., Hatch, W., & Lee, S. (1997). Asia in Japan's embrace: Building a regional production alliance. *International Journal, 52*(3), 535.

Yang, T., Long, R., Li, W., & Rehman, S. U. (2016). Innovative application of the public–private partnership model to the electric vehicle charging infrastructure in China. *Sustainability, 8*(8), 738.

Yin, R. K. 2009. *Case study research: Design and methods*: Sage.

Zhao, J., Xi, X., & Yi, S. (2015). Resource allocation under a strategic alliance: How a cooperative network with knowledge flow spurs co-evolution. *Knowledge-Based Systems, 89*, 497–508.

Zhao, Y., Han, X., Yang, X., & Li, Z. (2021). Interorganizational knowledge networks, R & D Alliance networks, and innovation capability: A multilevel network perspective. *Complexity, 2021*, 8820059.

Xiao Han received her Ph.D. degree from Shanghai University. She is a lecturer at the College of Business Administration, Ningbo University of Finance & Economics. Her current publications and research interests focus on innovation networks in organizations, knowledge management, and the Entrepreneurial Ecosystem. Her papers have been published in a variety of journals including Studies in Science of Science (CSSCI), R & D MANAGEMENT (CSSCI), Science Research Management (CSSCI), healthcare (SSCI), Frontiers in Psychology (SSCI), Complexity (SCI), etc.

Agile at Scale Adoption: New Perspectives from a Solely Remote Environment

Tatiana Lekýrová and Gabriela Antošová

Abstract Agility is a lever to achieve the entrepreneurial, innovative culture which allows companies to build close relationships with customers and quickly adapt to their environments. In this light, this study aimed to assess virtual scaled agile transformation. Qualitative research situated in a large software company based on 16 semi-structured interviews, observations and artifacts analysis was carried out to evaluate the studied agile adoption. Findings uncovered the challenges, strengths, innovative aspects, and the effect of the transformation on the firm's effectiveness. The study concludes with a set of recommendations for other organizations. The firm successfully utilized the full potential of the online environment, which shows that online interconnectedness provides a way to advance digitalization and the development of the whole digital ecosystem. The empirical evidence from this study demonstrates that it is possible to realize a scaled agile adoption solely remotely when the global pandemic does not allow for in-person meetings.

Keywords Scaling agile · Agile software development · Organizational change · Large-Scale Scrum

1 Introduction

Virtual agile transitions have multiple factors that companies can benefit from even in the post-COVID-19 world. Like agile adoptions in the physical space, purely remote change endeavors rely on effective bi-directional communication, frequent feedback sessions, transparency among all hierarchical company levels, and technical tools. Executing agile adoptions online has the advantage of cost savings. The disadvantage is perhaps the missing social aspect and the lack of in-person

T. Lekýrová (✉) · G. Antošová
Masaryk Institute of Advances Studies, Czech Technical University in Prague, Prague, Czech Republic
e-mail: tatianalekyrova@gmail.com; gabriela.antosova@cvut.cz

H. Pechlaner et al. (eds.), *The Clash of Entrepreneurial Cultures?*, FGF Studies in Small Business and Entrepreneurship, https://doi.org/10.1007/978-3-030-97050-5_12

interactions, however with the use of digital technology organizations can compensate for this factor to some extent.

Scaling agile to large companies comprises more complexity than in small teams. To make sense of this complexity and support innovation from the bottom up, companies can use agile scaling frameworks (Digital.ai, 2021; Ebert & Paasivaara, 2017).

In this study, a large software company adopted Large-Scale Scrum (LeSS). The researched company used the terms agile transformation and agile adoption in the following context. The transformation itself was a point in time when the studied product group transferred from one way of working into another. The agile adoption, or transition, had been an ongoing process of acquiring and improving the new selected way of working. The two terms are used with these meanings in the remainder of this paper.

Sixteen semi-structured interviews were conducted to map and examine the scaled agile adoption in this firm. Additionally, observations and artifact analysis provided another perspective on the aspects emergent from the interviews. Due to the global pandemic, the transformation itself as well as all parts of the research were realized online.

Academic research on fully virtual agile adoptions is scarce (Dikert et al., 2016; Paasivaara et al., 2018) and thus this study aimed to cover this area. The contributions of this chapter include empirical evidence of a scaled agile transition being carried out entirely remotely and online. The conducted study provides a set of recommendations and lessons learned, which the researched company as well as other firms undergoing change endeavors are encouraged to take into consideration.

The rest of this chapter is organized into sections that contain theoretical background for agile methodologies, research methodology the authors chose for the study, data analysis expanding on the outcomes of the research, implications for the academics and the industry, and conclusion with future research possibilities.

2 Theoretical Background

Basic agile methodologies include Scrum, Extreme Programming, or Kanban (Diebold et al., 2018). These elementary concepts are however not sufficient for large firms. Scaling agile has become prevalent in software companies in recent years (Diebold et al., 2018; Theobald et al., 2019). Multiple frameworks can be used to expand agility to scaled environments, such as Scaled Agile Framework, LeSS, Scrum of Scrums, Disciplined Agile Delivery, or Scrum at Scale (Conboy & Carroll, 2019; Diebold et al., 2018; Digital.ai, 2021; Ebert & Paasivaara, 2017).

The common challenges from agile adoption journeys include resistance to change, insufficient leadership, an imbalance between bottom-up and top-down approaches, agile immaturity, and cultural conflicts (Conboy & Carroll, 2019; Digital.ai, 2021).

This study is specifically focused on an agile adoption in the virtual environment using the LeSS framework. Large-Scale Scrum is a scaling framework based on Scrum (Larman & Vodde, 2008).

Scrum is an iterative empirical agile framework with the purpose to provide teams with concepts for better communication and cadence to deliver something of value to the customer. Scrum uses the Product Backlog to track work items (Schwaber & Sutherland, 2020).

LeSS principles include lean thinking, empirical adjustments, continuous improvement, transparency, and customer focus (Larman & Vodde, 2008). At the core of LeSS are the feature teams, which are cross-functional, self-organizing, customer-centric (Larman & Vodde, 2008, 2016).

Larman and Vodde (2016) introduce two schemes to choose from when scaling LeSS: (1) regular LeSS with up to eight teams, and (2) LeSS Huge scaled up to a few thousand employees. LeSS Huge uses requirement areas to categorize items in the Product Backlog and establish a structure that is needed to handle higher complexity (Larman & Vodde, 2016). LeSS and LeSS Huge transformations as well as conversion of teams to feature teams should be done gradually (Larman & Vodde, 2016).

Factors that determine successful agile adoptions include proportional time commitment, training, and collaboration with and understanding of the customers (Gandomani et al., 2015). To carry out agile adoptions or any kind of online collaborative activity, Singh (2020) suggests using tools with low barriers of entry. Further recommended are online whiteboards, using a moderator for the video calls and iterating over until the selected approach serves the team well (Comella-Dorda et al., 2020; Mancl & Fraser, 2020).

Metrics to evaluate agile adoptions can be divided into quantitative and qualitative (Bergqvist & Gordani Shahri, 2018; Mahadevan et al., 2019; Olszewska et al., 2016). Although quantitative metrics are prevalent (Digital.ai, 2021), qualitative metrics provide a way to a more in-depth understanding of a firm's employees' perspectives. They can be carried out via a direct inquiry about employee's engagement and well-being (Bergqvist & Gordani Shahri, 2018; Mahadevan et al., 2019). Employee Net Promoter Score (eNPS) is one of the qualitative metrics to measure adoption's success (Sedlak, 2020).

3 Research Methodology

This study used qualitative research to assess the agile transition in a department of about 100 employees within a large company from the software development field. The agile adoption was focused on merging two sub-departments together and gravitating toward a unified product while adopting Large-Scale Scrum. After the initial literature review, the authors formulated the following research question to evaluate the virtual agile adoption:

RQ: What shortcomings and accomplishments were present and what was their effect on product group's effectiveness during the agile adoption journey in the studied company?

To fulfill the research question, the authors used two main primary data sources and a supporting data source. Specifically, the authors relied on (1) semi-structured interviews with selected participants, and (2) observations of the team activities. The supporting data source consisted of an array of artifacts, such as communication channels, online video conferencing, and whiteboard collaboration tools. Once all data was collected, comprehensive data analysis followed, for which thematic analysis was used. Thematic analysis yielded results which were then synthesized into clusters according to research questions.

All the research activities were conducted in an online environment. Interviews were executed using the online video conferencing platform Zoom (2021) and were recorded with the consent of participants. In summary, 16 interviews were conducted in two rounds. In the first round, 5 participants were interviewed and in the second round, 11 participants were part of the semi-structured interviews. The second round included the same five participants already interviewed in the first round.

The interviewees were selected to construct a diversified sample from the product team, such that multiple roles, skill sets, seniority level, time zones, and cultural backgrounds were present. The first author collected and analyzed the data altogether. The second author helped to validate the findings and review the paper draft.

4 Data Analysis

All the recordings were transcribed in the SonixAI (2021) and f4transkript (2021) software. Thematic analysis was selected to analyze the data and was realized inductively, using the open-source data analytical tool Rampin et al. (2021). In the following sections are the outputs of the data analysis in relation to each aspect of the research question.

4.1 Shortcomings from an Online Agile Adoption Journey

4.1.1 Insufficient Cultural Readiness for Change

Transitions of any kind rely on the organizational culture. Culture affects how the employees will perform and what will be the company's reputation in the eyes of the customers (Cameron & Green, 2019). In the studied company, alignment of culture proved to be one of the biggest challenges. Cultural alignment was connected to unpreparedness for the transition of one of the sub-departments. The bigger sub-department conducted agile experiments during one and a half years prior to the LeSS transformation; however, there were no preparations carried out in the second sub-department.

> It is not only about the skills, it is also about the culture. . . . It is about the DNA that you have in the company. (Developer)

> We see perhaps that from the parts [of the sub department 1] which we did not work with, those who joined [the transformation], there were more pushbacks, there was a cultural misunderstanding and in fact some of the principles, many of those values have not got under their skin. ... Now we did this, when we formalized the organization, so it somehow connected and now we see where the differences are. And I think that it is a really nice example of how necessary cultural preparation is for organizational change. (Agile Coach)

4.1.2 Negligence of the Large-Scale Scrum Rules

LeSS practitioners advise to acquire LeSS Huge gradually by one requirement area at the time (Larman & Vodde, 2016). The studied product group disobeyed the step-by-step LeSS Huge adoption and thus some difficulties occurred in the initial weeks after the adoption began.

> We violated two big rules about the Flip and we did so knowingly. The first rule is that you first should do LeSS, regular LeSS and you should not do LeSS Huge, which we did, we took too many people. And the second rule is that the Flips take place in person. That means that all the people meet in one place for one week or a few days and there it takes place. We were not given this luxury. (Agile Coach)

Except for the non-gradual shift, the studied product group violated the recommended number of teams within one requirement area, which should be between four to eight (Larman & Vodde, 2016). The studied product group started with three requirement areas, which showed to be too much for a group of approximately 80 developers. Consequently, feature teams' members repeatedly concentrated on multiple requirement areas, which led to local optimization, lack of flexibility, and high amounts of Zoom (2021) meetings one had to attend.

> We are finding out after those two three sprints that the institute of areas is not bringing us anything extra or we do not know about a problem that it would solve for us and give us the reason why we want them. . . . The problem is that we do not have enough teams for the number of areas we have. . . . We are talking about cancelling these areas. (Agile Coach)

4.1.3 Initial Composition of Feature Teams

The studied department let feature teams self-design. A few rules had to be followed during the product group's team creation. The first one was the end-to-end aspect of teams as well as complete cross-functionality. Although complete cross-functionality was according to the theory (Larman & Vodde, 2008), the interview participants pointed out that this setup was unsatisfactory, and the teams could not deliver as a whole.

> With all the chaos that there was and how the teams self-organized, I do not think that they will be able to be autonomous and that is important to me. So, for the team to be autonomous,

> it is able to work, take the objective and finish it from A to Z. . . . I think this should be the goal. (Developer)

The studied department decided to abandon the original feature teams' setup and established new teams with a specific concentration, such as teams focused on the desktop side of applications. The focused teams maintained the cross-functional aspect by having multiple roles such as Quality Assurance engineers, User Experience designers or developers of various programming languages. Furthermore, the product group dissolved the three requirement areas and created only a single requirement area. All the changes happened after the third Sprint.

4.2 Accomplishments from a Virtual Agile Adoption

4.2.1 Online Environment

The COVID-19 pandemic caused neither two members of the product group being able to meet physically. The online means of communication and collaboration, such as Zoom (2021) for video conferencing, Miro (2021) as a collaboration whiteboard were beneficial for the transformation. The tools allowed for effective bi-directional communication between the managers, Agile Coaches, and the rest of the product team. Especially crucial were the digital tools during the week when the product team flipped from their old status quo to LeSS.

> Miro board visualization, the way how the cards [for the team creation] were prepared, that was pretty good to me. One could have a quick overview of what the other people have put there, like what skills they have and then it enabled [me] to quickly see who is where and what teams we have. (Developer)

4.2.2 Dry Run

The studied department carried out a Dry Run of a transformation a few months prior to the actual event when it shifted from one way of working to another. Dry Run helped to mitigate some problem areas before the transformation itself. Furthermore, the product group's members were able to get their questions answered and gain an overview into their future structure.

> Dry Run was interesting because it was a mirror for us. . . . If somebody asked me if Dry Run was a good thing, I would say hundred percent yes and I would maybe say on the contrary not one Dry Run, but even two, yeah, because preparation is key. (Product Owner)

4.2.3 Engagement Metrics

The researched department used two engagement metrics to inquire about their employees' well-being and work satisfaction. The first metric the product group

Table 1 Accomplishments found in previous research versus accomplishments innovative for the studied company

	Previous research	Novel in this study
Purely online environment	✗	✓
Dry run	✗	✓
Engagement metrics	Only eNPS	"Shovel index"
Breaking the silos	✓	✗

used is eNPS. The second metric focuses on employee autonomy and how much each employee feels they are in control of their work. The name that the department used for this metric can be loosely translated into English as "shovel index." The following excerpt expands on how the studied department measured success of the LeSS adoption and Table 1 summarizes the accomplishments.

> Via engagement. We got to eight out of ten, eight and a half on the shovel index and NPS. I would like to get to nine out of ten. . . . If this does not fail and if it stays and the engagement trend will be increasing and it will be so even in the new departments, then to me it shows that it is possible to do these transformations this way, when the bigger units are merged, that when one unit is bigger and prepared more . . . we are able to infect the smaller unit with the culture. Because if it works out, if it works then it shows the way for the company how to do it further. (Engineering Director)

4.2.4 Breaking the Silos

Prior to the LeSS transformation, there were silos between the two sub-departments. Although working on connected products, the two sub-departments shared information ineffectively. The LeSS adoption helped to eliminate this obstacle and allow a more transparent approach toward innovation.

> I mean John, my boss was like, yeah, I totally get it here. Let's go ahead and do it in the department. You guys can be like the kind of hotbed to test it in here. We will see how it works with you, see what we learn there. And if it works well, six months down the road, we can do the same Flip over in other departments as well to try to mirror what you have done and remove some of the hurdles or some of the downsides that we currently have here at the company given the previous structure, the siloed product-based structure. (Engineering Director)

4.3 Changes in Effectiveness

The immediate effect of the transformation was decreased productivity and effectiveness. This is a typical phenomenon of disruptions to the status quo (Cameron & Green, 2019).

> When we talk about the short horizon the effect is indeed negative. At the moment, everything is broken. (Developer)

However, over time the benefits of LeSS started to show. The effectiveness increase was correlated with the resolution of the initial struggles, such as original non-focused team setup or too many requirement areas.

> There would be a big slowdown if someone was sick, someone was out of work in training or left for the day, you name it. . . . there would be a big slowdown. Now after the Flip we are sharing all the knowledge and one person is not responsible just for one aspect. . . . When you share that knowledge to a variety of different engineers that slow down no longer occurs. So, I think that we will function much more efficiently. (Engineering Director)

The impact on the effectiveness started to become positive over time. The beneficial aspects included substitutability of certain roles, increased learning, improved quality of work, and siloes breaking down.

5 Implications and Recommendations

As the conducted study implies, scaled agile frameworks, such as Large-Scale Scrum have many benefits to large companies. Scaled agile frameworks bring structure, give innovation responsibility to the teams, and allow for ongoing improvement based on empiricism (Larman & Vodde, 2008). Qualitative research which the authors conducted in a large software firm yielded the following results.

The study identified three drawbacks that were identified during the study: inadequate culture readiness, negligence of the Large-Scale Scrum rules, and initial composition of feature teams.

Furthermore, four accomplishments aided to achieve successful LeSS adoption, one out of which can be found in previous empirical research (Ebert & Paasivaara, 2017)—the silos were breaking down. Purely online environment and a rehearsal of the transformation are two aspects novel to the researched company. One success factor, the selected engagement metrics, was scarcely included in the previous empirical research.

The authors recommend other companies do not have to wait for in-person meetings to carry out scaled agile transformations. The studied company is an example of a successful scaled agile adoption from a completely virtual environment. As a result of frequent feedback loops, continuous improvement, and testing, adjusting, and efficiently using the digital tools, the department was able to compensate for the physical setting.

The second recommendation is to rehearse the transformation. The half-day Dry Run event provided more insight and understanding of the forthcoming situation. Initial struggles were eliminated and feedback from the employees was considered in the planning of the actual Flip event. Furthermore, Dry Run allowed for testing the technology, fine-tuning of the selected technology, and educating the product team on how to use these tools.

The third recommendation is aligned with the previously existing research (Gandomani et al., 2015). The research from this chapter showed that adequate cultural preparedness for the change with certain agile maturity are necessary for a change effort of this scale. Experimental approach before the actual transformation is recommended.

6 Conclusion and Future Work

The new era of remote work is the era of change. Change in the technical tools and means of communication companies used to utilize in their daily work. Successful online adoption can be achieved even during this new age.

To assess the agile transition, qualitative research was conducted, where 16 semi-structured interviews, along with observations and artifact analysis were realized. This chapter fills in the gap in empirical research about fully distributed, virtual scaled agile adoptions. The contribution of this chapter to academia and agile practitioners lies in an empirical evidence that a successful scaled agile transition can be achieved fully remotely.

The adoption had some initial struggles, such as: inadequate culture preparedness, violation of the selected scaling framework's rules, and initial composition of teams. The initial struggles were resolved, and product group's newly stabilized position brought studied scaled agile adoption to fruition.

The accomplishments from the researched agile transition include online environment itself, rehearsal of the transformation, innovative employee engagement and autonomy metrics, and removal of the existing silos.

In terms of product group's effectiveness, the positive results started to show over time, such as improved quality of work, enhanced learning, the eradication of silos, and substitutability of certain roles.

Ongoing improvement is one of the principles central to agility. Organizations can benefit from establishing feedback loops and experimentally advancing the process, which can help them boost their performance. When scaling agile frameworks, ongoing improvement is the status quo. Companies can leverage timely feedback and adjust processes according to their needs. As future research the authors suggest two possible extensions to the conducted research. The first option is to re-evaluate the transition in the same software company after an extended period. The second alternative is to expand the research to multiple companies to provide more generalized results on fully virtual agile adoptions at scale.

This study implies that agility is a useful lever for large or small companies to be able to quickly react to their environments and adjust their strategies and business plans accordingly. The results from this study are beneficial for the whole digital ecosystem across Europe and Asia.

References

Bergqvist, J., & Gordani Shahri, N. (2018). *Large-Scale agile transformation: A case study of Volvo Cars' transformation process* (Master's thesis). https://odr.chalmers.se/handle/20.500.12380/255549

Cameron, E., & Green, M. (2019). *Making sense of change management: A complete guide to the models, tools and techniques of organizational change*. Kogan Page Publishers.

Comella-Dorda, S., Garg, L., Thareja, S., & Vasquez-McCall, B. (2020). *Revisiting agile teams after an abrupt shift to remote.* https://www.mckinsey.com/business-functions/organization/our-insights/revisiting-agile-teams-after-an-abrupt-shift-to-remote

Conboy, K., & Carroll, N. (2019). Implementing large-scale agile frameworks: Challenges and recommendations. *IEEE Software, 36*(2), 44–50. https://doi.org/10.1109/MS.2018.2884865

Diebold, P., Schmitt, A., & Theobald, S. (2018). Scaling agile: How to select the most appropriate framework. In *Proceedings of the 19th international conference on agile software development: Companion* (pp. 1–4). https://doi.org/10.1145/3234152.3234177

Digital.ai. (2021). *15th state of agile report.* https://explore.digital.ai/state-of-agile/15th-state-of-agile-report

Dikert, K., Paasivaara, M., & Lassenius, C. (2016). Challenges and success factors for large-scale agile transformations: A systematic literature review. *Journal of Systems and Software, 119*, 87–108. https://doi.org/10.1016/j.jss.2016.06.013

Ebert, C., & Paasivaara, M. (2017). Scaling agile. *IEEE Software, 34*(6), 98–103. https://doi.org/10.1109/MS.2017.4121226

Gandomani, T. J., Zulzalil, H., Ghani, A. A. A., Sultan, A. B. M., & Parizi, R. M. (2015). The impact of inadequate and dysfunctional training on agile transformation process: A grounded theory study. *Information and Software Technology, 57*, 295–309. https://doi.org/10.1016/j.infsof.2014.05.011

Larman, C., & Vodde, B. (2008). *Scaling lean & agile development: Thinking and organizational tools for large-scale scrum*. Addison-Wesley Professional.

Larman, C., & Vodde, B. (2016). *Large-scale scrum: More with LeSS*. Addison Wesley Professional.

Mahadevan, D., Paquette, C., Rashid, N., & Ustinov, E. (2019). *Building agile capabilities: The fuel to power your agile 'body'.* McKinsey Analytics. https://www.mckinsey.com/~/media/McKinsey/Business%20Functions/Organization/Our%20Insights/Building%20agile%20capabilities%20The%20fuel%20to%20power%20your%20agile%20body/Building-agile-capabilities-The-fuel-to-power-your-agile-body.pdf

Mancl, D., & Fraser, S. D. (2020). COVID-19's influence on the future of agile. In *International conference on agile software development. Springer* (pp. 309–316). https://doi.org/10.1007/978-3-030-58858-8_32

Miro. (2021). *An online whiteboard & visual collaboration platform for teamwork | Miro.* viewed 30 July 2021. https://miro.com/

Olszewska, M., Heidenberg, J., Weijola, M., Mikkonen, K., & Porres, I. (2016). Quantitatively measuring a large scale agile transformation. *Journal of Systems and Software, 117*, 258–273. https://doi.org/10.1016/j.jss.2016.03.029

Paasivaara, M., Behm, B., Lassenius, C., & Hallikainen, M. (2018). Large-scale agile transformation at ericsson: A case study. *Empirical Software Engineering, 23*(5), 2550–2596. https://doi.org/10.1007/s10664-017-9555-8

Rampin, R., Steeves, V., & DeMott, S. (2021). *Taguette (Version 1.0.0). Zenodo*. https://doi.org/10.5281/zenodo.5111814 .

Sedlak, P. (2020). Employee Net Promoter Score (eNPS) as a Single-item Measure of Employee Work Satisfaction an Empirical Evidence from Companies Operating in Poland. *Contemporary organisation and management*. Challenges and Trends, Michałkiewicz A. and Mierzejewska W. (eds), Wydawnictwo Uniwersytetu Łódzkiego, Łód, pp. 347–357. https://www.ceeol.com/search/book-detail?id=932552#page=348

Schwaber, K., & Sutherland, J. (2020). *The scrum guide.* viewed 3 November 2021. https://scrumguides.org/docs/scrumguide/v2020/2020-Scrum-Guide-US.pdf

Singh, V. (2020). Workshops are now required to be conducted remotely: Is this a bad thing? *Interactions, 27*(4), 52–54. https://doi.org/10.1145/3406102

Sonix, Inc. (2021). Automatically convert audio and video to text: Fast, *Accurate, & Affordable | Sonix.* viewed 30 July 2021. https://sonix.ai/

Theobald, S., Schmitt, A. & Diebold, P. (2019). *Comparing scaling agile frameworks based on underlying practices*. In International Conference on Agile Software Development (pp. 88–96).

Zoom Video Communications, Inc. (2021). *Video Conferencing, Cloud Phone, Webinars, Chat, Virtual Events | Zoom.* viewed 30 July 2021. https://zoom.us/

Ing. Tatiana Lekýrová holds an M.Sc. in Innovation Project Management and a B.Sc. in Knowledge Engineering, both from Czech Technical University in Prague (CTU). Tatiana did her master's degree at Masaryk Institute of Advances Studies at CTU and focused her research on scaled agile frameworks, change management, and Large-Scale Scrum. Her research interests include agile adoptions, organizational transformations, and employee engagement. During her studies, she organized a startup conference called Startup Start Now for young entrepreneurs at the Czech Technical University. Currently, she works as a Platform Specialist in the e-commerce field.

Ing. Gabriela Antošová Ph.D. holds a degree in Regional and Social Development in the Faculty of Economics and Management at University of Life Sciences in Prague. Currently Academic assistant at Czech Technical University, namely at Masaryk Institute of Advanced Studies. Good interpersonal relationships with a global approach to business, global strategy, and innovations. Scientific major interests are in innovations, strategic planning and development, business etiquette, and internationalization processes. Her last publication is the international book Innovative Strategic Planning and International Collaboration for the Mitigation of Global Crises.

Why and How Place Matters

Angelika C. Messner

> *This chapter is dedicated to Annelies Pechlaner, my outstanding teacher at high school in a little town in Northern Italy. I wish to thank Claudia Zimmermann for great many inspiring discussions and crucial inputs that make a difference.*

Abstract Recent decades produced progress and wealth for many, at the same time the inequalities grew alike. This is what the current historical conjuncture painfully reveals. Urgently asking for new paradigms of learning, trading and collaboration, the theoretical dimension of place is crucial. However, we do not know to see tangible, clear steps yet.

Moving at the crossroads of current transformative trajectories in the Eastern and Western hemisphere and at a global scale, this chapter shall offer a few foundational thoughts in this regard.

Keywords Space · Place · Location · Knowledge · Territoriality · Corporeality · Physicality · Subjectivity · New enlightenment

1 Moving through Space

Imagine you are moving through space. Wandering or flying without obstacles and without any physical or geographical limitations. It can be a carefree joyful wandering (遊) through landscapes. In the words of the great philosopher and poet Zhuangzi 莊子(365–290 BC), to "wander beyond the four sees" (遊乎四海之外) requires the ability to moving in a real, very concrete physical, mental and spiritual sense (莊子Zhuangzi 1/17.13, 2021). Therefore, trying to surpass one's corporeal boundedness *via* mental and cognitive means can be disastrous. With regards to the

A. C. Messner (✉)
China Centre, Kiel University, Kiel, Germany
e-mail: messner@sino.uni-kiel.de

H. Pechlaner et al. (eds.), *The Clash of Entrepreneurial Cultures?*, FGF Studies in Small Business and Entrepreneurship, https://doi.org/10.1007/978-3-030-97050-5_13

relation between the very place of life and knowledge he warns about having overconfidence in our knowledge: "Life is bounded. Knowledge is unbounded. Using the bounded to follow the unbounded is dangerous (吾生也有涯, 而知也无涯. 以有涯隨无涯, 殆已; 已而為知者, 殆而已矣)" (莊子*Zhuangzi* 3/1). We will come back to Zhuangzi and his explanation why place and the fact of the boundedness of life and place, its very territorial and corporeal disposition is essential for the dimension of knowledge and its implications for our planetary life.

In the late twentieth century, when the dream of globalization inspired millions of people on a global scale, we are told by the globalization guru Richard O'Brien (1992): "Geographical location no longer matters, or matters less than hitherto. Money, being fungible, will continue to try and avoid, and will largely succeed in escaping, the confines of existing geography" (O'Brien, 1992, 1–2).

Although this description lacks the notion of joyfulness, the idea of borderless moving through quantifiable and measurable geometric space is highlighted: money, things and commodities of any kind, people and animals, knowledge and believes, taste and style to be moving underground, on the earth, in water or in the air. In correlation with an immense growth of digital technologies borderless trading and learning were envisioned as instrumental tools for elevating education standards and life conditions of all. Eventually, people were expected to being freed from bad life conditions and from "backward" mindsets. Massive urbanization worldwide, moreover should foster the postmodern move towards cosmopolitanism (Appiah, 2006). However, in reality, billions of people did not become cosmopolitans but instead transformed into professional tourists and consumers, experiencing massive decentering. "Scattering of seeds" (the literal meaning of diaspora) is another name for the fragmentation of identities accompanying the intensive exchange and borderless movement of people and commodities. We see a strong move back to localism and regionalism, both at an individual as well as on a political level (McClay & McAllister, 2014). Currently, several factors (war, catastrophic implications of economic, ecological and cultural globalization, climate change) cause people to lose their homes.In order to protect homes and residences, maintain a sense of belonging and counteract migration, we see people drastically interfering with their environments and re-constructing nature when facing threatening climate change.[1] At the same time, in different places, urgent searching for new habitats in completely new environments for the sake of survival is present in some regions.[2] Therefore, place currently regains a significant role in a very existential sense.

[1] A brilliant case study about local community movements for place preservation in the Japanese contexts, is Saburo Horikawa. *Why Place Matters. A Sociological Study of the Historic Preservation Movement in Otaru, Japan, 1965–2017*. Cham, Switzerland, 2021.

[2] https://www.adaptation-undp.org/explore/asia-and-pacific/kiribati

2 Places of Knowing

As recognized in scholarly discussions, knowledge is diverse, proximate, situational and interpretative.[3] In fact, historians, anthropologists and sociologists started to focus on the entanglements and thus show strong evidence in doing justice between single regions, people, populations and countries. Controversially, academic writing on world histories does not represent entanglements, but rather depicts a crafted, additive conglomeration of different regional histories. In other words, conventional ways to research and present knowledge still follow an obsolete Eurocentric perspective and are hence far from recognizing entanglements and connectivity.Nonetheless revealing insights into the paths of connectivity that heavily shaped and continues to shape global history, however, the issue of periodization, e.g. the chronological ordering of time and place, still remains as an unsolved problem. The Hegelian dichotomy of the "universal" and the "particular" continues to inform world histories. Therefore, questions remain unanswered: How is historical time structured and being divided into periods? Whose perspective is being depicted?

Considering an exemplary category such as the "Middle Ages"—do "Middle Ages" apply to regions beyond the European regions?

Certainly not, as numerous "particular" histories in Asian and African societies show. Evidence is growing that only by recognizing area Studies (Asian and African) will we come to explore viable paths that could possibly lead out from hegemony and prioritizing a given epistemological framework that so far has mostly stemmed from European contexts (Maissen/Mittler 2018, 11-23). We will need to foster intensive dialogues between the disciplines and regions. As Phillippe Peycam puts it, Asian and African studies can act "as a unique vector of knowledge with is multiplier effects, not just in terms of scholarly research "impacts", or the direct benefits of training language and country or regions "specialists", but in its potential to formulate new methodologies (comparisons and connections), new pedagogies (transcending mental and institutional boundaries), and new relationships (between societies, between situated experiences, between the academic and the non-academic communities)" (Peycam, 2020, 3).

Whereas the notion of "total knowledge" is being presumed as a capsule, it is being transferred from teacher to student. However, there are forms of knowledge, such as multilingual practices that claim to be recognized as equally worthy for commitment and engagement as the so-called "total knowledge".

Today, Universities as unique places of academic research and education, are directed towards a new business model, which foundationally draws on the commodization of higher education with EdTech platforms. "Ivy League" US and UK Universities are among the first moving in this direction. This correlates with the belief among American well-to-do people, namely, that America would be the best

---

[3] See the long term symposia on this issue held in coordination with the University of Heidelberg from 2006–2022: https://www.geog.uni-heidelberg.de/knowledgeandspace/informations/index.html

place in the World, to study and to flourish in an environment of freedom and liberal democracy. However, people now begin to realize that these places actually primarily act as instruments for social segregation at a global scale. Academicians recently textualized an explicit claim for Universities to realize their existential role in social cohesion and moral advancement (Kupe & Wangenge-Ouma, 2020; D'Souza, 2020). Advocating the recognition of the situatedness of knowledge reveals it as a prerequisite for real collaboration. This again requires to refuse the conventional view of "total knowledge".

3 Knowing Has a Place

Place can be seen through its attachments to physical, social and emotional aspects. Another perspective on place is to see it as an anchor for historical remembrance and cultural heritage. It is what turns an unlimited space of cultural memory and past events into a vertical, limited physicality.Questions of human identity and the human need to search for belonging, such as by questions like "who am I"? or "where do I come from"? are inevitably to be answered without physical place. Thus identity and belonging are crucially associated with place.This identification forms knowledge on a personal level. Hence, place is essential for producing knowledge.

Zhuangzi (who was quoted at the beginning of this chapter), a philosopher who lived in the fourth century BC, discusses critical aspects of place, notably with Hui Shi, who was a well-known logician from the School of Names. The following passage provides deeper understandings for the relation of place, joy and delight:

"Zhuang and Huizi were wandering (you) along the bridge over the Hao River.

Zhuangzi said, "The minnows swim about so freely (you), following the openings wherever they take them. Such is the happiness (le 樂) of the fish".

Huizi said, "You are not a fish, so whence (an 安) do you know the happiness of fish"?

Zhuangzi said: "You are not I, so whence do you know I don't know the happiness of fish"?

Huizi said, "I am not you, to be sure, so I don't know what it is to be you. But by the same token, since you are certainly not a fish, my point about your inability to know the happiness of fish stands intact".

Zhuangzi said, "Let's go back to the starting point. You said, 'Whence do you know the happiness of fish?' Since your question was premised on your knowing that I know it, O must have known it from here, up above the Hao River" (莊子 *Zhuangzi* 17. 13).

Knowing, in this passage, derives from a special point "*here,* up above the Hao River". In a specific location "*on the bridge*" Zhuangzi experiences a concrete community with the fish, as the fish are not objects of knowledge, but in their wandering at ease they share the same reality with Zhuangzi in this very place and moment. Knowledge about the happiness of the fish emerges from the shared situation, the realization of the happy experience of wandering at ease. Thus Zhuangzi comes to know about the fish's happiness. Knowledge is thus proximate, situational, interpretative and participatory (Ames 1998a, b: 223). "Place" in terms of a social and geographical concrete space refers to a particular relational event. It is limited.

This is congruent with present day reasoning about place. Claiming we take the very perspective of the conceptualizing of knowledge seriously (Massey, 2005; Hinchliffe & Lavau, 2013).

In the face of the current growing inequalities at a global scale, these considerations on a tight relation between place and emergence of knowledge will contribute to reshaping the academic world of doing research, learning or teaching. In order to recognize the fact that knowledge is inseparable from place, practices and emotional features (Tsing, 2015, 277–78), we are asked to strive, not to stop, for moving beyond the current prescribed logic of competition in the places of learning.

4 Is There Room for Imagining Other Worlds?

The current historical conjuncture along the threats of the twenty-first century painfully reveals that Covid-19 is by no means an epidemiological issue alone (Hinchliffe et al., 2021, e230). The pandemic brought longstanding incongruences between paradigms of learning, trading and collaboration to the surface. Multiple contradictory voices, anxieties and fears, prompting vigorous political assertions and psychosomatic symptoms alike reveal as "emotion-related diseases". This situation urged the United Nations and WHO to warn about the devastating mental health indices affecting up to a billion people since the start of the pandemic: insomnia, depression, neurodermitis and digestive problems (Ärzteblatt, 2020; Bartens, 2019:14; Krammer et al., 2020:272:282).

What Is at Risk?

First of all, the radically fast increase of corporeal suffering due to emotional and social imbalances and asymmetries in the course of the pandemic reveals the necessity of looking closer at highly complex terrain of disease. Furthermore, the precarious situations are bound with evidence for the representational predominance of a few paradigms that fatally dominated and determined doing and thinking of World politics and related governance with regard to the vital corporeal disposition of humans.

What are these paradigms about? Firstly, there is the all-dominant belief that the only solution to all problems in modernity would be science, economy and technology. This belief has dominated peoples' thinking and reasoning since a hundred years by now, and it continues to determine the paradigms of learning, trading and collaboration. This superstition foundationally relies on the systematic exclusion of "subjectivity" from the paradigms of learning. In other words, to deny everything that is difficult to measure requires denying everything that is impossible to be transformed into numbers. The concept of knowledge underlying this paradigm is "knowledge as such", as it was differentiated in ancient Greek philosophy from other processes of understanding. Education systems, academic practice as well as ethical reasoning in the Western hemisphere, and thus, European enlightenment highlighted empiricism as the exclusive means of understanding and as constituting the objective reality (Eno, 1996:128). This way excluding everything considered as subjective, the emotions were systematically excluded from the knowledge canon, as they were considered as highly subjective, difficult to measure and to count.

However, as neurobiology showed only recently, emotions inherit a significant role for everything people imagine and do. In a nutshell, there is no cognition without emotions. This is why emotions are most recently considered as an analysing category in social and political science, just like the categories of gender, ethnicity and class (Messner, 2021a, b).

However, schoolbooks, everyday politics, as well as trading practices still feel obliged to act according to "knowledge as such". The exclusion of everything which does not fit into an "objective reality" continues. Repeatedly announced political dogmas make an incompatibility with regard to morals, economy and technology evident.

This contributes to a denial of feelings and moral facts from the existential reality. Last not least, the cynical quantitative logic of economy contradicts the necessity to invest in the ethical education of our children.

Besides these aspects, the global Covid-19 pandemic has formed the importance of place with regard to medical intervention and innovation (Ibata-Arens, 2021:133–160). Having argued earlier on the connection between belonging, identity and place, let us consider the connection between place and space.

In many parts of the Eurocentric world, work space, which has been connected to a specific workplace pre-Covid, became disconnected from its original place and shifted to firstly, a new place, mainly home-office. Therefore "home" as a place of intimacy, has received a second identity by turning into a working place.

Secondly, a shift to work from home included a shift to working online and virtual meetings and conferences. Thus the second shift from place happened towards virtual space and virtual communication.

After a beginning "high", the gain and growth of virtual communication has clarified the important entanglement of space and place. The sense of belonging and identity was challenged since human physical contact in place became limited. Emotional suffering and mental imbalance occurred as a consequence of limited place and growing space.

From this perspective, the more space we want, the more place is actually needed. Travel restrictions stopped physical movement and tourism. Whereas the virtual space and communication have grown and became unlimited.

Therefore Covid-19 has vertically grounded the cloudy qualities of space into the necessity of a very earthly place. The experience of the current pandemic has thus closed aspects of space and simultaneously the importance of physical, intimate place even increased.

Space is unlimited, it is like knowledge, ever growing and expanding. Place is concrete, physical, intimate, affects our belonging and is limited.

5 The Place of the Corporeal Life in a New Enlightenment

Devastating mental health diseases in our current pandemic world shows evidence for the urgent and real need for coherence—between doing and thinking, between longing and reality. In order to widen the framework in which reality currently is being perceived, an engagement for enhancing the intellectual and personal involvement with different voices and traditions from other worlds than the one of present day capitalism, is needed.

First of all, there is an urgent necessity to advocate an approach to subjectivity, to the corporeal reality of humans (Messner, 2012a, b) and the emotions as powers that substantially direct our reasoning, behaviour and doing. In other words, a new foundation of enlightening our learning practices, other than the enlightenment movement in the European contextualizes several centuries before, the new enlightenment in the twenty-first century accepts the fact that we share a common destiny at a global scale. New Enlightenment recognizes the manifold phenomena such as colours, meanings, values, emotional, corporeal and mental states and "vacant places" as integral parts of reality. The corporeal disposition of our lives[4] refers to the boundedness of life and knowledge as much as of the planet and its resources.

It engages with voices and traditions from ancient times in East and West, North and South and thus gives room for imagining new worlds.

Markus Gabriel (2020) recently pulled our attention towards "New Enlightenment". It recognizes the fact that emotions—just like local diversities differ and throughout are subjective (no objectivity) and advocates a radical realism. At the same time, new enlightenment encourages the elaboration of universal values, thereby dealing with the fallacies of the cosmopolitan ideal.[5]

New enlightenment advocates an intensive engagement with humanities due to the fact that culture, religiosity and philosophy is clearly not a matter of context.

New enlightenment recognizes the crucial role of place/regions for internally generated authenticities, defined by their difference from other places.

New enlightenment accepts the place of one's own body as the existential ground on which and through which the moral implications of our existence are put in practice. Knowledge, as already discussed earlier above, is always situational, proximate and locational.

---

[4] Here too, Chinese philosophical perspectives should be considered. See the brilliantly elaborated monograph on Embodied Moral Psychology by Seok, 2014.

[5] This is not the place here to discuss the highly controversial issue of the cosmopolitan ideals and universalism. See Tan et al., 2021 in *Journal of World Philosophies* 6 (Summer 2021): 99–138 and Messner, 2021b.

Following Zhuangzi we need to learn that knowledge is concrete, territorial and worldly (*here, over the river*). Knowledge is relational—grounded in a concrete place and in touch with the surrounding environment. New enlightenments insist that we learn to be moved and affected by things, by the vitality of our planet, by our environment (Latour, 2004, Donna Haraway, 2008). Opening up to learn about being affected requires to know how vitality grounds in relational situations. Vitality connects the intimate textile and fabric of our corporeality, our local and individual, particular situatedness.

This is what "place" does: Place is not about surfaces, nor about objects. It is about the entangled situatedness of humans and things. Place is a specific mix of materiality, knowledge and others. Recognizing these aspects of place is the prerequisite for new ways of dialogue at eye level, between East and West, South and North.

References

Ames, R. T. (1998a). *Wandering at ease in the Zhuangzi*. SUNY Press.

Ames, R. T. (1998b). Knowing in the Zhuangzi. From Here, on the Bridge, over the River Hao. In *Wandering at Ease*, ed. Ames, Roger, 219–230. Albany. SUNY Press.

Appiah, K. A. (2006). *Cosmopolitanism: Ethnics in a world of strangers*. W.W. Norton.

Ärzteblatt. (2020). Accessed Oct 1, 2021, from https://www.aerzteblatt.de/nachrichten/117137/WHO-erinnert-an-psychische-Auswirkungen-der-Pandemie

Bartens, W. (2019). *Was hat er bloß? Die Jahrestagung für Psychosomatik widmet sich der Frage, warum seelisches Leid so unterschiedliche Beschwerden hervorruft–und warum vielen Menschen der Zugang zu ihren Gefühlen verstellt ist,* Süddeutsche Zeitung, no. 72, March 14.

Tan, K.-C., Coutinho, S., Penman, Z., Tagore, S., & Valdez, I. (2021). Global ethics or universal ethics? *Journal of World Philosophies, 6*(1), 99–138. Retrieved from https://scholarworks.iu.edu/iupjournals/index.php/jwp/article/view/4547

D'Souza, R. (2020). *Zooming Toward a University Platform*. RAIOT Magazine, June 8.

Eno, R. (1996). Cook Ding's Dao and the limits of philosophy. In *Essays on Skepticism*, eds Kjellberg and Ivanhoe, 127–151.

Gabriel, M. (2020). *Moralischer Fortschritt in dunklen Zeiten. Universale Werte für das 21.* Ullstein.

Haraway, D. (2008). *When species meet*. University of Minnesota.

Hinchliffe, S., & Lavau, S. (2013). Differentiated circuits: The ecologies of knowing and securing life. *Environment and Planning D: Society and Space, 31*(2), 259–274.

Hinchliffe, S., Manderson, L., & Moore, M. (2021). Planetary healthy publics after COVID-19. *Lancet planet. Health, 5*, e230–e236.

Ibata-Arens, K. C. (2021). *Pandemic medicine. Why the global innovation system is broken, and how we can fix it*. Lynne Rienner Publishers.

Krammer, S., Augstburger, R., Haeck, M., & Martina and Andreas Maercker. (2020). Anpassungsstörung, Depression, Stresssymptome, Corona bezogene Sorgen und Bewältigungsstrategien während der Corona Pandemie (COVID-19) bei Schweizer Klinikpersonal. *Psychotherapie, Psychosomatik Medizinische Psychologie, 70*(7), 272–282. Accessed Oct 01, 2021, from www.zora.uzh.ch/id/eprint/189034/

Kupe, T., & Wangenge-Ouma, G. (2020). *Post-Covid 19: Opportunity for universities to have a rethink*. The Conversation.

Latour, B. (2004). *Politics of nature: how to bring the sciences into democracy*. (Transl. C. Porter) Harvard University Press.
Maissen, T., & Mittler, B. (2018). Why China did not have a renaissance–and why that matters. In S. Richter, M. Banerjee, S. Meurer, & L. Xuetao (Eds.), *An interdisciplinary dialogue*. Walther de Gruyter.
Massey, D. (2005). *For space*. Sage.
McClay, W. M., & McAllister, T. V. (2014). *Why place matters. Geography, identity, and civic life in modern America*. Encounter Books, New Atlantis Books.
Messner, A. C. (2012a). *Aspects of emotion in late imperial China*. In Angelika C. Messner (editor of the issue on emotions) Editor's Introduction to the Thematic Section. (= Asiatische Studien/ Études Asiatiques LXVI (4)): 893–913.
Messner, A. C. (2012b). Towards a history of the corporeal dimensions of emotions: The case of pain. *Asiatische Studien/Études Asiatiques LXVI, 4*, 943–972.
Messner, A. C. (Forthcoming 2021a). Anger, hate, aggression. In *The Routledge history of emotion in the modern World*, eds. Katie Barclay and Peter Stearns.
Messner, A. C. (Forthcoming 2021b). The cultural dimension in the BRI's background: "All-under-Heaven" as principle of Chinese culture. The "Kingly Way" as ancient guiding habit of trans-civilizational integration. In *China's "New Silk Road" Project and Europe. Towards a Critical Dialogue*, ed. Roland Benedikter. Springer Verlag.
O'Brien, R. (1992). *Global financial integration. The end of geography*. Royal Institute Affairs.
Peycam, P. (2020). Beyond the 'competitive' model. *The Newsletter IIAS (Leiden University), 85 Spring*, 3.
Seok, B. (2014). *Embodied moral psychology and Confucian philosophy*. Lexington Books.
Tsing, A. L. (2015). *The mushroom at the end of the world. On the possibility of life in capitalist ruins*. Princeton University Press.
莊子*Zhuangzi*. In: Chinese Text Project 中國 哲學書電子化 计劃. Edited by Donald Sturgeon. Accessed Oct 01, 2021., from https://ctext.org/

Angelika C. Messner , Professor of China Studies, Director of the Chinacentre at Kiel University. Born and educated in Italy, she studied Sinology, History of Medicine and Anthropology in Innsbruck, Vienna, Beijing and Freiburg. Currently she is PI of the MOST-DFG Joint Research Project: 2018–2023 "Materialities of Medical Culture In/Between Europe and East Asia 醫藥文化的物質頂: 介於歐洲與東亞之間", and of the Chinese Fund of Social Science Project „Kulturen und deren Philosophien im Ost-West-Vergleich 东西文化及其哲学 (2021–2023), Speaker of „Regionale Medizinkulturen"-Ag "Gesundheit für alle", Berlin Brandenburgische Akademie der Wissenschaften (2020–2023).

The manufacturer's authorised representative in the EU is Springer Nature Customer Service Centre GmbH, Europaplatz 3, 69115 Heidelberg, Germany. If you have any concerns regarding our products, please contact ProductSafety@springernature.com

Printed and bound by CPI Group (UK) Ltd, Croydon, CR0 4YY
30/09/2026
02225513-0017